British Pakistani Boys, E
and the Role of Religion

British Pakistani children are the second largest ethnic group in UK schools, yet little of their education and wider needs have been researched. *British Pakistani Boys, Education and the Role of Religion* seeks to rectify this, by investigating the educational achievement of British Pakistani boys and the importance of education both in the Pakistani community and in the wider religion of Islam.

The book draws on research undertaken by the author in three British state secondary schools to respond to the national policy on the education of ethnic minority children. It considers the meaning of education for Pakistanis, where religion plays an integral role, the gaps in education as well as the issue of representation – in governance and in the teaching workforce. The author concludes by discussing the possibility of responsive education better meeting the needs of Pakistani children by integrating Islamic religious education and education of the world.

British Pakistani Boys, Education and the Role of Religion will be vital reading for academics and both undergraduate and postgraduate students in the fields of Education and Sociology and specifically those studying inclusion, equality and diversity, or Asian, Muslim or Pakistani education. It would also appeal to education practitioners, policymakers and community activists.

Dr Karamat Iqbal is an Education and Diversity Consultant and a school governor within the Ninestiles Multi-academy Trust.

Routledge Research in Educational Equality and Diversity

Books in the series include:

For more information about this series, please visit: www.routledge.com/Routledge-Research-in-Educational-Equality-and-Diversity/book-series/RREED

British Pakistani Boys, Education and the Role of Religion

In the Land of the Trojan Horse

Karamat Iqbal

Routledge
Taylor & Francis Group

LONDON AND NEW YORK

First published 2019 by Routledge

2 Park Square, Milton Park, Abingdon, Oxfordshire OX14 4RN
52 Vanderbilt Avenue, New York, NY 10017

Routledge is an imprint of the Taylor & Francis Group, an informa business

First issued in paperback 2020

British Library Cataloguing-in-Publication Data
A catalogue record for this book is available from the British Library

Library of Congress Cataloging-in-Publication Data
A catalog record for this book has been requested

ISBN: 978-1-138-49662-0 (hbk)
ISBN: 978-0-367-48938-0 (pbk)

Typeset in Bembo
by Apex CoVantage, LLC

Contents

4   Meaning and importance of education for Pakistanis   84

5   The gaps in education   105

6   A diverse teaching workforce   134

Tables

Glossary

Adab   manners
Akhlaq   character
Allah taala   God
Aur   and
Barkat   blessing
Bud-tameez   disrespectful
Chaa pee ray   drinking tea
Deen   religion
Deeni   religious
Dunya   of the world
Dunyavi   worldly
Eid   Muslim festival
Farz   obligation
Iftari   meal at end of fast
Jamaat   preaching trip
Juma   Friday
Kameez   Pakistani shirt
Naik tareeqa   pious manner
Namaz   prayer
Ramadan   month of fasting in the Muslim calendar
Rehmat   mercy
Roohani waldain   spiritual parents
Salaam-alaikum   Muslim greeting; Peace be upon you
Salaat   prayer
Shalwar   Pakistani trousers
Tadib   culture
Tahaaraf   introduction
Talim   knowledge
Tarbiya   growth and development
Theek thaak   allright
Ustaadji   teacher
Wahabi   a sect of Islam
Wudu   ablution

Acknowledgements

In 2010 I went to see Steve Strand to explore possible work opportunities. While these were not forthcoming, he managed to sign me up for further study. Thus began my doctoral research journey. Throughout this period he generously supported me, often going the extra mile. For this I am deeply grateful. I am also thankful to the Teacher Training and Development Agency in helping me to pay some of my fees.

I am deeply indebted to the academic community whose contribution got me started on my journey. I hope others can similarly benefit from the work I have been able to produce.

I would like to thank the students and their parents and teachers for their generosity in facilitating my research. I hope I can do justice to their views and opinions and use the result to make some impact, however small.

I appreciated the proofreading help, given by Alison Davies, Razwan Faraz and Catherine Coyles, which led to my writing being much tighter.

Then there is my family. I thank my parents for their sacrifice when they parted with me and sent me to England so that I would have a better future. And my current family – Sue, Hannah, Adam and Owen – without whose on-going support and encouragement this long journey would not have been possible. So thank you for cheering me on.

Finally, I thank God for his blessing on what I have been able to achieve, especially after the health incident I faced in the middle of my study. I look forward to Him being there in my effort to try to make some impact.

1   Introduction

Autobiographical sociology

I bring to the research my personal experience and insight as both a first generation immigrant to the UK and an education practitioner. These have enabled me to understand the subject under study, within its context, identify the research questions and provided me with the ability to make sense of the data gathered.

Long before the education of Pakistani boys became a research topic, it was a personal experience, for I was one such boy. Gradually, it became a topic to observe, to learn about, to become concerned with and then, many years later, it became a problem to research. I provide here a brief sketch of my personal and professional journey.

I spent my early years in the Pakistani-controlled Azad Kashmir. My connection with Birmingham was established soon after I was born when my father had decided to come to the UK, known locally as *vilayat* (a derivative of Blighty). He was a part of the early cohort of people who had migrated from our country to the UK. After five years in Birmingham, he relocated back home.

In Kashmir, I attended the local primary school where I was a conscientious student. Soon after transferring to the secondary school my family decided to send me to live with my older sister in Birmingham, in the hope that I would have better opportunities for education and employment. I was 12 years of age at the time.

Upon arrival in Birmingham, in line with educational practice at the time, I was sent to an Immigrant Reception Centre so that I could be immersed in the English language and, soon after, I transferred to our neighbourhood secondary modern. My new school served its immediate working class community, previously White but now also Pakistani.

I continued to be a hard-working student, with a drive to learn and the determination to overcome any barriers I faced. I made good use of my local public library and joined a local evening institute for additional lessons in English. My hard work paid off. By the time I left school after three years, I had achieved a number of CSEs (Certificate of Secondary Education).

Soon after leaving school in 1974, I began to volunteer at a local Saturday School for Pakistani children. I was also a part of the Asian Youth Association which had been set up by Birmingham's Community Relations Council, to explore leisure provision for Asian young people. Later this became a full-time job when I was appointed as a Youth and Community Worker, through a Birmingham City Council Positive Action scheme.

After leaving school I continued my education through evening classes and day-release given by my employers. This enabled me to achieve the qualifications necessary to gain entry to university, six years after leaving school, to study for a Bachelor of Education.

Upon qualifying as a teacher I worked for Birmingham's Multicultural Support Service. In the school I was sent to teach, I recall the Pakistani pupils questioning my credentials as a teacher; so unusual it was for them to have a Pakistani in such a role. Many years later I found myself working for Birmingham Education, this time as an Education Adviser. My duties included researching educational underachievement of ethnic minorities. Later, I came to be known as a 'champion' of the White working class for my focus on their education. I produced a number of reports, one of which was used as the main text for an Adjournment Debate in Parliament. This work provided a foundation for my current study.

Pakistani-Birmingham;[1] development of a community

Following World War II there was a major labour shortage in Britain where the factories and foundries were busy helping to rebuild the country after the war. This led to a policy to encourage the arrival of migrants from countries within the British Empire, including the new nation of Pakistan, created after the Partition of India. Their entry was made easier by the passing of 1948 Nationality Act which "gave all imperial subjects the right to free entry into post-war Britain" (Winder, 2004, p. 332).

The national profile of the Pakistani community changed from a few thousand in 1950 to nearly three-quarters of a million at the turn of the century (Peach, 2006). While the majority of the Pakistanis were from Kashmir, significant numbers also came from areas such as Attock, Ghurghushti, Nowshera, Peshawar, Jehlum, Gujrat, Rawalpindi, Multan, Faisalabad and Sialkot (Dahya, 1973; Abbas, 2010).

As a major industrial centre, Birmingham has had many ethnic communities settling amongst its population leading to the city becoming 'superdiverse' (Rex & Moore, 1967; Vertovec, 2007). Similar to the national development of the Pakistani community, their presence in the city changed rapidly from the 1950s, reaching 40,565 by 1981 and constituting 4% of the city's total population (Anwar, 1996). By 1991, at 6.9%, Birmingham had the largest Pakistani population of any British city (Tackey et al., 2006). Having been the *largest* single ethnic minority group for some time, the community is predicted to make up 21% of the city's population by 2026 (Dorling &Thomas, 2008).

Upon arrival in Birmingham, as elsewhere in the UK, Pakistanis were faced with a difference-blind policy approach[2] of treating everyone the same even though people had different needs, circumstances and historical trajectories. According to Sutcliffe and Smith (1974) "the Government had to maintain that there was no difference between immigrant Commonwealth citizens and indigenous Britons" (p. 369). For Newton (1976) this is a problem of the pluralist theory which "tends to work on the assumption that each and every interest is equally capable of organising and defending itself" (p. 228).

Historically, given the vast majority of Pakistanis originated from rural and underdeveloped areas, their education level was much lower upon entry to the UK compared to many other migrant communities (Anwar, 1979). They, therefore, lost out to the more advantaged Indian community or the more organised and vocal Black Caribbean community. This poor educational start of the Pakistanis was to lead to the community remaining behind other ethnic minorities (Abbas, 2010). It also provides a critical backdrop to educational achievement of the community's young people.

The disadvantaged context of the Pakistanis was acknowledged by the Birmingham Stephen Lawrence Inquiry Commission (BSLC), which showed that there was under-representation of Pakistanis in the City Council's workforce, by 4.9% – indicated by the gap between their presence in the Council's workforce (2%) and in the local population (6.9%) (BSLC, 2001). My later research showed the gap had increased by 2012. While the Pakistani proportion in the workforce had nearly doubled, their presence in the local population had also doubled to 13.5%. This meant that the gap was now 9.6%. Abbas and Anwar (2005) pointed out that big Birmingham employers and service providers do not take race equality seriously. This was confirmed by my later research which showed that many organisations which claimed to have a diverse workforce often tended to employ other ethnic minority groups such as Black Caribbean and Indian (Iqbal, 2013).

Within the education sector, under-representation of Pakistanis was apparent amongst both the workforce and the composition of school governing bodies. For BSLC (2001), it was of fundamental importance that the teaching workforce and governing bodies reflected the ethnic composition of schools. Cox (2001) pointed out that people not fluent in English faced discrimination. They experienced an atmosphere that tended to favour educated professionals who had a better grasp of the jargon associated with the education process. He also pointed out that many people from ethnic minority communities felt that they were not taken seriously because their limited English often meant they were unable to put their point across effectively in meetings.[3] As a result, many only attended meetings infrequently and then drifted away.

Pakistani children; a neglected group

As researchers we are asked: why do we do educational research? For me the answer is quite clear: to impact on policy, to empower ourselves and the people we are researching and to search for truth. I have drawn on the work of a number of social justice–oriented writers and activists. Sivanandan (1982) has said:

> Knowledge is not a goal in itself, but a path to wisdom; it bestows not privilege so much as duty, not power so much as responsibility. . . . But the business of the educated is . . . to turn those skills to the service of their people.
>
> (p. 89)

In such a context our responsibility as researchers is clear; to serve the local community as well as policymakers and professionals. Eqbal Ahmad saw the function of knowledge to comprehend reality in order to change it (Babar, 2015). Following Stuart Hall's advice, I would like to tell people how reality really is – to look it in the face. For Basit (2013), the creation of knowledge and its dissemination was a moral act; she saw it as researchers' role to ensure that it leads to educational and social improvement by challenging unjust policies and practices. I especially agree with Angela Davis when she points out that knowledge is useless unless it assists us to question habits, social practices, institutions, ideologies and the state.[4] For her, new knowledge allows new questions to be asked. Drawing on Critical Race Theory, I do not wish merely to interpret and report on a social situation but to change it for the better. I would like to contribute new knowledge so to help for new questions to be raised. Following Gardner's advice (2011), I will strive to make my work accessible, relevant, persuasive, credible and authoritative in order to get my message across. I hope that the knowledge I produce helps to improve the education of Pakistani children and leads to some transformation, however small. I see the knowledge I have been privileged to acquire as having 'political implications' in contexts beyond the academic world. Ladson-Billings (2006) asks us as education researchers to help to find answers to pressing education questions. For me, the educational achievement and underachievement of Pakistani young people is currently one such pressing issue for which I hope to provide some possible answers.

The aim of making the knowledge one produces useful also raises questions about accessibility. While the language used in one's writing has to be credible within the academy, it has to be understood too by the wider community. I hope not to become mired in separatist language with 'alienating jargon' in what I write. Following Sivanandan's advice (1982), my aim is to create knowledge that is accessible for the wider community, expressed not in terms private to me and my academic peers, but in familiar language which can be accessed by the general community.

While the problem of ethnic minority underachievement in England was acknowledged by the government many years ago (Swann Report, 1985), the focus at the time, and for many years to come, remained on Black Caribbean young people. This was based on the assumption that Asian children were doing well in school. Some of the Asian neglect had resulted from their absorption into the 'Black' category (Modood, 2005) and Pakistani underachievement suffered further by being absorbed in the 'Asian' category, with its higher achieving Indian children. Although it was accepted that the Pakistanis were "the largest minority ethnic group" (DFES, 2006, p. 7), there continued to be relatively little detailed analysis of factors relating to their achievement (Gillborn & Gipps, 1996; Coles & Chilvers, 2004). It is my aim to help fill some of this information gap.

The Youth Cohort Study broke down the 'Asian' category into Indian, Pakistani and Bangladeshi, in 1991 (Strand et al., 2010). The work of Gillborn and Mirza (2000) made it clear that much of the high achievement of the 'Asian' group reflected the achievement of Indian children and that Pakistanis were underachieving compared to White children. They pointed out that "African-Caribbean and Pakistani pupils have drawn the least benefit from the rising levels of attainment; the gap between them and their White peers is bigger now than a decade ago" (p. 14). They showed, in 1997, 28% Pakistani pupils achieving five or more higher grade passes, compared with 44% for the White group. They also pointed out that social class was a significant factor in educational achievement with a far greater impact than race and gender. Demack et al. (2000) investigated variations of social class, ethnicity and gender and showed that the percentage with five high grade passes worsened for Pakistani boys, from 21% in 1988 down to 16% by the end of the study period, in 1995. They pointed out that the problem of Pakistanis was one of both race and social disadvantage.

According to DFES (2006) minority ethnic pupils usually begin with low levels of attainment but make good progress. "However, the continued existence of attainment gaps between these minority ethnic groups and the average for all pupils, shows that, on average, they do not completely catch up with their higher attaining peers" (p. 49). Here it is worth asking what happens to the gap in achievement between different groups of children; does it narrow, close altogether or become wider? The answer is this: it depends on the approach taken by education practitioners and policymakers and the intersection of effects of ethnicity and socio-economic status. Ceci and Papierno (2005) pointed out that where the gap-narrowing interventions are universalised – given not only to the group of children who most need assistance but also to the more advantaged group, the gap can get bigger; in their view to narrow the gap what is needed are interventions *targeted* at the children who have fallen behind.

> This is because . . . although the disadvantaged children who most need the intervention do usually gain significantly from it, the higher functioning or more advantaged children occasionally benefit even more from the intervention. The result is increased disparity and a widening of the gap that existed prior to universalizing the intervention.
>
> (p. 150)

While recognising that universal approaches are usually politically more accept-able, gaps between the advantaged and disadvantaged are only likely to close through focused and targeted interventions that boost the lower scoring group without adding to the higher scoring group's pre-intervention advan-tage. Gillborn (2008a) pointed out that while, between 1992 and 2004, Paki-stani pupils improved in their GCSE attainment, so did others, especially White pupils. Because the latter had improved their performance to a greater extent, it meant the gap between the two had become wider – from minus 11 in 1992 to minus 18 in 2004 (p. 58). One explanation for this was the range in practices between education authorities in relation to setting targets, some of which may have actually made the gap wider. Gillborn and Mirza (2000) outlined three typical approaches to addressing educational underachievement, through setting targets. Firstly, *inclusive targets*: the lower a group currently attained, the higher its improvement target was. This was the declared approach in Birmingham where the authority spoke of 'differential targets'. Secondly, *common improvement targets*: regardless of each group's current position, the same target was set for them. Contrary to its declared approach, it was this universal, difference-blind approach that was often adopted in Birmingham. Thirdly, *increase inequalities targets*: higher targets were set for higher achieving students with the result that, if the targets were achieved as set, it would cause the lower achieving groups to fall behind even further.

Table 1.1 illustrates how Pakistani progress improves but so does the progress of others, which means they continue to be below the national average, with a similar on-going gap between them and 'All pupils'. The gap appeared to con-tinue as pointed out by Strand (2014a):

> The most recent 2011 national data on attainment at age 16, using the threshold of achieving five or more GCSE passes at A–C grades including English and mathematics, indicates the performance of Black Caribbean (48.6%), Pakistani (52.6%) and Black African (57.9%) groups is below that of their White British peers (58.2%), while the achievement of Ban-gladeshi (59.7%) and Indian (74.4%) students is higher.
>
> (p. 132)

In an email communication (Overington, 2012), the Department for Edu-cation (DfE) let me know that it was a matter of concern for them that

Table 1.1 Achievement at GCSE and equivalent (including English and Mathematics) for pupils at end of Key Stage 4 – England

Pupil group	2009	2010	2011	2012	2013
All pupils	50.7	54.8	58.2	58.8	60.6
Pakistani	42.9	49.1	52.6	54.4	55.5
Gap	7.8	5.7	5.6	4.4	5.1

Source: (Strand, 2015)

there were attainment gaps between minority ethnic groups and their peers. With reference to Pakistani pupils, the DfE acknowledged that, as a group, they continue to underperform relative to their peers:

> In 2011 for example, 67.5% of Pakistani pupils achieved national expectations at the end of primary education, compared to 72.5% of all pupils, a gap of 6 (sic) percentage points. A similar gap exists at key Stage 4 where in 2010, 49.1% of Pakistani pupils achieved five or more good GCSEs including English and mathematics, compared to 54.8% of all pupils, a gap of 5.7 percentage points.

Pakistani pupil attainment; the situation in Birmingham

In the earlier stages of the post-war migration it was mainly the Black Caribbean community which had established a presence in the UK, including Birmingham (Phillips & Phillips, 1998; Grosvenor, 1997). According to Rose et al. (1969) and Sutcliffe and Smith (1974), in 1959, most of the approximately 1,000 ethnic minority pupils were West Indian.[5] Later, as shown in Table 1.2, the school population changed in favour of Asian, especially Pakistanis, as our fathers began to settle down in the city and call their wives and children to join them. It was during this phase that I arrived in the city, in 1970. According to the most recent data, we can see that Pakistani pupils had become the largest ethnic minority group, at 24.5%; second only to White British children.

Nationally, Pakistani children have also increased, as a proportion of the overall – from 2.7% of the pupil population in 2003 to 3.9% in 2013 (Strand, 2015).

For BSLC (2001), the success of minorities was linked to the prosperity of the city. "Education is one of the crucial means by which the city will develop the multi-cultural diversity agenda. However, the current educational experience of large sections of the minority ethnic communities is likely to impede real progress" (p. 17). With reference to Pakistani pupils, Birmingham local authority has been aware, since 1993, of their low levels of achievement, given their own data (Table 1.3).

The question that arises is whether enough has been done to remedy the situation. Latterly, the local authority has acknowledged that Pakistani pupils were one of the largest ethnic groups, so any improvements in their attainment

Table 1.2 Percentage of pupils in Birmingham schools from the top two ethnic groups; 1995, 2005, 2011

Ethnicity	1995	2005	2011
White British	60.2	51.0	37.9
Pakistani	16.7	18.9	24.5

Source: (BCC, 1995, 2005, 2011)

Table 1.3 GCSE results in Birmingham by ethnicity, 1993

Ethnic group	5 or more A–C grades	Above/below city average
White	32.9%	+3.4%
Pakistani	17.1%	−12.4%

Source: (BCC, 1993)

would have significant impact on Birmingham's overall performance. It was reported that, of the "6900 students not achieving 5 A*-C including English and maths, last year, 3100 were White British and 1300 were Pakistani heritage" (BCC, 2009, p. 2). Significantly, for the Pakistanis, the report pointed out that not only were they the largest non-White group, at 22%, the community was also much younger on average than the White British population and thus the "percentage of Pakistani heritage children attending Birmingham schools is increasing while the percentage of White British children is decreasing"(p. 2). This can be seen from the data in Table 1.4, which shows that the Pakistani proportion, as a percentage of those not achieving the benchmark qualifications, had actually increased. In 2006, the proportion was 18.6% but, by 2012, it had increased to 22.9%. While there was a continuing percentage improvement for the Pakistani pupils, the actual numbers of them leaving school without the benchmark qualifications only reduced marginally: from 1377 in 2006 to 1133 in 2012. The explanation for this can be found in the growth in numbers of Pakistani pupils in the city schools: 27,123 in 1995 and 42,558 in 2011 (BCC, 1995, 2011).

Table 1.4 Percentage of Birmingham pupils (overall and Pakistani) not achieving 5A*–C at GCSE, 2006–2012

	2006	2007	2008	2009	2010	2011	2012	Total
LA	7,388	7,384	6,996	6,428	5,566	5,110	4,934	43,806
	(59%)	(58%)	(55%)	(52%)	(45%)	(42%)	(40%)	
Pakistani	1,377	1,353	1,351	1,450	1,194	1,152	1,133	9,010
	(68%)	(64%)	(60%)	(58%)	(48%)	(46%)	(44%)	
Pakistanis as a proportion of the LA figures	18.6%	18.3%	19.3%	22.5%	21.4%	22.5%	22.9%	

Source: BCC, 'Report to the Children and Education Overview and Scrutiny Committee/Cabinet', 26 January 2011 (Table 7c), 27 February 2013 (Table 7d).

Pakistani boys; a particular problem

Attention has been drawn to the particularly low levels of attainment by Pakistani boys in Birmingham (Hewer, 2001; Warren & Gillborn, 2004). Early on, the matter had been brought to the attention of the local authority by the Pakistan Forum, a body that was concerned with representing the views and concerns of

Table 1.5 Birmingham Pakistani boys and girls achieving five or more A*–C at GCSE, 2006–2011

	2006	*2007*	*2008*	*2009*	*2010*	*2011*
Pakistani boys	29	33	35	37	47	50
Pakistani girls	35	39	45	48	57	58
Gap (between boys and girls)	6	6	10	11	10	8

Source: Scrutiny Report (BCC, 2008, 2013).

the Pakistani–Birmingham community (Akhtar, 1996). Later, the authority had acknowledged the problem: "By the end of key stage 4 over the last three years (1995–97) Pakistani boys achieving 5 or more A–C grades have remained 'stuck' on 20%.... The average for all boys is 30%" (BCC, 1998, p. 8).

According to the most recent data, it can be seen (Table 1.5) that, as a norm, Pakistani boys' achievement was generally behind that of Pakistani girls. Between 2006 and 2011 there was an average gap between them of 8.5%.

Education of minorities; policy responses

It is important to learn from the different phases of education of minorities (Parker-Jenkins et al., 2004; Race, 2005; Tomlinson, 2008). The first, 'do-nothing', phase (Tikly et al., 2005) operated within the wider social context of hostility and resentment towards the migrants (Dummett, 1984; Hiro, 1991). This was followed up by an emphasis on teaching immigrant children literacy and numeracy. Next came multicultural and the anti-racist education (Gill et al., 1992). The government's own comprehensive Swann Report (1985) summed up the situation thus: "central Government appears to have lacked a coherent strategy for fostering the development of multicultural education" (p. 220). However, the particular situation of groups such as Pakistanis was not about to get any better as the government policy shifted to the needs of "*all* (my emphasis) children, irrespective of race, colour or ethnic origin" as stated by the then Secretary of State for Education, Keith Joseph in his foreword to the Swann Report. This was an early example of a 'colour-blind' policy which would disregard differences in background of the pupils; something that would become more of a norm under the Coalition government, which came into power in 2010.

Later, Modood and May (2001) pointed out that there was little support, nationally for multicultural education, which they saw as being "patchily experimented with by some local authorities and schools" (p. 308). This was a particular problem towards the end of the century. Jenkins et al. (2004), in their research for the Teacher Training Agency (TTA), found that whilst there were many studies on equal opportunities, race and education in the 1980s and early 1990s, the post-1995 period revealed far fewer such studies. With some exceptions – the *Aiming High* strategy (DFES, 2003), which identified the characteristics of the successful school in tackling underachievement – from here onwards power and influence began to transfer to central government and schools directly (Brighouse, 2002), leading to a deprioritisation of local initiatives which had previously supported multicultural education. This was confirmed by Ollerearnshaw et al. (2003) in a report on the equality commitment of public sector organisations. I was part of their team of researchers and had investigated the situation in schools. Ofsted also began to ignore race equality in their inspections (Tikly et al., 2005).

Policy neglect of Pakistanis

It is necessary to point out that Pakistanis have been disadvantaged in much of the post-war policymaking related to ethnic diversity. In Britain, according to Modood (2012), "virtually nobody, policymakers, the media, or academics, talked about Muslims until the late 1980s, the time of the Salman Rushdie affair" (p. 49). For Muslims we can read Pakistanis, given that almost all follow Islam as their religion.

When it comes to race and education much of the attention has been focused on African Caribbean young people. According to Gillborn (2008a) this partly reflected the Black community's history of higher profile political mobilisation. In their government-commissioned report, Taylor and Hegarty (1985) had reported that Black parents "often vociferously complained about their children's educational experience" (p. 4) while pointing out that no such concerns were being expressed by the Asian parents. One expression of the Black demands was the publication of the pamphlet by Coard (1971), about how the West Indian child had been made educationally subnormal in the British education system.

The concerns of the Black community were recognised by the government, which led to a national policy debate on educational underachievement but one which "prioritized African Caribbean experience" (Modood & May, 2001, p. 310) as exemplified by the Swann Report (1985) and its predecessor, the Rampton Report (1981). Parekh (1992), who had contributed to the Swann Report, pointed out how the Committee's African Caribbean members were able to influence its work in favour of their own community; the Asians were not able to exert similar pressure. The 'prioritisation' of Black Caribbean pupils can also be seen in the publication of a number of government publications (DFES, 2004b; NCSL, 2004; DFES, 2005; Tikly et al., 2006; DFES, 2007; DCSF, 2009). There were a number of other, non-governmental, publications with the same focus (McKenley et al., 2003; LDA, 2004; Demie et al., 2006; Tomlin, 2006).

The needs of Pakistanis continued to be ignored, as acknowledged in a government report (Coles & Chilvers, 2004). "Over the years there has been almost no research regarding the position of Muslim pupils in the education system. Nor has there been much research concerning the dominant cultural groups that make up the Muslim communities, like Pakistani ... pupils" (p. 61). According to the authors, a system that relied on the enthusiasm of individual schools, teachers or LEAs (local education authorities) would not produce an effective curriculum reflecting the experiences and heritage of Muslim pupils. In their review for the TTA (Teacher Training Agency), most of the studies unearthed by Parker-Jenkins et al. (2004) were concerned with ethnicity rather than religion, which meant the exclusion of Pakistanis for whom religion was very important. The review recommended that more research should be conducted on the role of religion.

One possible reason for the exclusion of Pakistanis was the predication of policy on political blackness, which 'silenced' Asian communities (Hall, 1991). Modood (1998) pointed out that, unlike the Black Caribbean community for whom skin colour was prominent in the self-description of their identity, for South Asians it was their religion that had such prominence. He pointed out that this thinking was widely prevalent "as is reflected in virtually all CRE publications, local authorities' race discourse, academic texts, the 'quality' press, radio and television, as well as in documents of most central government departments and many large employers" (p. 47). For a period Birmingham also used 'black' to mean all ethnic minorities, including the label 'Black Asian' (BCC, 1996, 1997).

There was occasional focus on Pakistani pupils (DFES, 2003). DCSF (2008)[6] was particularly notable in this respect and may provide a model in the context of this study. Given that the majority of the pupils covered were from a Muslim background, the document was significant in its recognition of, and references to, religion:

- Characteristics of inclusive schools: to include a culture of mutual respect for pupils' cultures, religions and languages reflected in the school's curriculum.
- Identity and respect: leading to pupils experiencing a greater sense of belonging. Emphasis is placed on the development of staff and pupils' awareness of Islamic heritage as well as Islamophobia (Lopez, 2011) and racism.
- An inclusive curriculum: so pupils could see their cultural and religious heritages, histories and languages reflected in the curriculum. Examples were provided such as the inclusion of Muslim contribution to European learning and using Islamic content such as teaching calligraphy, mathematics, design technology, music and art.

The document stressed the positive potential of pupils' religion in raising their attainment. This can "contribute significantly to the moral climate of a school, encouraging high standards of respect and behaviour which are upheld by the religious belief systems of pupils' families" (p. 16). The document showed that, out of all groups, their religion was the most important for Pakistani pupils. Earlier, the government Swann Report (1985) had recommended that schools needed to do far more

> to respond to the pastoral needs of Muslim pupils, to ensure that there is a real respect and understanding by both teachers and parents of each other's

concerns and that the demands of the school place no child in fundamental conflict with the requirements of his faith.

(pp. 773–774)

Richardson and Wood (2004) explored the key factors underlying the success of British Pakistani learners, especially those of Kashmiri heritage. It pointed out how schools could capitalise on the pupils' diverse language skills, stressed the significance of home-school relationships and identified the implications for CPD.

At least on one occasion there appeared to be a deliberate neglect of Pakistanis. In a government report, Strand et al. (2010) pointed out that there was a particular problem with underachievement of Pakistani boys. "A slightly larger gap remains for Bangladeshi boys in comparison to White British boys (56.0% vs. 59.5%). However this gap is small compared to that between White British and Pakistani boys" (p. 65). For the Pakistanis, it was accepted that "they are an ethnic group with much in common with Bangladeshi students so some tables also include Pakistani students as a further comparison group" (p. 68). The data underlying their report (Table 1.6) removed any doubt that Pakistani attainment was low when compared with White British, even lower than Bangladeshi pupils. As to trends,[7] they presented data from 1991[8] to 2006, which showed the consistently low attainment of Pakistanis compared with White British. There was a particular problem with the low attainment of Pakistani boys when compared with White British boys.

In spite of this being the case, Pakistani children were left out of the analysis and subsequent discussion in the report, which had, as its focus, only pupils of Bangladeshi, Somali and Turkish heritage. Strand was my PhD supervisor, so I was able to investigate this matter during our meetings and have the information confirmed in emails. He (Strand, 2014b) explained to me that the Government was explicit that they did NOT (original emphasis) want Pakistanis to be included in the report. "They got anxious in case the underachievement was seen as a *Muslim* (original emphasis) problem; they got cold feet". Elsewhere, during a general query from me, he volunteered a comment on the situation in an email,: "It was the LSYPE 2007 rather than the drivers report that said the most about Supp School I think though worth checking the drivers, . . . but I was not allowed to talk about Pakistani pupils . . . only Turkish, Bangladeshi & Somali" (Strand, 2016). This would appear to be a case of a government attempt to massage the figures by deliberately leaving out the most underachieving group, the Pakistanis.

Table 1.6 Public exam results at age 16 by ethnic group (Strand et al. 2010, Table 24, p. 69)

Ethnic group	5 GCSEs A*–C	5 GCSEs A*–C inc English and Maths
White British	59%	48%
Bangladeshi	58%	41%
Pakistani	53%	40%

The Birmingham response to minority pupils

To respond to the education needs of its newly arriving minority pupils, Birmingham set up a department for the teaching of EAL (Rose et al., 1969; BABP, undated), including two Reception Centres for intensive English teaching. Upon arrival in the city as a 12-year-old, I attended one of these centres. The authority was also the first to issue guidance on the teaching of world religions (Cox, 1976). By the early 1980s, Birmingham had established a Multicultural Support Service. This was where I began my teaching career, in 1983.

Later, the LA published a strategy for underachieving groups, which included Pakistanis. It established two achievement groups – one for Asian and the other for African Caribbean pupils – with associated achievement plans (BCC, 2003, 2003a). The groups included, as members, head teachers, local authority advisers and members of minority communities. The strategy had the expressed aim to 'close the gap.' It set out "a planned reduction of 5% per annum of 'the equality gap' that exists between these groups and the overall averages. This was to be achieved by *differential* (my emphasis) target setting for individual schools" (BCC, 2002, p. 2).

The plans described underachievement as a 'systemic phenomenon'.[9] "Asian Heritage young people underachieve because they are educated in an education system . . . which exhibits aspects of racism" (BCC, 2004, p. 2). The plans committed the local authority to work with schools "as an external change agent", to provide services to underachieving groups and by providing strategic leadership and management in the city. Around this time Birmingham had set up its own Stephen Lawrence Inquiry. This had identified institutional racism in the city. In response the local authority devised policies to address racism within the provision of education, something that was highly commended by Ofsted (Holmwood & O'Toole, 2017). Birmingham was unusual among local education authorities, as Ofsted acknowledged, in collecting data relating to the differing performance of pupils from their different heritages, socio-economic groups and gender, which was effective in monitoring performance and directing support. An Ofsted report on the performance of the LEA in 2002 rated Birmingham's achievements as outstanding. It commented that:

> the LEA has done much, with its schools, to overcome the educational effects of this high degree of disadvantage. Since 1997, the attainment of pupils has risen at almost all levels at a rate faster than the national average. . . . (Birmingham) is one of a very small number of LEAs which stand as an example to all others of what can be done, even in the most demanding urban environments.
>
> (Holmwood & O'Toole, 2017, p. 133)

Similar to the national situation, Birmingham also prioritised the needs of African Caribbean pupils, as shown by its production of numerous reports (BCC, 2000; BCC, 2003b; Walker & Brown, 2000; Tomlin & Hatcher,

2002; Bean & Cham, 2003; Wisdom, 2006). This work was acknowledged by Ofsted (2002, para 149) who had cited examples of initiatives such as mentoring, Black History Month and a science club for African Caribbean pupils. This particular focus was in response to the activism of the local Black Caribbean parents (Warren & Gillborn, 2004). "No comparable influence by other communities was brought to our attention" (p. 53). Grosvenor (1997, p. 150) had similarly found the Caribbean community as 'confrontational', 'disrespectful' (of authority) who 'complained vociferously' and wanted equality with White people. They were able to articulate their case to the local authority in a way which was difficult to ignore (Newton, 1976). An illustration of this was provided by Brighouse (2008). He talked about a meeting he attended, as the Chief Education Officer, with the African Caribbean community. He referred to it as a 'baptism of fire':

> The hall was full of 300 or so people from the African–Caribbean community. All were angry. All felt let down by the education system. Most were in despair. It was difficult not to be defensive and almost impossible to persuade them that I would or could contribute anything.

For Newton (1976), the political system does not respond equally to different groups; some they are forced to respond to while others they can ignore without any cost. "The formal arrangements of liberal democracy ... do not ensure that each and every voice, or each and every interest is attended to with equal care, or that all voices are heard in the first place" (p. 236). As a consequence, "the system responds differentially to different interests according to the strength with which they can press their case" (p. 235). Later, he points out that when "interests are not articulated at all clearly or powerfully, decision-makers may be completely oblivious of them and quite unable to take them into account" (p. 237).

Unlike the African Caribbean community, Pakistanis generally did not participate in 'the politics of protest' (Dench, 1986, pp. 172–173) which meant their case has not been properly articulated or, in Newton's words, was "neglected, overlooked, ignored or denied" (p. 236). Pakistanis continued to be poorly represented at policy level. For example, when Birmingham Race Action Partnership (BRAP), the body whose role it was to promote equality for all groups in the city, was invited to give evidence on educational under-achievement in Birmingham to the Select Committee on Education and Skills, (House of Commons, 2002), its chief officer, Joy Warmington, reported that Bangladeshi pupils were the main underachieving group, making no mention of Pakistanis. Consequently, in Birmingham, there was a belief expressed that the problem of Pakistani underachievement would sort itself. "Pakistani pupils will soon show rapid improvement as generational factors work through" (BSLC, 2001, p. 17).

There was occasional focus on Pakistani pupils (Rashid et al., 2005; BCC, 2009; BCC, 2010), including in partnership between the LA and the local

Anjuman Taraqqi-e-Urdu, Society for the Advancement of Urdu, in order to facilitate Urdu teaching.

By the time I left my post as Adviser, in 2011, much of the LA's equality-related work in education had ceased and the Black and Pakistani staff, who would normally lead on such initiatives, were made redundant in response to funding cuts, leaving a handful of mainly White staff in post. While the Council's Scrutiny Committee continued to receive reports (BCC, 2013) on who was underachieving in the local schools, beyond this, the authority appeared to lack the resources to take any action as schools now controlled much of the funding.

Back to colour-blind education policy

From the turn of the century the work in Birmingham generally began to take a colour-blind approach. Warren and Gillborn (2004) pointed out that

> school improvement and effectiveness does not necessarily embody a meaningful concern with race equality. Research elsewhere (and Birmingham's own recent statistics) suggest that pursuing "effectiveness" without a conscious and explicit focus on race equality will not narrow the "equality gap".
>
> (p. 49)

Indeed, Gillborn (2008b) has argued that unless a policy is consciously designed to challenge race inequalities, it is likely to reinforce those inequalities (p. 244). In his case study of Birmingham, Newton (1976) explained that a 'neutral' policy meant that discriminatory practices were given free rein. Warren and Gillborn (2004) also drew attention to an 'implementation gap'. While the authority has made a bold and important commitment to closing the existing 'equality gap', its schools are equally dominated by national initiatives and professional concerns and who have "promoted 'improvement' strategies that are known to detrimentally affect minority ethnic pupils" (p. 60).

Towards the end of my time as a Schools' Adviser with Birmingham I had been informed by senior colleagues that it was unnecessary to take targeted and differentiated approaches to addressing needs of particular underachieving groups. This had resulted from the policies of the then Coalition Government. In an email communication (Overington, 2012), I was informed that the "Coalition Government believes that every child can succeed with the right support and that no barrier should ever be allowed to hold a child back from fulfilling their potential". It was pointed out that, unlike the previous Government, who had developed a number of centrally driven, targeted interventions for Black and minority ethnic pupils – including one aimed specifically at raising the attainment of Pakistani, Bangladeshi, Somali and Turkish Heritage pupils[10] – the current Government's approach to tackling inequality involved moving away from "treating people as groups or 'equality strands' in need of special treatment". Instead, the Government intended to act as a "catalyst for change by developing frameworks that will help create fairness and opportunities for *everyone* (my emphasis)". It was further pointed out that teachers and head teachers would take a stronger lead in tackling the underperformance of disadvantaged and vulnerable pupils.

The 'de-racialised' (Troyna, 1994) approach on educational inequalities is premised on the assumption that all pupils have the same contextual backgrounds and needs and omits issues such as ethnicity or racism from educational discourse and, instead, relies on the ethnocentric 'everyday world' of teachers. For Gillborn (1997) adopting such discourse removes from the policy agenda concerns for ethnic inequalities of achievement and opportunity. For Crozier (1999), this leads to ignoring the unequal terrain upon which different young people experience their education. "It also implies that all children are the same, with the same needs and desires … it ignores the heterogeneity of society … and thus provides a justification for ignoring the politics of difference" (p. 86).

In their evaluation of Aiming High, a government education initiative, Tikly et al.(2006) pointed out that colour-blind ethos within schools had acted as a barrier to what was being implemented. Gillborn (2008b) explained that the colour-blind approach in education policy led to institutional racism.[11] "Because of the existing race inequalities in society, and because of the racist assumptions that most Whites bring into school, every single education policy is likely to impact on minoritized groups differently" (p. 244). Policies are, therefore, likely to have a disproportionately negative impact on particular groups, such as Pakistani students. He goes on to point out that unless a policy is consciously interrogated for race equality impacts, it is likely to disadvantage minorities. This view was supported by the government. Its education department (DfEE, 2000) pointed out: "A colour blind approach can mean that factors important to the education of minority group pupils are overlooked" (p. 24). The importance of treating children *differently* was also stressed by the TTA (2000). It had advised ITT (initial teacher training) providers to enable teacher trainees to develop their understanding of the importance of an inclusive curriculum:

> An inclusive education cannot be achieved by treating all pupils in the same way. To be effective, schooling has to take account of the often very varied life experiences, assumptions and interests of different pupils and different groups, including sometimes their differing responses to schooling itself.

Elsewhere, the guidance pointed out that not to acknowledge *difference* was racist, as it would encourage White children to think of their culture as superior and minority children to think they were "outside the 'norm' and therefore less acceptable and of less value" (p. 40).

As an illustration of the current colour-blind policy approach is the recent use of the umbrella 'Asian' category. use of the umbrella 'Asian' category. This hides Pakistani *underachievement* by including it with the higher achieving Indian pupils. Under the previous government (DCSF, 2007 – SFR/38) it was pointed out that "Pakistani pupils perform below the national average across all Key Stages" (p. 2). They were reported to be 9 percentage points behind the national average for 5+ A*–C grades at GCSE, including English and mathematics. A similar picture was presented later (DCSF, 2010 – SFR 34). Here, Pakistani pupils were reported to have an attainment gap of 7.8 percentage points. This was supported by Strand (2007) who pointed out that, alongside their Black and Bangladeshi counterparts, "Pakistani pupils consistently achieve lower examination scores than White British" (p. 13). Instead, under the Coalition government it has been reported (DfE, 2012 – SFR 03) that "Pupils from an Asian background performed above the national average" (p. 3). SFR 05 (DfE, 2014) and SFR 06 (DfE, 2015) make a similar statement.

The different systems of funding for minority pupils also help us to understand government approaches to educational policy. Under Section 11[12] local authorities were supported in their work with ethnic minority pupils. This was later rebranded as the Ethnic Minority Achievement Grant (EMAG), and its scope was widened to the raising of achievement of minority ethnic groups (Tikly et al., 2005). The funding was ring-fenced; to be spent specifically on the pupils concerned. A minimum of 85% of the funds were devolved to schools (Jones & Wallace, 2001; Arnot et al., 2014). DFES (2003) consulted LAs and then issued guidance (DFES, 2004a), advising LAs to embed minority underachievement within the school improvement systems. The guidance recommended that there should be clear strategies for enhancing the achievement of minority ethnic pupils and that this should be "undertaken in a context where issues of equality and diversity are central to the school's basic systems and processes" (p. 8). It encouraged the development of links between schools and their communities.

> In particular, sharing of experience and knowledge between mainstream and supplementary schools can bring significant and mutual benefits to both, e.g. through better cultural awareness, curriculum enrichment and coordinated support in and out of school that focuses on the needs of the child.
>
> (p. 11)

For a number of years Birmingham accessed substantial EMAG funding. In 2004, it amounted to £9,110,045 (BCC, 2004a). The centrally held part of this was spent on schemes such as the MERITT (Minority Ethnic Recruitment in Initial Teacher Training) scheme and raising achievement initiatives.

Under the Coalition government, EMAG was absorbed into the Dedicated School Grant (DSG). This was explained to me in an email (Overington, 2012):

> In relation to schools, Ministers are clear that teachers and headteachers should take a stronger lead in tackling the underperformance of disadvantaged and vulnerable pupils. That is why ... the Government decided to mainstream ... Ethnic Minority Achievement Grant – into schools' own

budgets. Schools now have the freedom to spend it themselves, in whichever way they feel will have the greatest effect.

Here it is worth pointing out that, in Wales, there has continued to be specific funding for ethnic minority children (Welsh Government, 2014, p. 2).

In order to respond to the needs of disadvantaged pupils, the Coalition Government decided to pay schools a Pupil Premium, on the basis of the numbers of free school meals (FSM) children. According to Chowdry et al. (2010), the FSM indicator was chosen because schools would not be able to manipulate it to gain a financial advantage. However, they pointed out that there are other indicators which could be considered, such as having EAL or belonging to a low-achieving ethnic group. Chowdry and Sibieta (2010) suggested that low attainment at KS2 was another possible lever to redirect funding towards secondary schools whose pupils were low achievers at primary school. According to Carpenter et al. (2013), some schools used their freedom to target pupils they deemed to be most in need, such as those who were EAL.

Notes

1 Saeed et al. (1999) discussed the issue of hyphenation in identity. They used the hyphenated identity label 'Pakistani-Scots' upon which I have based 'Pakistani-Birmingham'.
2 Also referred to as 'colour-blind' which is based on the assumption that differences such as racial, group membership do not make a difference to outcomes (Tarca, 2005; Bonilla-Silva, 2010). Such a belief among dominant White people can be traced to a lack of personal understanding about how race shapes life experiences – how it privileges some and disadvantages others. For Cose (1997), colour blindness is presented as a way of equalising race-related inequalities though in reality it acts as a 'silencer' – a way of quashing questions about the continuing racial stratification of the society. A related concept is 'de-racialised' (Crozier, 1999), explained later.
3 It is worth pointing out here that, alongside the aforementioned group of governors, there are now a growing number of second or third generation Pakistanis, who, having been brought up in the UK and educated here expect more from the education system. They are also capable of assertively and confidently articulating their views on governing bodies and in other situations.
4 The 17th Steve Biko Memorial Lecture at University of South Africa https://www.youtube.com/watch?v=_8t_qxgDF2o downloaded 2.3.2018
5 This was how Black Caribbeans were described at the time.
6 Significantly, this was archived by the Coalition government's DES and "not to be considered as government policy".
7 See Strand et al., 2010, Figure 4 (p. 64) and Figure 5 (p. 66). http://dera.ioe.ac.uk/828/1/DCSF-RR226.pdf.
8 Prior to this no distinction was made within the overall Asian group.
9 Described in these words: "the education system is not always as effective as it might be in meeting the needs of some learners. In particular, the curriculum does not always take account of the heritage, cultures and concerns of minority ethnic groups" (BCC, 2004a, p. 1).
10 I was referred to this resource on the following web link: www.education.gov.uk/schools/pupilsupport/inclusionandlearnersupport/mea/a0013246/ethnic-minority-achievement. However, on 8 January 2013, the resource was archived by the then current government. They had similarly done so with a wide range of resources which were produced by the out-going Labour government.

11 Defined by Macpherson (1999) as the collective failure of an organisation to provide an appropriate and professional service to people because of their colour, culture or ethnic origin. It can be seen or detected in processes, attitudes and behaviour which amount to discrimination through unwitting prejudice, ignorance, thoughtlessness and racist stereotyping which disadvantage minority ethnic people.

12 Of the Local Government Act 1966.

Bibliography

Abbas, T. (2010). The British Pakistani diaspora. *Orient* 2.

Abbas, T. & Anwar, M. (2005). An analysis of race equality policy and practice in the city of Birmingham. *Local Government Studies* 31(1) 53–68.

Akhtar, J. (1996). *Pakistanis in Britain in the 1990s and beyond.* Birmingham: Pakistan Forum.

Anwar, M. (1979). *The myth of return.* London: Heinemann.

Anwar, M. (1996). *British Pakistanis.* Warwick. CRER (Centre for Race and Ethnic Relations).

Arnot, M., Schneider, C., Evan, M., Liu, Y., Welply, O. & Davies-Tutt, D. (2014). *School approaches to the education of EAL students.* Cambridge: University of Cambridge.

Babar, K. (2015). The intellectual's intellectual. *The Friday Times,* 22 May.

BABP *(Building achievement for bilingual pupils).* (Undated). Birmingham City Council. Education Advisory Service.

Basit, T. (2013). Ethic, reflexivity and access in educational research: Issues in intergenerational investigation. *Research Papers in Education* 28(4) 506–517.

BCC. (1993). *Needs analysis for the three projects-detached duty project.* BCC. Education Department.

BCC. (1995). *Schools data.* BCC. Education Department.

BCC. (1996). *Equal opportunities in employment: Report of the Chief Education Officer.* BCC. Personnel Committee, 18 January.

BCC. (1997). *Summary of information on school based staff: Equal opportunities in employment annual report 1997.* BCC. Personnel and Staffing services.

BCC. (1998). *The achievement strategy for the city's four major underachieving groups.* BCC. Education Department.

BCC. (2000). *The way forward: Raising African Caribbean achievement in schools; conference report.* Birmingham City Council. Education Advisory Service.

BCC. (2002). *The fourth annual report on raising the achievement of pupils most at risk of underachieving (Education Development Plan Priority 4).* BCC. Education Department.

BCC. (2003). *Asian heritage achievement action plan: 19 December 2003 revision.* BCC. Education Department.

BCC. (2003a). *African Caribbean achievement action plan: 19 December 2003 revision.* BCC. Education Department.

BCC. (2003b). *Raising African Caribbean Achievement.*

BCC. (2004). *Action plans for African Caribbean and Asian heritage achievement – subject and brief summary of proposals.* BCC. Education Department.

BCC. (2004a). EMAG budget 2004/05 – allocations for 15% strategic initiatives. BCC. Education Department.

BCC. (2005). *Schools data.* BCC. Education Department.

BCC. (2008). *Examination and assessment results 2008.* BCC. Overview and Scrutiny Committee, 26 November.

BCC. (2009). *Raising the achievement of Pakistani and White disadvantaged children.* BCC. Report to the Children and Education Overview and Scrutiny Committee, 22 April.

BCC. (2010). *Raising the achievement of groups at risk of underachieving.* BCC. Report to the Children and Education Overview and Scrutiny Committee, 24 March.

BCC. (2011). *Schools data.* BCC. Education Department.

BCC. (2013). *Examination and Assessment Results 2012.* BCC. Overview and Scrutiny Committee, 27 February.

Bean, S. & Cham, M. (2003). *Young, gifted and Black-and that's a fact: The raising African Caribbean achievement project handbook for parents.* Birmingham City Council. Education Advisory Service.

Bonilla-Silva, E. (2010). *Racism without racists.* MD: Rowman & Littlefield.

Brighouse, T. (2002). The view of a participant during the second half: A perspective on LEAs since 1952. *Oxford Review of Education* 28(2–3) 187–196.

Brighouse, T. (2008). Hope has to be the new Black. *Times Educational Supplement,* 16 October.

BSLC (Birmingham Stephen Lawrence Commission). (2001). *Challenges for the future-race equality in Birmingham.* Birmingham City Council: Report of the Inquiry Commission.

Carpenter, H., Papps, I., Bragg, J., Dyson, A., Harris, H., Kerr, K., Todd, L. & Laing, K. (2013). *Evaluation of Pupil Premium Research Report, July 2013.* Department for Education.

Ceci, S. & Papierno, P. (2005). The rhetoric and reality of gap closing-when the 'have-nots' gain but the 'haves' gain even more. *American Psychologist* 60(2) 149–160.

Chowdry, H., Greaves, E. & Sibieta, L. (2010). *The pupil premium: Assessing the options.* London: Institute for Fiscal Studies.

Chowdry, H. & Sibieta, L. (2010). *Introducing a pupil premium: IFS researchers' response to government consultation on school funding arrangements.* London: Institute for Fiscal Studies.

Coard, B. (1971). *How the West Indian child is made educationally subnormal in the British school system: The scandal of the Black child in schools in Britain.* London: New Beacon Books.

Coles, M. & Chilvers, P. (2004). *Curriculum reflecting experience of African Caribbean and Muslim pupils.* Department for Education and Skills.

Cose, E. (1997). *Colour-blind.* New York: Harper Collins.

Cox, E. (1976). Does it do as it says? *Learning for Living* 15(4) 125–126.

Cox, G. (2001). *The causes of minority ethnic underrepresentation as school governors in East Birmingham.* East Birmingham *Plus* Parents Association.

Crozier, G. (1999). The Deracialisation of initial teacher training: Implications for social justice. *Race Ethnicity and Education* 2(1) 79–91.

Dahya, B. (1973). Pakistanis in Britain: Transients or settlers? *Race and Class* 14 241–277.

Demack, S., Drew, D. & Grimsley, M. (2000). Minding the gap: Ethnic, gender and social class differences in attainment at 16, 1988–95. *Race Ethnicity and Education* 3(2) 117–143.

Demie, F., Mclean, C. & Lewis, K. (2006). *The achievement of African heritage pupils: Good practice in Lambeth schools.* London: Lambeth Council.

Dench, G. (1986). *Minorities in the open society.* London: Routledge & Kegan Paul.

DCSF (Department for Children Schools and Families). (2007). *SFR 38/2007): First release: National curriculum assessment, GCSE equivalent attainment and post-16 attainment by pupil characteristics.* London: DCSF.

DCSF. (2008). *Raising the attainment of Pakistani, Bangladeshi, Somali, and Turkish heritage pupils: The national strategies: Secondary.* London: DCSF.

DCSF. (2009). *Gifted and talented Black pupils' achievement: Continuing Professional Development (CPD) module and briefing pack.* Nottingham: DCSF.

DCSF. (2010). *SFR 34/2009: Key stage 4 attainment by pupil characteristics, in England 2008/09.* London: DCSF.

DfE. (2011). *Teachers' Standards: Guidance for school leaders, school staff and governing bodies.* www.gov.uk/government/uploads/system/uploads/attachment_data/file/301107/Teachers__Standards.pdf Accessed 10.3.2016.

DfE. (2012). *SFR 03/2012: GCSE and equivalent attainment by pupil characteristics in England, 2010/11*. London: DfE.

DfE. (2014). *SFR 05/2014: GCSE and equivalent attainment by pupil characteristics in England, 2012/13*. London: DfE.

DfE. (2015). *SFR 06/2015: GCSE and equivalent attainment by pupil characteristics, 2013 to 2014 (revised)*. London: DfE.

DFEE. (2000). *Removing the barriers: Raising achievement levels for minority ethnic pupils*. London: DfEE.

DFES. (2003). *Aiming high: Raising the achievement of minority ethnic pupils*. London: DFES.

DFES. (2004a). *Aiming high: Supporting effective use of EMAG*. London: DFES.

DFES. (2004b). *Ensuring the attainment of Black boys: Key stage 3 national strategy*. Norwich: DFES.

DFES. (2005). *Ensuring the attainment of Black pupils: Secondary national strategy for school improvement*. Norwich: DFES.

DFES. (2006). *Ethnicity and education: The evidence on minority ethnic pupils aged 5–16*. London: DFES.

DFES. (2007). *Ensuring the attainment of Black pupils*. Nottingham: DFES.

Dorling, D. & Thomas, B. (2008). *A short report on plurality and the cities of Britain*. Birmingham: Barrow Cadbury Trust.

Dummett, A. (1984). *A portrait of English racism*. London: CARAF.

Gardner, J. (2011). Educational research: What (a) to do about impact! *British Educational Research Journal* 37(4) 543–561.

Gill, D., Mayor, B. & Blair, M. (1992). *Racism and education: Structures and strategies*. London: Sage Publications.

Gillborn, D. (1997). Racism and reform: New ethnicities/old inequalities? *British Educational Research Journal* 23(3) 345–360.

Gillborn, D. (2008a). *Racism and education: Coincidence or conspiracy?* London: Routledge.

Gillborn, D. (2008b). Coincidence or conspiracy? Whiteness, policy and the persistence of the Black/White achievement gap. *Educational Review* 60(3) 229–248.

Gillborn, D. & Gipps, C. (1996). *Recent research on the achievements of ethnic minority pupils*. London: Ofsted.

Gillborn, D. & Mirza, H. (2000). *Educational inequality*. London: Ofsted.

Grosvenor, I. (1997). *Assimilating identities*. London: Lawrence and Wishart.

Hall, S. (1991). Old and new identities, old and new ethnicities in King, A. (ed.) *Culture globalization and the world-system*. Binghamton: Macmillan.

Hewer, C. (2001). Schools for Muslims. *Oxford Review of Education* 27(4) 515–527.

Hiro, D. (1991). *Black British, White British*. London: Grafton books.

Holmwood, J. & O'Toole, T. (2017). *Countering extremism in British schools? The truth about the Birmingham Trojan Horse affair*. Bristol: Policy Press.

House of Commons. (2002). *Education in Birmingham*. The Stationery Office: Education and Skills Committee.

Iqbal, K. (2013). *Dear Birmingham*. Bloomingdale: Xlibris.

Jenkins, M., Hewitt, D., Brownhill, S. & Sanders, T. (2004). *What strategies can be used by initial teacher training providers, trainees and newly qualified teachers to raise the attainment of pupils from culturally diverse backgrounds?* EPPI-Centre University of London.

Jones, C. & Wallace, C. (2001). *Making EMAG work*. Stoke-on-Trent: Trentham Books.

Ladson-Billings, G. (2006). From the achievement gap to the education debt: Understanding achievement in U.S. *Educational Researcher* 35(7) 3–12.

LDA (London Development Agency). (2004). *The educational experiences and achievements of Black boys in London schools 2000–2003*. London: LDA.

Lopez, F. (2011). Towards a definition of Islamophobia: approximations of the early twentieth century. *Ethnic and Racial Studies*, 34(4) 556–573.

Macpherson Report (1999). *The Stephen Lawrence Inquiry.* London: TSO.

McKenley, J., Power, C., Ishani, L. & Demie, F. (2003). *Raising achievement of Black Caribbean pupils: Good practice in Lambeth schools.* London: Lambeth Council.

Modood, T. (1998). Anti-essentialism, multiculturalism and the 'recognition' of religious groups. *The Journal of Political Philosophy* 6(4) 378–399.

Modood, T. (2005). *Multicultural politics: Racism, ethnicity and Muslims in Britain.* Edinburg: Edinburgh University Press.

Modood, T. (2012). *Post-immigration 'difference' and integration: The case of Muslims in Western Europe.* London: British Academy Policy Centre.

Modood, T. & May, S. (2001). Multiculturalism and education in Britain: An internally contested debate. *International Journal of Educational Research* 35 305–317.

NCSL (National College for School Leadership). (2004). *The aiming high: African Caribbean achievement pilot project: Summary of leadership learning.* Nottingham: NCSL.

Newton, K. (1976). *Second city politics.* London: Clarendon Press.

Ofsted (2002). *Inspection of Birmingham Local Education Authority.* https://reports.ofsted.gov.uk/sites/default/files/documents/local_authority_reports/birmingham/012_Local%20Authority%20Inspection%20as%20pdf.pdf Downloaded 22.3.2018.

Ollerearnshaw, S., Walmsley, A., Jackson, J., Iqbal, K. & Schneider, R. (2003). *Towards racial equality: An evaluation of the public duty to promote race equality and good race relations in England and Wales (2002).* London: Commission for Racial Equality.

Overington, A. (2012). *Email from improving pupil performance division.* 2.7.2102. Reference: 2012/0007010.

Parekh, B. (1992). The hermeneutics of the Swann Report in Gill, D., Mayor, B. & Blair, M. (eds.) *Racism and education: Structures and strategies.* London: Sage Publications.

Parker-Jenkins, P., Hewitt, D., Sanders, T., Brownhill, S., Lall, R. & Keeling, J. (2004). *What strategies can be used by initial teacher training providers, trainees and newly qualified teachers to raise the attainment of pupils from culturally diverse backgrounds?* University of London.

Peach, C. (2006). Demographics of BrAsian settlement, 1951–2001 in Ali, N. (ed.) *A Postcolonial people: South Asians in Britain.* London. Hurst & Company.

Phillips, M. & Phillips, T. (1998). *Windrush: The irresistible rise of multiracial Britain.* London: Harper Collins.

Race, R. (2005). Analysing the historical evolution of ethnic education policy-making in England, 1965–2005. *Historical Social Research* 30(4) 176–190.

Rampton Report (1981). *West Indian Children in Our Schools.* http://www.educationengland.org.uk/documents/rampton/ Accessed 16.8.2016.

Rashid, N., Naz, I. & Hussain, M. (2005). *Raising achievement of Pakistani and Bangladeshi boys.* Birmingham City Council.

Rex, J. & Moore, R. (1967). *Race community and conflict.* London: Oxford University Press.

Richardson, R. & Wood, A. (2004). *The achievement of British Pakistani learners.* Stoke-on-Trent: Trentham Books.

Rose, E., Deakin, N., Abrams, M., Jackson, V., Peston, M., Vanags, A., Cohen, B., Gaitskell, J. & Ward, P. (1969). *Colour and citizenship.* London: Institute of Race Relations.

Saeed, A., Blain, N. & Forbes, D. (1999). New ethnic and national questions in Scotland: post-British identities among Glasgow Pakistani teenagers. *Ethnic and Racial Studies* 22(5) 821–844.Sivanandan, A. (1982). *A different hunger.* London: Pluto Press.

Steve S., de Coulon, A., Meschi, E., Vorhaus, J., Frumkin, L., Ivins, C., Small, L., Sood. A., Gervais, M-C., & Rehman, R. *Drivers and challenges in raising the achievement of pupils from*

Bangladeshi, Somali, and Turkish backgrounds. Research Report DCSF-RR226. http://dera.ioe.ac.uk/828/1/DCSF-RR226.pdf

Strand, S. (2007). *Minority ethnic pupils in the longitudinal study of young people in England.* London: DFES.

Strand, S. (2014a). Ethnicity, gender, social class and achievement gaps at age 16: Intersectionality and 'getting it' for the White working class. *Research Papers in Education* 29(2) 131–171.

Strand, S. (2014b). Personal email. 4 March.

Strand, S. (2015). *Ethnicity, deprivation and educational achievement at age 16 in England: Trends over time.* London: Department for Education.

Strand, S. (2016). Personal email. 1 February.

Strand, S., Coulon, A., Meschi, E., Vorhaus, J., Frumkin, L., Ivins, C., Small, L., Sood, A., Gervais, M. & Rehman, H. (2010). *Drivers and challenges in raising the achievement of pupils from Bangladeshi, Somali, and Turkish backgrounds.* London: DCSF.

Sutcliffe, A. & Smith, R. (1974). *Birmingham 1939–1970.* Oxford: Oxford University Press.

Swann Report. (1985). *Education for all.* London: HMSO.

Tackey, N., Casebourne, J., Aston, J., Ritchie, H., Sinclair, A., Tyres, C., Hurstfield, J., Willison, R. & Page, R. (2006). *Barriers to employment for Pakistanis and Bangladeshis in Britain.* London: Department of Work and Pensions.

Tarca, K. (2005). Colorblind in control: The risks of resisting difference amid demographic change. *Educational Studies* 38(2) 99–120.

Taylor, M. & Hegarty, S. (1985). *The best of both worlds . . .?* Berkshire: NFER-Nelson.

Tikly, L., Osler, A. & Hill, J. (2005). The ethnic minority achievement grant: A critical analysis. *Journal of Education Policy* 20(3) 283–312.

Tikly, L., Haynes, J. & Caballero, C. (2006). *Evaluation of aiming high: African Caribbean achievement project.* London: DFES.

Tomlin, C. (2006). *An analysis of high attaining Black students: Factors and conditions that affect their achievement levels.* London: Multiverse.

Tomlin, C. & Hatcher, R. (2002). *The personal and academic development of vulnerable African Caribbean pupils.* Birmingham: University of Central England.

Tomlinson, S. (2008). *Race and education.* Berkshire: Open University Press.

Troyna, B. (1994). The 'everyday world' of teachers? Deracialised discourses in the sociology of teachers and the teaching profession. *British Journal of Sociology of Education* 15(3) 325–339.

TTA (Teacher Training Agency). (2000). *Raising the attainment of minority ethnic pupils: Guidance and resource materials for providers of initial teacher training.* Surrey: TTA.

Vertovec, S. (2007). Super-diversity and its implications. *Ethnic and Racial Studies* 30(6) 1024–1054.

Walker, C. & Brown, G. (2000). *Raising African Caribbean achievement.* Birmingham City Council. Education Advisory Service.

Warren, S. & Gillborn, D. (2004). *Race equality and education in Birmingham.* Birmingham City Council and Birmingham Race Action Partnership.

Welsh Government. (2014). *Minority ethnic achievement in education in Wales.* Cardiff.

Winder, R. (2004). *Bloody foreigners.* London: Abacus.

Wisdom, P. (2006). *The context of African Caribbean education and employment in Birmingham: Research report.* Birmingham: Partnership for Achievement.

2   In the land of the Trojan Horse

Exclusion and consequences

For the media and the wider public the term 'Trojan Horse' has become synonymous with Muslim takeover of British schools in order to promote their own agenda. While initially centred on Birmingham, over time it has come to be seen as a wider problem that could surface across the UK towns and cities with a significant Muslim presence. This was as a result of events taking place mid-way during my doctoral research.

In November 2013, Birmingham city council received correspondence in the form of a photocopy letter. It appeared to be between Muslims who were attempting to takeover local schools with the aim of running them according to Islamic principles. The letter contained a strategy which was called 'Operation Trojan Horse'. It outlined a step-by-step guide on how to achieve the desired goals, beginning with identifying vulnerable schools where most of the pupils were Muslim. The next step involved encouraging agitation by a group of sympathetic parents for an Islamic agenda. It also involved putting in place additional governors with conservative Islamic beliefs and encouraging Muslim staff to disrupt the schools from within. Finally, the letter suggested steps to get rid of the current head teacher and replacing her/him with a more sympathetic person who would be supportive of the Islamic agenda.

The city council passed the letter to the Department for Education (DfE) and the Home Office. Soon after the letter was leaked to the media and began to give rise to headlines which spoke of 'Islamist plot' 'radical teachers' and 'extremist curriculum'. Like the media, the DfE and Ofsted, the inspection body, continued to behave as if the letter was real.

The letter mentioned six schools which were allegedly being targeted by the so-called Islamist activists. These were the following:

- Adderley School Primary
- Regents Park Community School Primary
- Park View (Academy) Secondary
- Saltley Specialist Science College Secondary

- Highfield School Primary
- Springfield School Primary

In response, the DfE ordered Ofsted to inspect five of the six schools. One, Springfield, had been spared this as the incident which was included in the Trojan letter about the school was supposed to have taken place over 20 years ago. In addition to the five schools, the inspections targeted 16 other schools. Their only 'crime' appeared to be that they served majority Muslim pupil populations. According to Holmwood and O'Toole (2017), of the 21 schools that were inspected by Ofsted, only 14 had had any allegations made against them. Three of the five which were subjected to full inspection had been recently inspected, with two being rated 'outstanding' (Park View and Oldknow) and one as 'good' (Saltley School). This was based on the significant increases in their pupils' attainments. When they were re-inspected after the Trojan allegations, they were downgraded to 'inadequate'. The pretext for this was their poor 'safeguarding' and 'leadership and management' practices.

The Trojan effect had gone further than Birmingham. Ofsted conducted a number of unannounced inspections of other schools in areas of the UK which had a significant Muslim population. In particular, five schools were inspected in the Tower Hamlets area of East London, which had a majority Bangladeshi Muslim population (Adams, 2014).

According to Miah (2017), the way the inspections were ordered and conducted made it clear that the Trojan letter was being used by the government to fulfil a broader agenda in relation to its Muslim communities. He pointed out that the inspections were not focused on the quality of teaching and learning, nor on children's safety and well-being, but on security matters. He cited the inspection of Golden Hillock School as evidence. During their inspection of the school, alongside interviewing pupils, teachers and governors, Ofsted interviewed the local police and members of the Prevent Team. More generally for him Ofsted reports simply redefined extremism to equate with Muslim cultural conservatism. Holmwood and O'Toole (2017) also supported this view and pointed out that the 'Trojan Horse affair' had been used by the government to indicate the need for its new counter-extremism strategy.

Upon conducting all the inspections Ofsted concluded that there was no evidence of extremism. This was confirmed by the Head of Ofsted, Michael Wilshaw, when he appeared in front of the House of Commons Education Committee:

> We did not see extremism in schools. What we did see was the promotion of a culture that would, if that culture continued, have made the children in those schools vulnerable to extremism because of [...] the disconnection from wider society and cultural isolation.
>
> (House of Commons, 2015, p. 6)

Parallel lives; by choice or circumstance?

The 'disconnection from wider society' and 'cultural isolation' have been long-standing gripes of liberal society against Muslims. These were first raised by the Cantle Report (2001), published after the riots in a number of Northern British communities. He had coined the phrase 'parallel lives'. The accusatory finger was pointed clearly at the Pakistani communities who were seen to self-segregate and be culturally isolated. It is worth pointing out here that, while there may be segregation of communities, the problem cannot be understood ahistorically and without considering its context. The segregation was not a problem necessarily of the Pakistani community's making. Its origins lay in the historical development of communities following the post-war migration to places such as Birmingham (Iqbal, 2013). For Sivanandan (1982) racism played a critical part in the process. Newly arriving communities, such as the Pakistanis, were welcome in many areas of the city for their labour but not as neighbours. There were other contributory factors too. For example, council houses, in the mainly white areas, were often not available to the incoming migrants due to the five-year rule of residence. In addition, there was the tradition amongst minorities to own their place of residence, rather than live in rented accommodation. In order to achieve this, many found it easier to buy houses in inner city 'immigrant' areas where properties were affordable. The few who did try to venture out to the mainly white areas were discouraged by estate agents who refused to sell them the property in question. Another factor that inadvertently contributed to the segregation in the city's communities was the practice by the mainly white schools and their parents to keep their communities separate from the immigrant areas. This was one reason why Birmingham as a local authority had not implemented the 'bussing' policy[1] (Sutcliffe & Smith, 1974). Some of the segregation continues to this day, not just due to the behaviour of Pakistanis or Muslims generally. During my research on the educational achievement of the White working class in Birmingham, I recall suggesting to the Head Teacher of an Outer Ring school that he should consider twinning his mainly White school. Before I had the chance of saying who with, he said, "as long as we don't have to link up with one of those schools in Saltley or Sparkhill – mainly Pakistani areas" (Iqbal, 2013, p. 120). I said nothing since that is exactly what I had in mind; thinking that both sets of school communities would equally benefit from such a relationship.

Early warnings of Trojan Horse

Boyes was seen as a central character in the Trojan Horse affair. He is an educationalist with many years of experience in Birmingham schools, many of which were located in Pakistani communities. A few years before the affair became known as such he had made a presentation to the DfE (2015). At the time he was the head of Queensbridge School and had been asked to take-over Moseley School where there were a number of problems involving the school governors. The starting point of his presentation was what he described as the preconditions for school-community disconnect. These were weak leadership, low standards and school community disconnect. He accepted that there was a lot wrong in some of the schools and parents were justified in complaining. In his view some head teachers had not paid enough attention to the standards agenda; something that the government had wanted and also what the parents had wanted. He cited the example of Moseley School where, in 2008, 74% of the children had not achieved the benchmark qualification of 5 A*–C at GCSE. He also spoke of Golden Hillock School where the head had not paid "enough attention to the standards agenda. This was what the government wanted and what the parents wanted".

This clearly added fuel to the fire amongst some of the parents. He explained that his motivation in the presentation was not to point a finger at key individuals in the Pakistani community. "My number one issue was that education policy was out of touch with places such as Birmingham" (Boyes, 2018). In this he agreed with Tahir Alam (2015) for whom the missing link in Birmingham education was the community where "the schools operate as 'islands', run by commuter teachers". In his interview with me, Boyes confirmed the 'broader agenda' in these words: "To the Secretary of State, Michael Gove, and to Michael Wilshaw" (Head of Ofsted), Birmingham is only about Trojan Horse even still. And that is not because of Tahir Alam (Abbas, 2017) but because of Paris and Islamic State. Elsewhere, he pointed out that Trojan Horse "wasn't about Tahir Alam, it was about terrorism; Syria and Prevent. The Prevent agenda is huge". For him, Trojan Horse was also the focus of power games between Gove and Wilshaw, two macho men (he described it as 'willy waving'). "Trojan Horse is now a euphemism for any challenge from the Muslim community" (Boyes, 2016).

One section of Boyes' presentation was entitled 'Parallel Lives in Schools and Neighbourhoods'. He had spoken of 'declining white population' and 'highly segregated wards' with schools that were not properly preparing children for mainstream British life. According to the press reports the problem for such segregation lay with Muslim communities living in ghettoes (Oldham, 2014). Boyes had been reported as saying that Trojan Horse was not about Islamic extremism; "it is about schools unhelpfully locked into the closest parameters of their neighbourhoods". For Holmwood and O'Toole (2017), such 'parameters' are understood to be those of conservative values, self-segregation and deprivation. However, what was not reported was the possible response that could be made to this situation. Boyes explained that he had advocated greater capacity of local authorities to support schools. He explained that this was why he had started the Birmingham Education Partnership "so schools are not isolated and doing their own thing". In his view the monocultural nature of schools in particular neighbourhoods was a fundamental system problem; that was compounding underachievement, introspection and community narrowness. As a response Boyes suggested a programme for the linking of mainly white schools with those that are mainly Pakistani. "Such twinning needed to be a priority for the Department for Education who should facilitate the programme". In his presentation, Boyes had pointed out a lack of cultural competence amongst some Birmingham headteachers; his slide had said: "dynamic female head completely ill equipped from the shire". The head of a mainly Muslim school had come from Warwickshire. "She had only ever worked in white environments". He also warned about internationally funded Islamic activities. This was with reference to John Ray, a Birmingham community activist, though Boyes did admit to me that this was an area he knew the least about. "John would say that there are internationally funded activities that are much more serious ... but I don't know about that. I talked about John. I took with me copies of letters which John had written to Baroness Cox in the early 90s and John always had that kind of perspective". More broadly, for Boyes, the Trojan Horse affair was a clash of values between parents from Pakistan or Kashmir and the liberal education being offered in Birmingham. "If I was to describe some of the community attitudes and values that I saw in Diyaraan Mohra or in Sorakhi (areas of Kashmir he had visited some years ago) I wouldn't want my children in a state-funded school being governed by those kinds of attitudes". Summing up why he had made his presentation, Boyes said:

> my number one issue was that education policy wasn't understanding how communities and cities were working. That the segregation of schools, the monocultural nature of schools' neighbourhoods was a fundamental system problem, that was compounding underachievement and introspection and community narrowness and lack of mobility. That was number one.

Trojan reports

Within a few months of the letter being received by the city council, Michael Gove, Secretary of State for Education, ordered Peter Clarke to head an investigation into the Trojan horse allegations. This appointment of the former head of the Metropolitan police's counter-terrorism division removed any ambiguity about how the government viewed the Trojan affair. The decision received some criticism at the local Birmingham level. Sims, the Chief Constable of West Midlands (which covered Birmingham) warned of the potential damage to community relations. In his view the appointment would send the wrong signals to the Muslim community as they would draw 'unwarranted' conclusions from Clarke's former role as national co-ordinator for counter-terrorism (Pidd & Dodd, 2014).

Birmingham City Council ordered its own investigation into the affair. This was carried out by the educationalist, Ian Kershaw. He had been asked to coordinate his investigation with Clarke. As a result, relevant evidence was shared between them. Between them, Clarke and Kershaw interviewed more than 70 witnesses and generated more than 2,000 pages of transcripts. According to Holmwood and O'Toole (2017), both Clarke and Kershaw accepted the narrative of Trojan Horse, as if the letter was true.

The summative report on the Trojan Horse affair was the one produced by the House of Commons Education Committee (House of Commons, 2015). This was the result of receiving evidence from, amongst others, Clarke, Kershaw, Nicky Morgan (who was the new Secretary of State at the DfE) and, the Head of Ofsted, Michael Wilshaw. Like Ofsted, their report also concluded that there was no evidence of direct radicalisation or violent extremism. However, they did acknowledge that some people in positions of influence in Birmingham schools had a restricted and narrow interpretation of their faith (meaning Islam) and were not promoting British values.

The myth of Ofsted neutrality

Ofsted was established by the government in 1992 as an impartial body with the aim of inspecting and regulating the education sector. It is run by senior civil servants which is meant to protect it against political influences or biases. However, this independence was brought into question by the way the organisation behaved and how it was used by politicians, especially the DfE during the Trojan Horse affair.

The Key[2] is a trusted organisation in the education sector. Teachers and governors subscribe to it for reliable and up-to-date information. Soon after the Trojan Horse affair they conducted a survey amongst 1,180 school leaders on a range of education issues: 81% of their respondents stated that they would like to replace Ofsted with "a body independent of central government". McInerney, the editor of their in-house journal, *Schools Week*, was quoted as saying: "I suspect the desire for Ofsted to be 'independent' actually shows a disgruntlement with the way Ofsted has been used by politicians".[3] For Miah (2017) when politicians point out concerns about a school, as it had happened in relation to the 21 schools in the Trojan Horse affair, and Ofsted later finds it wanting, then there is the charge that politicians have used the inspection body for their own agenda. During a presentation at a seminar at the Centre for Research in Race and Education (14 February 2018), Miah reiterated this position and stated that Ofsted had gone beyond their core purpose of inspection and had instead assisted the government's own agenda in constructing a particular narrative on Muslims, schools and security.

A number of educationalists with deep knowledge of Birmingham expressed concern about Ofsted's role and failure to be impartial and independent.[4] This included a letter which had been signed by, amongst others, Sir Tim Brighouse who had been the Chief Education Officer in Birmingham for many years (Brighouse et al., 2014) In their view those conducting the inspections had been poorly prepared and had a pre-set agenda that called into question Ofsted's claim to be objective and professional.

Others have similarly questioned Ofsted's impartiality. MG Khan (2014), an academic who was the chair of the governing body at Saltley School, one of the Trojan Horse schools, pointed out that Ofsted was being used to destabilise governing bodies in Muslim majority schools "through snap inspections that would find these governing bodies unfit for governance, caricaturing them as driven by ideology rather than student needs". Arthur (2015), a Professor of Education from the University of Birmingham, also pointed out that Ofsted appeared to be open to political interference by government. Sudworth (2014)[5] is a religious activist in the inner city of Birmingham. He is an academic who is also a vicar within the Church of England covering the area of Sparkbrook, a mainly Muslim parish and where he chaired a mainly Muslim Church of England primary school. He has spoken of DfE politicising the Ofsted process with a pre-set agenda. "At grassroots, many school leaders feel that the process has been manipulated to achieve an ulterior end of exposing Islamisation of schools".

We can understand the role of Ofsted by looking at the example of two schools: Parkview and Oldknow. In 2012 Ofsted inspected Parkview and decided it was 'outstanding' under their new inspection guidelines. They singled out the school's excellent provision for social, moral, spiritual and cultural education. Soon after Michael Wilshaw, the head of Ofsted visited the school and said "you can see a good school as soon as you walk in" (Shackle, 2017). Following this a number of national newspapers published adulatory profiles of the school. Here it is interesting to note that, upon being appointed Chief Inspector in 2011, Wilshaw had made a speech where he had criticised local authorities that accepted low academic achievement, especially in schools in disadvantaged areas. He argued that good leadership by a head teacher supported by strong governors could produce dramatic improvement: exactly what had been accomplished at Park View (Holmwood & O'Toole, 2017).

Soon after, Park View became an academy. It set up the Park View Educational Trust. They now had greater autonomy and could decide the school's curricula. The academy programme had been introduced by Labour in 2000 and expanded by the government that followed. By 2013, there were 3,444 academies, all of them accountable not to the local authority but to the DfE. In 2012 Faraz was appointed Deputy Head at Nansen Primary, the feeder school for Park View. A few months later the school converted to academy status, joining the Park View Educational Trust. The Trust was run by a mixture of Muslims and non-Muslims: Tahir Alam, Monzoor Hussain, Hardeep Saini (who is Sikh) and Lindsey Clark. Within a few months of being established, the Trust was running two schools: Park View and Nansen. The following year it had been invited by the local authority and DfE to takeover a third school, Golden Hillock. Furthermore, at the time of the Trojan Horse scandal, the Trust had been approved to takeover two further schools.

Brighouse and others pointed out that it was:

> beyond belief that schools which were judged less than a year ago to be 'outstanding' are now widely reported as 'inadequate', despite having

the same curriculum, the same students, the same leadership and the same governing body.

(Adams, 2014a)

According to Holmwood and O'Toole (2017), this was the case with Park View school; that is, what was, following the alleged Trojan plot, seen as problematic had been commended in the earlier reports. This can be further illustrated by the case of Oldknow Academy. It was inspected on 16–17 January 2013 and given an outright 'outstanding' across the five areas of overall effectiveness, achievement of pupils, quality of teaching, behaviour and safety of pupils and leadership and management. The academy was re-inspected 7–8 April 2014. This time it was rated as 'inadequate' because of the failings in behaviour and safety of pupils and leadership and management. Presented in Table 2.1 are a few extracts, comparing the two inspection reports.

Table 2.1 Oldknow Academy; comparison of pre- and post-Trojan Horse affair Ofsted (2013, 2014) reports

Pre-Trojan Horse (2013)	*Post-Trojan Horse (2014)*
Contribution to pupils' spiritual, moral, social and cultural development	
The academy's contribution to pupils' spiritual, moral, social and cultural development is exceptionally good. The very wide range of different cultures is celebrated. . . . . . . the academy respects different faiths and cultures. . . . The academy is a friendly and racially harmonious place, where discrimination of any kind is not tolerated.	Pupils and staff are poorly equipped to understand, respond to or calculate risks associated with extreme or intolerant views. Leaders do not take sufficient action to prevent discriminatory language. . . . The academy does not meet the requirements of the Equality Act 2010. Plans are in place to train staff on all issues of equality. The curriculum is inadequate because it does not foster an appreciation of, and respect for, pupils' own or other cultures. It does not promote tolerance and harmony between different cultural traditions.
Safeguarding	
The academy has rigorous procedures to ensure that pupils are kept safe and that all newly appointed staff are suitable to work with children.	The academy's work to keep pupils safe is inadequate. The governing body does not give pupils' safety a high enough priority. They are unable to ensure that pupils are kept safe from any extreme or radical views they encounter.
Trip to Saudi Arabia	
The academy does all it can to remove any barriers to learning and to ensure that every pupil has equal opportunities to succeed. The large amount of pupil premium funding is used to . . . subsidise uniforms, trips and even large-scale trips, such as the ones to Saudi Arabia, to ensure that any pupil is able to participate.	Leaders have not assessed adequately the risks to pupils associated with trips, visitors and links with other institutions. For example, the academy has links with a school in Saudi Arabia but could not tell inspectors whether risk assessment had been carried out on the people or materials that pupils may come into contact with.

(Continued)

Table 2.1 (*Continued*)

Pre-Trojan Horse (2013)	Post-Trojan Horse (2014)
They feel they are fortunate to be in an academy which offers them opportunities such as the week-long visit for 40 pupils to participate in a trip to Saudi Arabia. For pupils who spoke to the inspectors, last year's trip had clearly been a life-changing experience.	Governors have used the academy's budget to subsidise a trip to Saudi Arabia for only Muslim staff and pupils. The choice of destination meant that pupils from other faiths were not able to join the trip. Governors who accompany the trip are paid for from the academy budget. Inspectors were told that in 2013 a relative of the academy's governor joined the trip from Pakistan without the necessary checks having been made.

The school farm

The very wide range of additional activities and extracurricular opportunities motivates the pupils and results in extremely positive attitudes towards school.... Pupils love the academy's farm and the opportunity to look after and interact with a range of animals from goats and rabbits to snakes and geckos.	The grounds of the academy are secure but parts are unkempt. Although fenced off, parts of the farm area are full of broken wooden furniture, fencing and overgrown vegetation.

Behaviour and safety of pupils

Behaviour and safety of pupils was seen as 'inadequate' even though the 2014 Ofsted report found:

- Pupils' behaviour is outstanding. They have highly positive attitudes to learning and are extremely proud of their achievements.
- They understand how to behave well and take a pleasure in doing so, in class and as they move around the building.
- Pupils are polite, respectful and courteous to their friends, to staff and visitors. They have a clear knowledge of what is expected of them and are keen to live up to the academy's high expectations.
- Exclusions are low.
- Parents who spoke to inspectors during the inspection were confident that their children are safe.
- Pupils report they feel safe and well cared for and know any adult will support them in times of need.

Leadership and management

Leadership and management were found to be 'inadequate', in 2014, in spite of:

- The academy's leaders and governors have high expectations for the pupils' academic achievement. They ensure that pupils are prepared very well, academically, for the next steps in their education.
- The monitoring of teaching and learning is regular and systematic. Governors receive regular reports on the quality of teaching and on the performance of all staff.
- The governing body holds the academy to account for the achievement of pupils and the quality of teaching. Governors are very aware of teachers' performance.
- Governors know how the pupil premium funding is spent and how well pupils for whom the academy receives the additional funding are doing. The academy's website lists a wide range of measures on which the funding is spent.

Inspectors noted the above average standards of education for children when they left the school at the end of Year 6. Pupils were reported as feeling safe in the academy.

Underachievement; a personal matter

In her review into Opportunity and Integration, Dame Louise Casey noted that "Discrimination and disadvantage was feeding a sense of grievance and unfairness, isolating communities from modern British society and all it has to offer" (Casey, 2016, p. 5). This is the general context for more specific concerns about educational underachievement. As well as Boyes, the question of standards being central to the Trojan Horse affair had been acknowledged by another senior Birmingham education practitioner. Chris Quinn was an Executive Head Teacher at the time of Trojan. She was later appointed as the Regional Schools Commissioner for the West Midlands. In an interview she acknowledged that "some of the demands made (by Muslim parents) were entirely reasonable and based on the premise that Pakistani Muslim children had previously been very poorly served by the city's schools" (Pidd, 2014).

Underachievement has been a long-standing concern of communities such as Pakistanis in Birmingham. During his time as Chief Education Officer in Birmingham (1993–2002) Sir Tim Brighouse regarded such underachievement amongst ethnic minority pupils as one of the most important issues of his tenure. It was an issue that Pakistani heritage parents had brought to his attention. They "were concerned about a range of schooling issues – in particular what they perceived, I discovered rightly, as low standards and expectations within some of the schools which their children were attending in east Birmingham" (Holmwood & O'Toole, 2017, p. 133). But then later such work had become deprioritised. For Abbas (2017a), the Trojan Horse affair was a case study of Muslim-minority experiences in relation to ethnic and religious identities in Britain. He pointed out that after 70 years of post-war immigration, Muslim-minority communities continue to face racism and discrimination which affected educational outcomes. For him education managers in Birmingham City Council had been

> complicit in overlooking the realities facing young Muslims in education over the years. Decade upon decade of underachievement, in particular for men, inevitably means that some enter into criminality, and even extremism. These schools were mismanaged, with aspirations of young people thwarted.

Here it is worth looking at how parents are sometimes seen by schools, especially those from a minority background who may challenge the school leaders. Raihani and Gurr (2011) undertook a case study of an Australian Islamic school's strategies to involve parents in their children's education. The findings showed three 'types' of parents. The 'silent' type had a passive relationship with the teachers whom they respected and who they deferred to as experts. The 'managed' type were perceived as a threat to teachers' professionalism and thus needed to be carefully managed. The 'activist' parents were fully engaged and saw decision-making in school as a joint venture between them and teachers as equals. For Lareau and Horvat (1999), the 'ideal' parent from a school's perspective is one who is positive but deferential. According to Warren et al. (2009), when working with parents, especially those from disadvantaged backgrounds, teachers can be guilty of exercising 'unilateral power' – power over the parents. It is possible that in Birmingham, there may have been a case of teachers trying to slot Pakistani parents into the 'silent' or 'managed' category but who, in reality saw themselves as 'activist'. Furthermore, for disadvantaged and less articulate Pakistani parents, teachers might be guilty of exercising unilateral power, instead of 'relational power' – power to get things done collectively. There is also the concept of 'storming parents' (Ranson et al., 2004); these are parents who feel strongly about the education of their children, especially where there has been a failing on the part of the school. Could it be that in the 'Trojan Horse' controversy schools and minority ethnic families saw things differently? Maybe they were travelling on 'parallel tracks' when it came to education priorities (Ran, 2001)?

Here it is worth looking at the concept of 'participation'. In 1969 Sherry Arnstein produced a 'ladder of participation'. Building on this, Wilcox (1994) has identified five stances which can be translated to the Trojan Horse context. It begins with one-way communication, where schools provide parents information. Second the school may occasionally consult with parents in order to seek their views. The third stance is where parents and schools decide together on matters of mutual concern. The fourth stance involves them acting together, and the fifth stance is where independent community action is supported. In my view all schools act on the first stance and some do so on the second, with the parents being 'passive recipients'. With the occasional tokenistic gesture, such as one or two parents being involved on the school governing bodies, this is as far as it goes, leaving some parents frustrated given that they want more. It is likely that some Birmingham Pakistani parents wanted to become 'active participants' in the education enterprise. They wanted to decide together with the schools on matters of importance to their children's education. With both parents and school leaders having a different conception of running education which, with hostile media and politicians, resulted in the situation described as the Trojan Horse affair.

And then there is the racial dimension! It is bad enough when schools' leaders are challenged by parents of their own ethnic and social class background. How much worse is it when a white head teacher is challenged by a middle-class and educated Pakistani parent? Archer (2010) pointed out that schools are more accepting of White parents' assertiveness than that which is expressed by minority ethnic parents. Alternatively, what about a Pakistani parent whose English is not sophisticated enough or who is not up on the English niceties of communication and appears to be quite pushy or aggressive? The work of Spivak (1988) has some relevance here. She asked "Can the subaltern speak?" Similarly, women in leadership often have a difficult time when they challenge stereotypes. Their behaviour may be interpreted as angry or emotional even when they report that they were not being so but were simply not deferential (AAUW, 2016). Maybe those Pakistani community activists accused of challenging school leaders were not expected to speak at all or to do so more deferentially? Was their assertive behaviour interpreted as aggressive and found too challenging? Another possibility is the likely conflict between how the (Pakistani) parents and the (mainly White) teachers perceived of their own and the other's status. If the parents thought of the teachers as 'public servant' who are there to serve and be accountable to the parents while the teachers thought they were superior, to the parents, because of their race or education then this could have been a possible source of conflict in their interaction.

For some of the current crop of Pakistani education activists, poor educational standards in the schools that serve their community is a personal matter. These are the schools they themselves attended and where their own children and the children of their wider family and community attend. We can see this from just two of the actors from Trojan Horse, individually and collectively as both knew each other. Razwan Faraz was one of the people who appeared in front of the professional conduct panel of the National College of Teaching and Leadership. He was a deputy head at Nansen School, located next door to Parkview School, which was seen as the epicentre of Trojan Horse. He had attended Golden Hillock School where low standards of education and poor exam results was the norm. It was quite common for fewer than 10% pupils to achieve 5 A*–C grades at GCSE. In an interview with Shackle (2017) Faraz spoke about the poor education he had been provided. He also pointed out a lack of coherence and continuity in his life. Home and school were separate worlds where the staff were mainly White and students mainly Pakistani. In 2004 his paths crossed with Tahir Alam, another community activist. According to Shackle (2017), Alam provided Faraz a role model. The encounter helped him to discover his passion for education. He became a governor at his old school, Golden Hillock, and began to challenge its poor educational standards. He questioned some of the old thinking of the school's teachers, especially their low expectation of Pakistani children. His journey as education practitioner continued when later he trained as a teacher. During this time he worked at Park View, where Alam was the chair of governors.

Tahir Alam had attended Parkview when it was known as Naseby School. Wanting to make a difference to education in his community Alam became involved as a governor, at a time when standards of education were poor. In an interview (Abbas, 2017) he pointed out:

> In Park View School ... when I became a governor in 1997, the results were just 4% (5+ GCSE A-C). This was a school that I went to myself as a pupil and I decided to get involved.
>
> (p. 6)

He saw there was a problem of low expectation by teachers, something he set out to change through revisions in the curriculum and by employing more competent staff. Shackle (2017) quoted Marius Felderhof, a theology professor at the University of Birmingham, who knew Alam very well. In his view Alam was "committed to improving the education of Pakistani boys in particular, because he thought the Pakistani community was being disadvantaged". Alam also had a belief that within education, children should not be expected to leave their faith or culture outside the school door. Therefore, in this school and others they took over later, they instigated inclusive practices such as accommodation of the Pakistani Muslim community's religion and culture:

> providing washing facilities, prayer facilities, conducting Islamic service for children in the morning, making special arrangements for children that are fasting during Ramadan . . . introducing community languages, for example Urdu and Arabic alongside Spanish and French.
>
> (Abbas, 2017, p. 7)

The schools empowered young Muslims to know their religious character.

> It equipped pupils to appreciate the depth and nuances of Islam, bestowing young people with the courage and wisdom to counter the narratives propounded by the likes of Islamic State.
>
> (Abbas, 2017, p. 14)

More broadly they practised a belief that poor schools create poor neighbourhoods, not that poor schools were a function of children coming from poor backgrounds. The school then hired Lindsey Clark, a non-Muslim head teacher. She and the governing body, led by Alam, worked to improve standards for each student through effective monitoring and tracking. The benchmark results improved and within a few years had gone up to 41%. The improvement continued and reached more than 70% by the end of the decade.

Throughout my time as Education Adviser for Birmingham City Council I was aware of Alam being employed within the authority's Governor Support Service. His role was to help increase governing body participation by ethnic minorities, especially Pakistanis and Muslims. Amongst the wider community too there were efforts to encourage greater diversity amongst teachers and school governors. Much of this happened during a time when the New Labour government, as a part of its Aiming High strategy, was committed to improving diversity in school staff and leadership. What was being implemented at Parkview was seen as positive and non-controversial. In 2007, in recognition for his work, Alam was invited to Downing Street to meet Tony Blair, the Prime Minister. Clark was also recognised for her work in transforming the school and was awarded an Order of British Empire.

Importance of religion

The role of religion appears to have been overlooked in understanding the Trojan Horse affair. We have been reminded that while there is a decline in religion in the population as a whole, there is an increase in religion amongst some ethnic minority groups, especially those in Birmingham (Iqbal, 2013; Holmwood & O'Toole, 2017). Arthur (2015) also pointed out that, while religion was something seen to be problematic in the context of secular liberalism, it was not unusual. He saw the problem to be the differential treatment of Muslims. "Muslim parents are not alone in questioning these processes in schools as many of Christian and Jewish faith share the concerns of Muslim parents about certain educational approaches and curriculum content" (p. 316).

Religion also played quite a significant role at Parkview. Soon after Alam's involvement as a governor the school applied for permission from the local Standing Committee on Religious Education (SACRE) so they could draw on Islamic values for their school's daily assembly. This is an option open for all schools if they wish to opt-out of the legal requirement to have a wholly or broadly Christian daily act of worship. The decision was based on the view that incorporating children's home culture into their school lives helps to create coherence and improves their behaviour and attainment. Religion also came into the school in other ways. Islamic texts were used in school assemblies to address a number of themes. Like a number of other Birmingham schools, Parkview accommodated the students' religious needs by making available a prayer room for them. The use of the facility was particularly noticeable on Fridays when an increasingly large number of students participated in the *Juma*, Friday congregational prayer. Even the school's critics acknowledged that religion served to create an ethos of hard work and a sense of community as Muslim teachers and students prayed together and shared a meal at the end of fasting during the Muslim month of Ramadan. These practices were all in line with government recommendations (DCSF, 2008).

System failure

For Brighouse (2014) a major contributory factor in the Trojan Horse affair was the broken system of school governance which had contributed to the situation in Birmingham. He pointed out that in his experience it is quite normal for school governors to misbehave. However, when they do so, usually their colleagues remind them of the respective roles of governors and school professionals. If they still continue with their agenda the local authority would step in, as had happened on a few occasions during his time as the chief education officer. The local authority would work with all the stakeholders to sensitively find a way forward that was the best for the interest of the children and the wider school community.

> As senior officers, with the help of local councillors and the Cabinet Member concerned, we would spend many evenings in schools, community venues and Balti houses seeking better understanding of the way forward with both governors and community members on the one hand and head-teachers on the other.

However, Brighouse pointed out that such a response was no longer possible. He cited two reasons for this. One was the cuts in local authority expenditure which meant that local authorities did not have the resources or the expertise to respond in this way. As a participant–observer in this process, I had first-hand knowledge of what was going on. As a result of these cuts I and a number of my colleagues were made redundant from our education roles. Some of us were those people who might have previously been called upon to intervene in malpractices in school governance. For Brighouse, the second problem arose out of the government's academisation programme. This took schools out of local authority control and handed it over to lay people and professionals. This, for him, created "an open season for lay people and professionals keen to pursue their own eccentric ideas about schooling". They work with like-minded people in their own networks. "When trust or governor vacancies occur, some perpetuate the very English tradition of inviting friends to join them". The key for him was not what happened but where. "When the community is white it doesn't cause much comment. In mono–ethnic east Birmingham, however, it is seen as a Muslim plot to expose pupils to an undefined 'extremism'". Brighouse laid the blame for Trojan Horse at the DfE. He reminded us that five of the six schools which were labelled as inadequate were academies. More specifically, he singled out the then Secretary of State for Education, Michael Gove, for his failure to use his powers to investigate what was going on in the schools in question, by sending in officials to governing body meetings. For Brighouse, such central control of education meant that communities such as Birmingham were being "treated as a colonial outpost of London". Both the Clarke and Kershaw reports had also identified the acdemisation programme as a contributory factor to the Trojan affair.

Trojan and its aftermath

Fast forward to 2017. One of the outcomes of the Trojan affair had been the decision by DfE's professional body, the National College for Teaching and Leadership to discipline Razwan Faraz, Lindsey Clark, Hardeep Saini and Monzoor and Arshad Hussain. However the case was dropped due to the failure of the government's lawyers to share crucial evidence from the Clarke inquiry. In the eyes of the disciplinary committee this had "brought the integrity of the process into disrepute". In total, 14 teachers had been charged. After four years and spending much public money all, except one, had had their cases overturned or dropped. The one teacher – the former acting head of Oldknow – has had any disciplinary charges upheld.

One thing that is clear from the Trojan Horse affair is how the media see Muslims. For Miah (2017) Muslim communities are seen as racialised outsiders and as folk–devils that display a moral panic. This is nothing new. For British Pakistanis this outsider status has always been a problem. In the Birmingham context the Pakistanis were already excluded from opportunities and centres of power (Iqbal, 2013). This was also true of the city's Muslims whose exclusion was acknowledged by Joly (1987).

So, while the debate continues in the Birmingham and wider Muslim community, how would I summarise the Trojan Horse affair? I believe I have been able to remain neutral throughout the Trojan Horse controversy. I have maintained relationships with a number of the key actors on both sides of the 'fence' – a term used by Boyes to describe the relationship between Birmingham schools and the Pakistani Muslim community. This included some of the people who were charged with wrongdoings.

So was there any substance to the Trojan Horse grievances that Boyes and others had spoken of? Salma Yaqoob (2014), a long-standing Birmingham community activist, is on record accepting some of the criticism from the Clarke report which had pointed out that a number of individuals were involved in promoting an intolerant Islamic ethos in some of the schools. For her there should be no place in the schools for such intolerance and division. However, she also pointed out that such problems are capable of being solved in more conducive ways, similar to the approach taken in Birmingham during the period when Brighouse was head of education. Elsewhere she pointed out that where people on governing bodies had overstepped their remit they needed to be challenged.

Through social media, I noted that Ansir Khan, a parent of a child at Oldknow School, appeared to be quite critical of some of the Trojan Horse practices. When I approached him, he was happy to share his perspective with me in response to questions from me. He pointed out that although "there was no extremism in the terrorist sense" there were philosophical problems such as Christian[6] children being denied the opportunity to celebrate Easter and have a Christmas tree; "basically trying to undermine their faith and putting Islam first". He informed me that the Christian parents had complained, at a parents' meeting, of their children's faith being excluded: why weren't they allowed to celebrate when it was OK for Muslim festivals to be celebrated? He also believed that there was a group of parents who held secret meetings at which school policy decisions were made. In his view some of these parents bullied other parents as well as staff. He spoke of 'Islamification' of the school. As examples he referred to tombola being banned at a school event, because it was gambling which is banned in Islam. He said he had noticed his daughter coming home from school and talking about God, which he found curious. "The first time I thought nothing of it, but she did it again a couple of times. I wondered why she was talking about God more than maths or English or science. It just seemed religion was being discussed more and became more prominent".

Holmwood and O'Toole (2017) have argued that there were no egregious practices in the Trojan Horse affair. However, whatever did happen had been amplified and given an excessive response. This was also how Head Teacher Richards, at Community, saw the Trojan Horse situation. His was one of the three schools I had used as site of my research. Although he was not implicated in the Trojan Horse affair and his school was not included amongst the 21 schools subjected to inspection by Ofsted, he nevertheless knew what had happened during the whole affair. He said to me during one of our meetings that, regardless of what had been done by the Trojan-accused schools and personalities within them, the system had been unfair in its over-reaction in the punishment it meted out to them. And then there was the press and the media; giving rise to a moral panic which then created the conditions for the central government to fulfil its broader agenda than the education of children.

In Birmingham, the trust deficit – when measured in the context of relationships between Pakistani Muslim parents and the school system – is very low as a result of the Trojan Horse affair (YouTube, 2014). The affair has caused rifts and alienation between the education system and the Pakistani Muslim community (Panjwani, 2014). Arthur (2015) has pointed out that in the light of Trojan Horse, Birmingham's Muslim population is being treated "as a 'suspect community' or even the 'enemy within'" (p. 320). Boyes has been quoted as saying "Trojan Horse has been unhelpful for Birmingham in so far as a lot of people have been hurt by it, a lot of fears and myths have been fed by it and a lot of heat has been generated off it". "We need to build trust and relationships, a sense of togetherness". He said the city's education sector had suffered 'irreversible' damage in the wake of the scandal (McKinney, 2015). Tahir Alam (2015a), the previous chair of the governing body at the then Parkview School, one of the schools implicated in the Trojan Horse affair, has said:

> Crucial teacher–pupil trust relationship has been violated. Soon Muslim parents may have no choice but to advise their children not to trust teachers and schools. A tragic loss for what education should be – engendering mutual trust and confidence.

This view was supported by Boyes. He pointed out that the biggest legacy of Trojan Horse is the number of Muslim families who would rather send their children to independent Muslim schools rather than the state system because they don't trust the system anymore. The growth of home schooling, independent schooling and under-the-radar schooling is a massive problem in Birmingham. It has grown *massively* (original emphasis). He alluded that one reason for this was the focus by some schools on teaching about sexual orientation. He referred to Welford School, where the majority of the children were Muslim and where, during the Trojan Horse controversy, there had been trouble between parents and the head teacher. He also referred to similar work being done currently at the nearly all Muslim Parkfield School.

Another consequence of the Trojan Horse affair so far has been fewer local Muslims volunteering to be school governors (Awan, 2018). This is at a time when my research has found an under-representation of governors from this community. Others (Holmwood & O'Toole, 2017; Abbas, 2018) have argued that significant damage was done to the representation of

British Muslims in the popular imagination and, in particular, within educational settings. This led to Muslims being mistrusted. So, according to Tim Boyes, if Pakistani Muslim parents and the wider community ever challenge[7] a head teacher over school performance, or make otherwise reasonable demands such as request prayer or other facilities to help meet their children's religious and cultural needs, they are likely to face the accusations of Islamification, as occurred most recently in Oldham. Abbas (2018) has pointed to the development of a possible vicious circle about the nature of exclusion and the community's response to it. In his view, the higher the fence keeping the community well outside the school the more likely they are to respond to marginalisation and exclusion with actions that might disconnect them further from the mainstream. According to Abbas (2018) ethnic minority groups respond to marginalisation and exclusion with actions that might disconnect them further from the mainstream. It is this kind of distance between the education system and the communities it is meant to serve that can create the conditions for controversies such as Trojan Horse. I asked Boyes whether Trojan Horse could happen again. His response was an emphatic 'yes'. As an aside he pointed out that a mark two Trojan Horse had already happened though not referred to as such. This was what had been done at the Perry Beaches group of schools, under the leadership of Liam Nolan, who was later discovered to have practised financial irregularities. "when you get people who've learnt how to cheat the system, to manipulate it to get good results and they are *praised* by the Secretary of State or by HMCI we've got a big problem". Boyes went on to explain: "Liam Nolan was the second version of the same problem. Because he became a monster heralded by Gove and by David Cameron as a success because he was delivering amazing English and maths results. But in an environment that was values-flawed". Going back to my question, he explained that the 'vulnerabilities' of the kind he had drawn attention to in his DfE presentation in 2010 had increased and little had been done about problems such as the segregation of schools. Moreover, he pointed out that school community disconnect had worsened within the free-market world of education. The curriculum in schools and the inspection framework were as narrow as before, "moving us away from good education". Furthermore the notion of school as community-owned, community-led and belonging in a locality had been undermined by academisation, "where there are arrogant, narrow, limited technicians sitting now in some headteacher seats who know how to get good results but have got a very limited sociological understanding of their school and its locality and its communities". To this we could add under-representation of Pakistanis in the school workforce, especially at leadership levels, and on school governing bodies. Boyes informed me that out of some 70-plus secondary schools in Birmingham only one had a Pakistani head teacher. Furthermore, unlike before, there are even fewer culturally and politically competent staff at the local authority level who could intervene. This situation had been arrived at after continuous central government funding cuts which appeared to be part of a deliberate strategy to centralise education and remove local democratic accountabilities.

Notes

1 Encouraged by the government, this was a policy designed to keep an ethnic balance in schools. Once a school had admitted a third of its children from ethnic minority background it could refuse the others, expecting them to be bussed to other schools. For further details, see Iqbal (2013).
2 https://schoolleaders.thekeysupport.com/
3 https://insights.thekeysupport.com/2015/04/30/what-does-an-independent-ofsted-actually-mean/
4 On its website Ofsted claims "We report directly to Parliament and we are independent and impartial": www.gov.uk/government/organisations/ofsted/about Downloaded 20.11.2017.
5 www.presenceandengagement.org.uk/trojan-horse-conversation-still-waiting-happen
6 The school had a very small number of Christian children, possibly 10.
7 Such behaviour is in line with government regulations (DfE, 2014). According to these role of governors includes this: to hold the head teacher to account for educational performance. Elsewhere it is stated: "To create robust accountability, governors need to ask challenging questions".

Bibliography

AAUW. (2016). *Barriers and bias: The status of women in leadership*. Washington: AAUW.

Abbas, T. (2017). The "Trojan Horse" plot and the fear of Muslim power in British schools. *Journal of Muslim Minority Affairs*.

Abbas, T. (2017a). The 'Trojan Horse' affair was about power, politics and racism, not students. *Middle East Eye*, 1 June. https://doi.org/10.1080/13602004.2017.1313974

Abbas, T. (2018). Reconfiguring religious identities. *British Journal of Sociology of Education* 39(2) 161–165.

Adams, R. (2014). Schools accused of failing to protect children from extremism. *The Guardian*, 19 November.

Adams, R. (2014a). Education experts voice fury over Ofsted's 'Trojan Horse' schools inquiry. *The Guardian*, 3 June.

Alam, T. (2015). Personal interview at Midland Arts Centre. 9 September.

Alam, T. (2015a). Facebook post, 7 December.

Archer, L. (2010). 'We raised it with the Head': The educational practices of minority ethnic middle class families. *British Journal of Sociology of Education* 31(4) 449–469.

Arthur, J. (2015). Extremism and neo-liberal education policy: A contextual critique of the Trojan Horse affair in Birmingham schools. *British Journal of Educational Studies* 63(3) 311–328.

Awan, I. (2018). 'I never did anything wrong' – Trojan Horse: A qualitative study uncovering the impact in Birmingham. *British Journal of Sociology of Education* 39(2) 197–211.

Boyes, T. (2016). Personal interview at the offices of the Birmingham Education Partnership. 29 January.

Boyes, T. (2018). Personal interview at his home. 2 May.

Brighouse, T. (2014). Trojan Horse affair: Five lessons we must learn. *The Guardian*, 17 June.

Brighouse, T. et al. (2014). Ofsted credibility at stake over 'Trojan Horse' schools inquiry. *The Guardian*, 3 June.

Cantle Report. (2001). *Community cohesion: A report of the independent review team.* Home Office.

Casey, L. (2016). *The Casey Review-a review into opportunity and integration.* London: HMSO.

DCSF. (2008). *Raising the attainment of Pakistani, Bangladeshi, Somali, and Turkish heritage pupils: The national strategies: Secondary.* London: DCSF.

DfE. (2014). *The school governance (roles, procedures and allowances) (England) regulations 2013.* Department for Education.

DfE. (2015). *Review into possible warnings to DfE relating to extremism in Birmingham schools.* Department for Education.

Holmwood, J. & O'Toole, T. (2017). *Countering extremism in British schools? The truth about the Birmingham Trojan Horse affair.* Bristol: Policy Press.

House of Commons. (2015). *Extremism in schools: The Trojan Horse affair: Seventh report of session 2014–15.* The Stationery Office.

Iqbal, K. (2013). *Dear Birmingham.* Bloomingdale: Xlibris.

Iqbal, K. (2014). Working out what to do with us immigrants – religion, belief and life-chances in a West Midlands city. *Race Equality Teaching* 32(2) Spring.

Joly, D. (1987). *Making a place for Islam in British Society: Muslims in Birmingham.* University of Warwick Research Papers in Ethnic Relations No.4, Centre for Research in Ethnic Relations.

Khan, M. G. (2014). The so-called 'Trojan Horse' document is being used to destabilise Muslim-majority schools. *Times Educational Supplement,* 27 March.

Lareau, A. & Horvat, E. (1999). Moments of social inclusion and exclusion: Race, class and cultural capital in family-school relationships. *Sociology of Education* 72 37–53.

McKinney, E. (2015). Trojan Horse One Year On: Headteacher who warned the government five years ago reveals plans to create 'families' of schools. *Birmingham Mail.* 23 April.

Miah, S. (2017). *Muslims, schooling and security.* Switzerland: Palgrave.

Ofsted. (2013). *Oldknow academy: School report.* London: Ofsted.

Ofsted. (2014). *Oldknow academy: School report.* London: Ofsted.

Oldham, J. (2014). Trojan Horse investigation: School head warned over signs of extremism four years ago. *Birmingham Mail,* 31 May.

Panjwani, F. (2014). Beyond the saga of the 'Trojan Horse': Some reflections on teaching about Islam in schools. *The Middle East in London,* October–November.

Pidd, H. (2014). Invention or not, tactics in alleged Birmingham school plot are familiar. *The Guardian,* 14 March.

Pidd, H. & Dodd, V. (2014). Police chief condemns appointment of terror officer over 'Islamic schools plot'. *The Guardian,* 15 April.

Raihani, D. & Gurr, D. (2011). *Parental involvement in an Islamic school in Australia.* www.aare.edu.au/10pap/1797RaihaniGurr.pdf Accessed 15.2.2012.

Ran, A. (2001). Travelling on parallel tracks: Chinese parents and English teachers. *Educational Research* 43(3) 311–328.

Ranson, S., Martin, J. & Vincent, C. (2004). Storming parents, schools and communicative inaction. *British Journal of Sociology of Education* 25(3) 259–274.

Shackle, S. (2017). Trojan Horse: The real story behind the fake 'Islamic plot' to take over schools. *The Guardian,* 1 September.

Sivanandan, A. (1982). *A different hunger.* London: Pluto Press.

Spivak, G. (1988). Can the subaltern speak? in Nelson, C. & Grossberg, L. (eds.) *Marxism and the interpretation of culture.* London: Macmillan.

Sudworth, R. (2014). *Trojan Horse: A conversation still waiting to happen.* www.presenceandengagement.org.uk/trojan-horse-conversation-still-waiting-happen Accessed 9.3.2018.

Sutcliffe, A. & Smith, R. (1974). *Birmingham 1939–1970*. Oxford: Oxford University Press.

Warren, M., Hong, S., Rubin, C. & Uy, P. (2009). Beyond the bake sale: A community-based relational approach to parent engagement in schools. *Teachers College Record* 111(9) 2209–2254.

Wilcox, D. (1994). *The guide to effective participation*. York: Joseph Rowntree Foundation.

Yaqoob, S. (2014). Stigmatising Muslims won't solve problems in Birmingham school. *The Guardian*, 22 July.

YouTube. (2014). *Islam in British schools: The Trojan Horse letter*. TV debate. 6 September. www.bing.com/videos/search?q=trojan+youtube+islamic+schools&view=detail&mid=9B71A2288922533A702F9B71A2288922533A702F&FORM=VIRE Accessed 10.7.2016.

3   A note on the research

Insider–outsider role in research

Who we are as researchers is intertwined with our personal and professional identities. The debate on who is qualified to research whom is particularly well-rehearsed in terms of gender (Ramazanoglu, 1992; Hammersley, 1994), race (Rhodes, 1994) and social class (Mellor et al., 2013). However, it remains a contested issue, with the debate being "multidimensional, continuous and inclusive" (Shah, 2004, p. 556). A researcher focusing on people of the community he is also a member of is described as an 'insider', as opposed to an 'outsider'. At the outset I had to explore where I fitted in. Was I an insider given my ethnicity and place of birth or had I become an outsider given my life's journey?

It is worth pointing out that just being a co-ethnic with the people one is researching is not sufficient to make one an insider. Nor is the possibility ruled out, forever. So, people of the same heritage may in some situations be alike while in other situations be different (Ali & Holden, 2006).

Given the unique ways in which our lives progress, our initial commonalities, such as sharing the same heritage, can become less significant and, in their place, differences come into greater prominence. It is important to recognise that none of us is a "complete insider or outsider". Relevant also are concepts 'outsider within' and 'relative insiders' (Griffiths, 1998; Watts, 2006). Shah (2006), a British Indian professional disabled woman, expecting herself to be an insider when researching disabled people, realised that only a part of her life history resembled that of her respondents. Mellor et al. (2013) also make a similar point when discussing the issue of working class researchers studying working class people and expecting somehow to be insiders. They concluded that shared class position does not necessarily equate with similar life experiences, or enable a strong rapport with, or understanding of, working class people's lives. Song and Parker (1995) have spoken of the limitations of the insider-outsider binary and advised against applying too rigidly the commonalities and differences between the researchers and their target audience. For them a diversity of experience, involving many different types of differences, can be found in such encounters. They spoke of cultural differences which may exist between the interviewer and interviewees in spite of their membership of the same racial or national group. For them, researchers were neither total insiders nor total outsiders.

Shared identities, between researcher and the researched, are said to bring certain benefits such as facilitating access to certain groups and engendering trust and a willingness to discuss certain issues (Francis & Archer, 2005). According to Shah (2004), it is advantageous throughout the research process – access, conducting interview and making meaning – for the researcher to understand their respondents' culture. For her, the insider-researcher is "better positioned to understand responses and to make meaning as a participative activity" (p. 564) and that "a cultural insider has a definite advantage of 'shared cultural experience', which facilitates understanding and interpretation of what the research participants share" (p. 569). Abbas (2002) pointed out that a researcher with shared ethnic characteristics was less likely to pathologise or stereotype and more likely to remain 'ethnically correct'. Archer (2002) suggested that responses given by ethnic minority respondents to White interviewers may be less valid, compared with those given to interviewers of their own ethnicity. She pointed to the possibility that cultural differences between researchers and participants may lead to the researcher being unable to generate 'meaningful' data, due to not having a shared understandings and cultural knowledge of the participants.

Being a partial-insider/outsider can have its advantages too. For Shah (2006), as researchers, parts of our life history may resemble that of the respondents, yet allowing us to be different and 'outsider' enough so that we are able to retain a fair level of objectivity. Griffiths (1998) pointed out that relative insiders have to face the charge that they are too distanced from the community which they have researched. For Bondi (2003), on the other hand, being a partial-insider is advantageous. It enables the interviewer to be emotionally present and reactive to the interviewees' responses while simultaneously staying in touch with, and reflecting on his/her own feelings. In this way, there is not a danger of the interviewer becoming unconsciously overwhelmed by the respondents' stories reacting to, rather than reflecting on, what is going on, and blurring the interviewer/interviewee boundary.

Being an insider-researcher can have problems too. For Kanuha (2000), while one is able to

> enhance the depth and breadth of understanding a population that may not be accessible to a non-native scientist, questions about objectivity, reflexivity and authenticity of a research project are raised because perhaps one knows too much or is too close to the project and may be too similar to those being studied.
>
> (p. 444)

Francis and Archer (2005) warned of the dangers that researchers from similar social positions as their respondents might conflate experiences or distort responses in order to fit their own experiences. For Reay (1996), the closer we are to the subject matter, the more likely our beliefs would influence the shape of our work, the questions we pose and the way we interpret the responses. Dimmock (2002) made a case that it was better for a researcher to be an outsider as it can help bring a fresh perspective to the situation being studied.

Peshkin (1988) warned against subjectivity in the research process. However, for him it was almost an impossibility to rid oneself of it; "one's subjectivity is like a garment that cannot be removed" (p. 17). For him, the only option is for the researcher to become aware of his/her subjectivity. Hall (2017) similarly had reservations about the division between the 'objective' and the 'subjective'. For him even the most abstract theories are informed by their subjective conditions of existence. Like Hall, I will try to draw out what connections I can between my 'life' and my 'ideas'.

Me and my position

In the context of the above discussion, I would describe myself as a 'relative insider'/'outsider-within'. One advantage of my particular life trajectory – working class who became middle class while maintaining close ties with the working class in the Pakistani community – has been that it enabled me to build rapport with parents from very different education and social class backgrounds; from the doctors and business parents living in big houses as well as the labouring parents in their low-paid factory jobs.

My life's journey and my professional trajectory have placed me at various locations along the insider-outsider continuum. This has resulted in a range of identities, some of which enabled me to get alongside and develop rapport with my research participants. Having begun as an insider, I became an outsider. I then decided to 'go back home' for the research, applying an outsider's perspective to the situation on the inside. While straddling the status of insider-outsider, it is my aim to bring a level of understanding to the subject matter and the community being researched while at the same time bringing a fresh perspective.

Reay (1996) drew attention to problems associated with men interviewing women, including, as in the present study, the particular issues surrounding an Asian male researcher interviewing Asian female participants. However, Abbas (2002), a Pakistani male, who had conducted his research amongst Pakistani Muslims and other Asians in Birmingham had found no such problems with interviewing Muslim females. Following his experience, I expected there to be no problems and, as far as I am aware, I did not encounter any. During my interviews with the Pakistani female parents, although I was conscious of our gender differences, I believe it did not create any barrier of communication. It certainly appeared to make little difference when interviewing female teachers, where the focus appeared to be on a professional, rather than gender-based, encounter.

Culturally competent research

The research encounter requires a certain level of cultural competency and sensitivity on the part of the researcher (Das, 2010). This, according to Colombo (2005), is the ability to understand diverse perspectives and appropriately interact with members of other cultures. Atim and Cantu (2010) described cultural competence as the ability of researchers to take "into account the culture and diversity of a population when developing research ideas, conducting research, and exploring applicability of research findings" (p. 6). Briscoe (2003) reminded us that "the goal of culturally competent research – or culturally competent intervention – is to always preserve and enhance the interests, dignity and integrities (of people being researched)" (p. 11). They also advised researchers wishing to adopt a culturally competent perspective to investigate their own beliefs, knowledge and information about the community being studied. Stuart (2004) suggested that researchers should develop skills in discovering the unique cultural outlook of the researched, acknowledge and control personal biases, develop sensitivity to cultural differences and show respect for the beliefs of the researched.

I was mindful that there was likely to be wide diversity amongst the parents I was interviewing, in terms of their level of education and social class. I consciously tried to be adaptable, depending on which parent I was meeting. Rhodes (1994) spoke of our linguistic and cultural 'equipment' which researchers may have. Here I was conscious of personal resources which I was able to draw on, such as cultural understanding and being able to speak Urdu and its various dialects; resources a non-Pakistani or even a non-Urdu-speaking Pakistani may not have had. During the interviews there were occasions when such linguistic connection enabled me to reach a deeper level of understanding or quickly pick up on the linguistic clues. For example, very early on, one of the parents used the phrase 'deen aur dunya', meaning religion and 'of the world'. It is likely that he may not have used the phrase with a cultural or linguistic outsider. Where I spoke English during parent interviews, then this was free of jargon. If their mother tongue was spoken, then this was the 'common and accessible' variety, including dialects as opposed to 'educated and complex' Urdu. Where the interview was conducted in English I used the occasional Urdu words, in order to both optimise the level of understanding and to "establish and maintain a good rapport with the interviewee" (Cohen et al., 2007, p. 362). Academy parent Najeeb, who sounded quite well educated, explained to me that he had participated on school governing bodies at his children's schools but had found that the English language was a barrier (Cox, 2001).

> I frequently felt unable to participate in meetings. I could understand what was going on but it was hard to contribute to the discussion. What might take someone with English half hour would take me forty five minutes. It was hard to find the right words to express myself. I could not speak fluently.

This was not something I had raised or invited him to discuss. So, it is unlikely that, with a non-co-ethnic researcher, he might have raised this personal barrier.

Religion and culture are said to be closely interwoven (Halstead, 2007). On a few occasions 'religio-cultural' (Abbas, 2003)[1] needs arose during my research which required an appropriate response from me as the researcher. For example, it became necessary to remove my shoes, in the hallway, before entering the parents' space for the interview. On other occasions, knowing that, as a male researcher, it would not be appropriate to do so, I did not offer to shake hands with the female parents interviewed. In most households, I was offered refreshments. Being prepared, I would always ask for a glass of water. In this situation it would have been rude not to accept a drink but would have taken time, away from the interview, to accept a hot drink. On a couple of occasions, a hot drink arrived without me being asked. This I accepted; not to do so would have been rude.

Being aware of my 'insider-outsider' position in relation to the Birmingham Pakistani community, to each interview with a parent, I went prepared with a script for my encounter. It included the questions I had agreed with my supervisor. But my script also included: I must listen, not talk; I must be grateful to them for giving me their time and for inviting me into their space; I must show them respect, for their knowledge and opinions and that I must remain friendly, yet businesslike. I also had a script for what I would say to them when we first met: why I was there, the university where I was studying, that I was not from their son's school so they could speak freely. I also made sure that I reiterated the assurance on confidentiality. And the question: 'who are you?' I knew this would come up so I had a response already worked-out. This was in multiple parts. Part one would be for when we first met. I had decided that beyond my name and where I was studying, I would say little else as I did not want to influence their thinking in any way. Being direct, I would attempt to, as quickly as possible, get started with the interview. Part two of the answer would be ready for the post-interview conversation, if it seemed necessary and if they were interested in my opinions and my background.

Henry (2003) asks: how can a researcher who exists on both the 'inside' and 'outside' of South Asian cultural identities simply label and name herself? Or occupy positions of power and privilege in the 'field'? I particularly needed a script for this part of the encounter with the interviewees. I knew I couldn't just walk away. I had to say something. But what would I say, how much, about which topics and which topics I would stay clear of? I knew if I did not have a mental script, things could go wrong here and I could start talking too much and about the wrong topics. So, as an example, just as we finished the interview, one parent asked me to do a proper *tahaaraf*, introduction. So, I was able to oblige with further details of my background: which district of Kashmir I was born in (from the way I spoke, he had worked out that we were from the same region), how long I had been in Birmingham etc. It turned out that we had both attended the same school upon arrival in

Birmingham. I was able to manage the discourse and conclude it appropriately and depart.

This study is being conducted within a particular context. Ringeisen et al. (2003) advise that by having some understanding of that context and its different levels it helps the researcher to explain and understand the meaning being generated by the study. There are three levels for the study: the individuals (children, parents, teachers); the organisations (the schools) and the government (local and national). Outlined next are the third and second of these levels.

My research and its context

Birmingham City Council is the largest local authority in England with an estimated population of 274,478 children and young people (BCC, 2011). This represented around a quarter of the city's overall population. Of this, Pakistani children were the largest ethnic minority, at 24.5%, and Muslims the largest pupil religious group, at 36%. Within England, the authority has been reported to have the highest percentage of children (40%) for whom English was not their mother tongue (McKinney, 2016, p. 11).

The Pakistani community in Birmingham is very large. They currently make up about 14% of the overall population of the city. The community is spread across the city, with at least 10% Pakistanis present in half of the 40 electoral wards (Iqbal, 2013). There is also diversity amongst the community; people originate from across Pakistan and in turn have settled in different parts of Birmingham. Therefore, in order to capture the heterogeneity of the community, I sought three secondary schools located in different parts of Birmingham.

Having worked as a Local Authority schools Adviser for 10 years (2001–2011), I knew what different types of schools there were in the city; in terms of their social and ethnic make-up, type of school and their location in the city. Utilising this knowledge, I approached three schools. In my email to the head teachers I referred to my past research on the White working class young people and pointed out that my focus had now shifted to the education of Pakistani boys in the city. I explained that the research was a part of my PhD and, therefore, would be governed by the rigours of higher education and its rules on ethics and confidentiality. A timeline for the recruitment of schools and conducting the research is provided (Appendix 1).

School portraits

Given below are details of the three schools. Much of the information was drawn from their most recent Ofsted inspection report, with other data supplied by the schools themselves. Details of the schools are summarised in Table 3.1.

Academy: a large secondary school, offering education for 1500 children. The school is located in the South East of the city. It served its immediate locality but also attracted students from other areas of the city. The school had 27%

Table 3.1 Schools as sites of research

School	Location/recruitment	Type	Size	Pakistani pupils	FSM
Academy	South East Birmingham	11–18 semi-selective	1,500 approx	29%	27%
Community	North of Birmingham	11–18 comprehensive	1,500 approx	43.9%	44%
Grammar	City-wide	Selective	1,000 approx	12.8%	6%

free school meals (FSM) pupils which is a proxy for children from poorer families. It had 29.3% Pakistani students. The school employed around 140 full-time equivalent staff, out of which 3.8% were Pakistani.

Community: a large comprehensive school, offering education for 1,500 children. It is located in the north of the city. The school had 44% FSM pupils. Almost all of the school's students were from ethnic minority backgrounds – 43.9% Pakistani and 35% Bangladeshi. The school staffing was diverse, of whom 8% were Pakistani.

Grammar: a grammar school which offers education for 1,000 boys, who came from across the city as well as some who travelled in from neighbouring local authorities. Entry was through passing the 11+ test. 12.8% of the boys were Pakistani. Students joined the school with above average attainment. The proportion of FSM students was very low, at 6.5%. The majority of the school's staff were White British. It employed one, part-time (0.6% full-time equivalent), Pakistani member of staff.

Schools were asked for access to Year 11 students; all of them for the questionnaire and up to 10 Pakistani boys to be interviewed, on a one-to-one basis. It was requested that the interviewees should be a mixture of abilities, i.e. some who were expected to achieve the benchmark qualification and some who were not. I requested that some of these interviewees should be FSM. In addition, schools were asked to nominate two teachers who could be interviewed, if possible, one of whom should be Pakistani. It was requested that one of the teachers should be someone who had a good understanding of Year 11 pupils such as a Pastoral Head of Year.

Schools were requested to put me in touch with parents of the boys being interviewed. The schools were supplied letters to the relevant people. Copies of these are provided in Appendix 2.

Conducting the research

In gathering primary data, I utilised a questionnaire with all Y11 pupils and structured interviews, with Pakistani boys, their parents and teachers. I decided that gathering data from all pupils would provide me with an opportunity to compare and contrast Pakistani pupils with White pupils and any others as necessary.

The questionnaire consisted of 17 questions. The start of the questionnaire was designed to gather general data on pupil characteristics such as gender, ethnicity and their eligibility for free school meals. The remainder of the questionnaire had questions on the following:

- Home and family
- Attitudes to learning
- Religion
- Teachers
- Post–16 aspirations

Within these categories, there were a number of statements, using a four-point Likert scale. The mid-point, neutral, option was not included in order to discourage the respondents to 'sit on the fence' (Cohen et al., 2007, p. 327). It also had a number of dichotomous and multiple choice questions. According to Newby (2010), "because self-completion questionnaires cannot probe respondents to find out just what they mean by particular responses, open-ended questions are a less satisfactory way of eliciting information" (p. 249). Therefore, such questions were kept to a minimum.

The questionnaire was designed to look "easy, attractive and interesting rather than complicated, unclear, forbidding and boring" (p. 258). It was administered electronically. Following advice from Cohen et al. (2007) and Robson (2011), I tried to avoid certain pitfalls, i.e. no leading, highbrow, complex or irritating questions. The language of the questions was kept simple yet not condescending. Questions were kept short, jargon was avoided, as were double-barrelled questions.

A total of 219 pupils, out of a possible 480, had completed the questionnaire: an overall response rate of 46%. They did so during normal lesson time. Through the Contact Teacher, the students were sent an email link to enable them to access the questionnaire. At appropriate intervals, the Contact Teachers were reminded to chase the pupils so to achieve the maximum respondents. Pupils at both Academy and Grammar had been asked by the tutors to complete the survey in good time before their exams. A 46% return rate was achieved at Academy while a much higher, 74%, return rate was achieved at Grammar. At Community the response rate was only 29%. It was explained that it had been left too late and the students had left the school in order to prepare for their exams. A copy of the questionnaire can be found in Appendix 3.

Interviews

According to Cohen et al., the interview is a "social encounter, not simply a site for information exchange" (2007, p. 350). The effective interviewer for them was "not only knowledgeable about the subject matter but also an expert in interaction and communication. The interviewer would need to establish an appropriate atmosphere such that the participant can feel secure to talk freely" (p. 361). Here, I was able to use my general communication skills, my ability to converse with diverse people, my professional knowledge – of education, especially within the Birmingham context and of the British Pakistani community – and experience, such as interviewing people in my role as a Diversity Consultant. This enabled me to structure the interviews appropriately, ask the right questions, offer the necessary prompts and explanations, all with the clear aim of stimulating a response in order to achieve my goals.

For Robson (2011), the interview is a flexible and adaptable way of finding things out. "The human use of language is fascinating both as behaviour in its own right and for the virtually unique window that it opens on what lies behind our actions" (p. 280). Following his advice, the interviewees were informed that the interview would take around 45 minutes. I generally managed to keep to this. As expected, on a few occasions, interviewees wished to talk beyond the interview. Here, I was able to use my skills to appropriately pull away without seeming rude. A phrase such as "I am sorry I have taken enough of your time already" often helped. I was also able to stick to Robson's advice, i.e. "listen more than you speak" (p. 282). If the interview was taking longer than planned and the process was generating useful data, then it was worthwhile to continue.

Following advice from Lofland et al. (2006), at the start of the interview I thanked the interviewees for giving me their time and explained the purpose and nature of the study. I assured them that the data would be anonymised and that neither they, nor the school, would be identifiable in any reports generated and their responses would be treated in strictest confidence. This was particularly necessary within the Pakistani context where there can be a fear that information given may be shared with others in their community especially where the researcher is also a Pakistani.

During the interviews, most of the discussion was conducted with the aid of open-ended questions. Use was made of *funnels* and *filters* (Oppenheim, 1992: ch.7). For example, all students were asked: "Do you go to the mosque?" If they answered 'yes' then there would be relevant follow-up questions, e.g. how long they spent there, how often they went. If they said 'no' then they would be asked whether they had done so in the past.

Given that the encounter with teachers and students took place at their school, an environment familiar to them, there was little 'settling in' needed. All it required was for me to thank them, explain what I was doing, the nature of the research being conducted and to reassure them of complete confidentiality. There was little extra effort involved for me, given that I had conducted many such one-to-one interviews during my many years as an education and equalities practitioner. The interviews with parents required a little more conscious preparation. Of particular relevance to my interviews were attributes of interviewers, drawn from ethnography, covering areas of trust, curiosity and naturalness (Woods, 1986).

The foundations of the 'relationship' with the parents and the teachers were laid by the first communication they received from me, in the form of a letter which had been sent to all the likely research participants. The communication with student interviewees was through the Contact Teacher at the school. Although different letters were written to students, teachers and parents, they had the same basic information (who I was, what I was doing, details of my university affiliation and, for teachers and parents, my phone and email contact).

In all three schools, I was allocated a quiet room for the interviews. The boys appeared at regular intervals according to the timetable that had been drawn up. Where they failed to attend such as through absence from school, they were rescheduled. All interviewees were happy for the interview to be audio-recorded.

At the start of each interview, during the settling in process, I would check to make sure the boys understood who I was and what I was doing, namely: that I was not a teacher but a researcher – explaining what PhD meant – and that I would keep all information confidential by using pseudonyms for schools and interviewees.

When I met the boys, I asked them if they thought their parents would be happy to be interviewed, explaining that I would conduct the interview at a place, time and in a language of the parents' choosing.

Most of the boys said that their parents would be happy to be interviewed. In this case, I asked the boys for the parents' contact details. One school, Community, provided me with a chart containing the name and address of the pupils, parents' names and contact number.

At the end of the interview, I would ask the boys to let their parents know that I would be contacting them to arrange an interview. I would reiterate that the anonymity for the parents would be the same. Here, I also explained that I would not divulge the boys', their parents' or the real names of the schools amongst my family, friends or the wider community so that no one would know the true identity of who had been interviewed and which school they attended.

Expecting the boys to go home and talk about the interview, I phoned the parents the same day or soon after, while the subject was fresh for them. By this stage, I had already established, through the students, whether the parents would prefer speaking in English or Urdu. The phone call to parents offered a further opportunity to develop my relationship with them. It was likely that, having signed the consent form for their son, they would remember who I was and the research I was conducting.

In conducting the parental interviews, I met the parents in their homes, at a time of their choosing. Two interviews were conducted on Saturday afternoons. Most of the rest of the interviews were conducted during the week at daytime and a few were conducted in the evening.

In terms of the language used at the interview, two of the four parent interviews at Academy were conducted in their mother tongue; one in Pahari and one in Punjabi. Four of the seven parent interviews at Community were conducted in their mother tongue, two in Pahari and two in Punjabi. All interviews with parents at Grammar were conducted in English. The language of the interview was an indicator of the parents' level of education; the more educated were likely to be more confident in their ability to speak English.

The schools provided two or more teachers for the interviews. At Community, I was also able to make use of interviews with four other members of staff which had been conducted as a part of a consultancy assignment I was undertaking at the school.

Between the three schools, in total, I conducted 52 one-to-one interviews – 24 Pakistani boys, 16 parents, and 12 teachers, 4 of whom were of Pakistani heritage. A full breakdown of the interviewees is provided in Appendix 4. The interview schedule for interviews with pupils, parents and teachers is provided in Appendix 5.

I managed to achieve the diversity I set out to do, amongst the Pakistani community, as indicated by the make-up of the parents interviewed. During my meetings I was able to gather that amongst the sample of 16 interviewees the following Pakistani towns and cities were represented as places of origin for the interviewees:

- Faisalabad (1)
- Gujar Khan (2)
- Gujrat (1)
- Gurgushti (1)
- Jehlum – ex-Mirpur[2] (1)
- Kashmir (6)
- Lahore (2)
- Lala Moosa – ex-Mirpur (1)
- Multan (1)

Making sense of the data

In the context of my research, the analysis of both quantitative and qualitative data were considered of equal importance (Cohen et al., 2007). I interrogated both the questionnaire and the interviews in order to draw out trends in what the respondents were saying.

The questionnaire responses from students needed to be considered in terms of percentages of pupils who gave a particular response. I needed to compare responses between boys and girls and to see how different ethnic groups responded to particular questions. I was able to make use of the analysis facility offered by the SurveyMonkey website, whose questionnaire design I had used. In addition, I undertook some additional manual analysis, such as working out percentages, combining data, such as agree/strongly agree or disagree/strongly disagree.

The analysis of the qualitative data was a bigger challenge. The task facing me was what to do with interview responses from over 50 people, which had resulted in some 150 pages of content.

A number of authors have provided useful advice on how to make sense of qualitative data. For Cohen et al. (2007), "qualitative data analysis involves organising, accounting for and explaining the data; in short, making sense of data in terms of the participants' definitions of the situation, noting patterns, themes, categories and regularities" (p. 461). They also state that there is no one single or correct way to analyse and present qualitative data. According to Basit (2003), most qualitative researchers analyse their own data and we are encouraged to draw on whatever understanding of analysis we bring from our previous work and the conventions of our respective disciplines and professions. This enabled me to work out my own method for analysis and draw on my many consultancy assignments where I had undertaken qualitative research. I found that the data analysis was not a discrete procedure carried out at the final stages of research but something that began with the interview and continued throughout the life of the study. The data gathered through the interviews were personal to me. It felt I had entered into a relationship, with my subjects, through the interview meeting, as I transcribed, analysed and interpreted what had been shared by the interviewees. I did not take short cuts but allowed plenty of time and energy to the task. As I listened to the interviews many times during the analysis, it became an enjoyable activity.

Lofland et al. (2006) suggest that the researcher should undertake an initial read through text data, identify specific segments of information, label the segments to create categories, reduce overlap and redundancy among the categories and create a model incorporating most important categories. For me, the process began with the literature review which had given rise to a number of questions which I felt required to be answered for Pakistani boys. It could be argued that a process had gone on even before the literature review which had helped me to decide what to read and why but that would mean writing a full personal and professional autobiography, something neither possible nor necessary here.

The resulting questions were ordered according to my experience of such situations, e.g. settling in/opening; the main body; concluding and then post-conclusion, e.g. "Is there anything else you would like to say?" My experience had shown that often this question can generate extremely useful data. It can also place the interviewees in a more powerful role as they have the opportunity to give an opinion about any of the issues under discussion.

All interviews were recorded on a Pearlcorder Dictaphone which would usually be placed on a table in front of the interviewee. Following advice from Lofland et al. (2006), I decided to transcribe the interviews myself. I felt quite possessive of the humans and their voices, inside the tape recorder. I set out to systematically listen to the interviews and type up the information, one individual at a time. Each interview 'file' on the Ipad could be identified by a four-word name: 'PhD', 'name of school', 'pupil/teacher/parent' and 'personal name' (a pseudonym which had been allocated to all participants to protect their and their school identity). For example: PhD Academy pupil Hussain.

Transcribing the interviews was a lengthy and complex process. But it was not a tedious activity; it did not feel like a chore to complete. In my mind, people had given me their time and opinions; I owed it to them to listen to their every word and do something with it. I would listen to one sentence, stop the tape and type it. Occasionally, I would need to listen a second, maybe even a third, time to the same information in order to capture it accurately. I would then move on to the next sentence. However, in order to arrive at the correct position in the interview, often it was necessary to rewind the tape which meant listening, again, to a few of the words of the previous sentence. Some of the interviews needed to be translated into English from the community languages in which the interviews were conducted. Consequently, by the end of the transcribing process, I felt as if I had listened to the interview three, maybe even four times over.

Having met the interviewees, listened to their opinions in person and now, again and again, on the Dictaphone, felt as if their voice was well and truly embedded inside of my head. I now knew what the whole, the sum total of all the interviews, looked like; what had been said, by whom, in which school community.

Given that qualitative data are textual, non-numerical and unstructured, coding is said to be crucial in the analyses of such data to organise and make sense of them. According to Basit (2003) coding allows the researcher to communicate and connect with the data, to facilitate the comprehension of the emerging phenomena and to generate theory grounded in the data. She identifies a number of stages of this process which include noticing relevant phenomena and analysing the data in order to find commonalities, differences, patterns and structures.

Cohen and Manion (1994) advise that in the case of small surveys analysis can be achieved manually. This was what I did as I did not think it was necessary to use a computer programme.

Based on the focus of my research and the research questions I had generated from the literature review I was now able to identify 33 codes:

- Deen
- Dunya
- Educated
- Message
- Adab
- Ikhlaaq
- Respect
- Teacher understanding
- Benefits of teacher understanding
- CPD
- Madrassah attendance

- Routine
- Madrassah impact
- Links
- Accommodation
- Prayer
- Wudu
- Relationship
- Diversity
- Minority teachers
- Pakistani teachers
- Male teachers
- Female teachers
- Mosque at school
- Pakistaniness
- Tuition
- Quran
- Family
- Siblings
- Role models
- Extracurricular
- Cohesion
- Religion-culture

I then went back to the text and inserted the codes where I identified units of meaning as appropriate for that code. I had already organised each transcript by naming it as one of the three schools and as 'pupil', 'parent' or 'teacher'. In this way I was able to access and aggregate all relevant data in respect to each code and identify the interviewees concerned. This enabled me to get an overview of responses; for example, to conclude that students and their parents were equally split on whether it was important for schools to employ Pakistani teachers. It also allowed me to zoom in on particular instances and draw out extracts which could be used as quotations.

The analysis was a lengthy and complex process. This involved listening to the interview tapes; transcribing the interviews, including translating parental interviews, which were in community languages, into English. I then read the transcripts a number of times: summarising the transcripts and choosing categories; coding statements; linking themes; selecting quotations and, ultimately, generating a theory grounded in the data and writing it up in a coherent fashion.

Generally, it is recognised that it is difficult to quantify data from within a qualitative process (Cohen et al., 2007). However, following (Abeyasekera, undated) the dichotomous nature of a few of the questions made this possible, for example, the numbers of students who, currently or in the past, attended a madrassah.

The overall interview data file was marked for 'track changes'. Having recently published a book (Iqbal, 2013), the writing process for me did not seem an overly daunting task. Depending upon what the writer within me felt like writing, I would pick a theme and start drawing, 'cutting' out all of the content, using the 'Find' facility in Word. 'Teacher Understanding' was the first theme on which I decided to write. As I cut the relevant content out of the script, it would be shown up in red and with a line through it. This enabled me to see, at any given time, what content had already been made use of; my aim being that little of it should be left unused by the end of the writing process. I felt obligated to use the data which people had given me; this was the least I could do.

Appendix 1

Research timeline

The following timeline lists the activities undertaken along my research journey with the schools concerned:

3.10.2011   Introductory and exploratory email sent to a number of Birmingham schools.

4.10.2011   Academy[3] responded, expressing their willingness to become a research site.

17.10.2011   Meeting held with Acting Headteacher at Comprehensive. They agreed to discuss amongst their Senior Leadership Team whether to participate in the research.

18.10.2011   Comprehensive agreed to participate in the research.

19.1.2012   Acting Headteacher at Comprehensive moved to another school.

27.3.2012   Introductory and exploratory email sent to Grammar.

28.3.2012   Headteacher at Grammar replied, expressing their willingness to participate in the research.

8.10.2012   Email sent to all schools, outlining my specific research requirements, i.e. (for the interviews) eight Pakistani Year 11 boys (mixture of FSM/Non-FSM), their parents and one or two teachers who knew the boys. If possible, one of the teachers was requested to be of Pakistani heritage. It was explained that the interviews would take about 45 minutes. In addition, schools were requested to ask all Year 11 pupils (boys and girls, across all ethnic groups) to complete an online questionnaire, which would take them about eight minutes to complete.

8.10.2012   Grammar requested that pupil interviews should be no longer than 30 minutes. This was agreed. They also informed me that I would need to obtain a new CRB clearance. The other schools had not raised this as a requirement and were happy with my existing CRB clearance which I had as an Education Consultant.

11.10.2012   Ethical approval given, to proceed with research. I informed the schools of this.

26.11.2012   New contact at Comprehensive requested further information about my research. This was supplied.

29.11.2012   Comprehensive requested to know the purpose of my research. This was explained.

18.12.2012   I received upgrade. The three schools were informed of this. I provided them letters for the interviewees (Appendix 2).

21.12.2012   Comprehensive wrote, informing that they were no longer willing to participate in the research, in the following words:

> I am sorry to inform you that we will not be able to assist you in your research, due to the fact that it is just targeted at one ethnic group. We only contribute to external requests for survey information if they allow equality of opportunity and access.

6.2.2013   At Academy, interviews with the Pakistani boys commenced. Parallel with these I also began to interview their parents and the teachers.

6.2.2013   Replacement for Comprehensive found, with Community, a school where I was undertaking consultancy, willing to participate in the research.

10.2.2013   Link sent to Academy for the online questionnaire to be completed by their students.

11.2.2013   I informed Grammar that I had obtained CRB clearance.

27.2.2013   At Community, interviews with the Pakistani boys commenced. Parallel with these I also began to interview their parents and the teachers.

27.2.2013   Link sent to Community for the online questionnaire to be completed by their students.

17.4.2013   At Grammar, interviews with the Pakistani boys commenced. Parallel with these I also began to interview their parents and the teachers. Link sent to their students for the online questionnaire to be completed by their students.

23.4.2013   Community raised a query about the online questionnaire; was it all pupils or just the ones who were interviewed. This had already been made clear to them that it was all pupils. I reiterated the information.

30.4.2013   Community informed me that the questionnaire was being completed that week. However, they pointed out that some students were now on study leave and would not be able to complete the questionnaire.

3.6.2013   Grammar informed me that they had done their best to encourage their students to complete the online questionnaire. Also that after this date I should not expect any more to do so as they were now involved in examinations.

Appendix 2

Letters to research participants

Letter to contact teacher

Pakistani boys' educational achievement in Birmingham schools

Dear teacher

I am in the process of looking into the educational achievement of Pakistani boys within Birmingham schools.

The research

The research I am carrying out is a part of my PhD course at Warwick University. Therefore, all my work is being carried out within the rules and regulations of the University where I am being supervised by a Professor.

I have already carried out a review of existing literature on this subject in order to learn from others who are experts in this subject. This has helped me to identify the gaps in knowledge which I hope my own research will help to fill.

I am hoping to talk to a number of Pakistani boys in three different schools across Birmingham.

Interviews with students

I would be grateful if you would help me to interview 4 Pakistani Y11 boys who are on FSM and 4 who are not FSM. It would be good to have a mix of abilities e.g. those who are expected to achieve 5 A*–C and those who are not or are expected to do less well.

The interview will take no more than 45 minutes of your student's time. I am keen to arrange the interview at a time which does not take the student away from something really important.

To make sure that I don't miss anything, the interview will be recorded. However, I will only use the recording for my own purpose and will not share it with anyone else.

The student's rights

The students' views are very important but it's up to him whether to take part in this research. Nothing negative will happen if he decides not to take part. During the interview, if he says something he wishes he hadn't, he can ask for this to be withdrawn.

Also, if he starts talking to me and then decides that he does not want to be part of the research then he can change his mind. Any information he has already provided will be destroyed without being used.

Student Questionnaire

In addition, I would be grateful if all Y11 students would complete an online questionnaire for me. This will take under 10 minutes.

Interviews with teachers

I would be grateful if I could interview 2–3 teachers who teach Y11 students, including those I am to interview. It would be helpful if at least one of the teachers was of Pakistani background.

Confidentiality

The discussion will be kept confidential. When the information is written up, names of interviewees will not be used so that no one will know who said what. The name of the school will also be kept confidential.

If you have any questions, please feel free to contact me:
0798 xxxxxxx
Karamat@forwardpartnership.org.uk

Letter to teachers as interviewees

Pakistani boys' educational achievement in Birmingham schools

Dear teacher

I am in the process of looking into the educational achievement of Pakistani boys within Birmingham schools. I am writing to ask you whether you are willing to take part in my research and answer some questions.

The research

The research I am carrying out is a part of my PhD course at Warwick University. Therefore, all my work is being carried out within the rules and regulations of the University where I am being supervised by a Professor.

I have already carried out a review of existing literature on this subject in order to learn from others who are experts in this subject. This has helped me to identify the gaps in knowledge which I hope my own research will help to fill.

I am hoping to talk to a number of Pakistani boys in three different schools across Birmingham. In addition, I am hoping to interview the boys' parents and teachers.

The interview

This will take no more than 45 minutes of your time. I am happy fit around your timetable.

To make sure that I don't miss anything, the interview will be recorded. However, I will only use the recording for my own purpose and will not share it with anyone else.

Confidentiality

The discussion will be kept confidential. When the information is written up, your name will not be used so that no one will know who said what. The name of the school will also be kept confidential.

Your rights

Your views are very important but it's up to you whether to take part in this research. During the interview, if you say something you wish you hadn't, you can ask for this to be withdrawn.

Also, if you start talking to me and then decide that you do not want to be part of the research then you can change your mind. Any information you have already provided will be destroyed without being used.

If you have any questions, please feel free to contact me:
0798 xxxxxxx
Karamat@forwardpartnership.org.uk

Letter to parents asking them to take part in the research as parents

Pakistani boys' educational achievement in Birmingham schools

Dear parents

I am in the process of looking into the educational achievement of Pakistani boys within Birmingham schools. I am writing to ask whether you as parents would be happy to meet me and answer some questions about your son's education.

The research

The research I am carrying out is a part of my PhD course at Warwick University. Therefore, all my work is being carried out within the rules and regulations of the University where I am being supervised by a Professor.

I have already carried out a review of existing literature on this subject in order to learn from others who are experts in this subject. This has helped me to identify the gaps in knowledge which I hope my own research will help to fill.

I am hoping to talk to a number of other Pakistani parents who have boys in three schools across Birmingham.

The interview

This will take no more than 45 minutes of his time.

To make sure that I don't miss anything, the interview will be recorded. However, once I have listened to the interview and taken all the information from it, I will destroy the recording.

Confidentiality

The discussion will be kept confidential. When the information is written up, your name will not be used so that no one will know who said what. The name of the school will also be kept confidential.

Your rights

Your views are very important but it's up to you whether to take part in this research. Nothing negative will happen if you decide not to take part.

During the interview, if you say something you wish you hadn't, you can ask for this to be withdrawn.

Also, if during your conversation with me you decide that you don't want it to be part of the research then you can change your mind. Any information you have already provided will be destroyed without being used.

If you have any questions, please feel free to contact me:
0798 xxxxxxx
Karamat@forwardpartnership.org.uk

Letter to parents

Pakistani boys' educational achievement in Birmingham schools

Dear parent

I am in the process of looking into the educational achievement of Pakistani boys within Birmingham schools.

I am writing to you for two reasons:

1   To request your permission as parents to talk to your son at his school and ask him some questions about his education.
2   To ask if you would be happy to be interviewed yourself as parents

I have attached two sets of information on the following pages.

Please note that I have CRB clearance at an enhanced level.
If you have any questions, please feel free to contact me:
0798 xxxxxxx
Karamat@forwardpartnership.org.uk

Requesting parents' permission for their son to participate in the research

The research

The research I am carrying out is a part of my PhD course at Warwick University. All my work is being carried out within the rules and regulations of the University where I am being supervised by a Professor.

I have already carried out a review of existing literature on this subject in order to learn from others who are experts in this subject. This has helped me to identify the gaps in knowledge which I hope my own research will help to fill.

I am hoping to talk to a number of Pakistani boys, their parents and teachers in three different schools across Birmingham.

Confidentiality

The discussion will be kept confidential. When the information is written up, the real name of the interviewee will not be used so that no one will know who said what. The name of the school will also be kept confidential.

The student interview

This will take no more than 45 minutes of your son's time. I will work with the school to make sure that my meeting with your son takes place at a time which does not take him away from something really important.

To make sure that I don't miss anything, the interview will be recorded. However, I will only use the recording for my own purpose and will not share it with anyone else.

Your son's rights

Your son's views are very important but it's up to him whether to take part in this research. Nothing negative will happen if he decides not to take part. During the interview, if your son says something he wishes he hadn't, he can ask for this to be withdrawn.

Also, if he starts talking to me and then decides that he does not want to be part of the research then he can change his mind. Any information he has already provided will be destroyed without being used.

Requesting parents to participate in the research in their own right as parents

It is very important that as well as students, I interview you as their parent.

The parent interview

This will take no more than 45 minutes of your time. I will be happy to meet you at a time and place of your choosing.

To make sure that I don't miss anything, the interview will be recorded. However, I will only use the recording for my own purpose and will not share it with anyone else.

Your rights

As with your son, nothing negative will happen if you decide not to take part in this research. During the interview, if you say something you wish you hadn't, you can ask for this to be withdrawn.

Also, if you start talking to me and then decide that you do not want to be part of the research then you can change your mind. Any information you have already provided will be destroyed without being used.

Educational achievement of Pakistani boys in Birmingham
consent form for parents/carers

Name of pupil_____

I have received a letter giving me details of the above research.

I agree/do not agree for my son to take part in a single one-to-one interview.

I agree/do not agree to take part in the research myself.

Signature of parent/carer: _____Date:_____

Letter to students inviting them to take part in the research

Pakistani boys' educational achievement in Birmingham schools

Dear student

I am in the process of looking into the educational achievement of Pakistani boys within Birmingham schools. I am writing to you to ask whether you would be willing to take part in this research and be interviewed, on your own.

The research

The research I am carrying out is a part of my PhD course at Warwick University.

I have already looked at what others have written about this subject. This has helped me to identify the gaps in the knowledge which I hope to fill through my research.

My plan is to talk to a number of Pakistani boys in three different schools across Birmingham.

The interview

This will take about 30 minutes of your time. I will work with your school to make sure that my meeting with you takes place at a time which does not take you away from something really important.

To make sure that I don't miss anything, the interview will be recorded. However, I will only use the recording for my own purpose and will not share it with anyone else.

Confidentiality

The discussion will be kept confidential.

When the information is written up, your name will not be used so that no one will know who said what. The name of the school will also be kept confidential.

Your rights

Your views are very important. It is up to you whether to take part in this research. Nothing negative will happen if you decide not to take part. During the interview, if you say something you wish you hadn't, you can ask for this to be withdrawn.

Also, if you start talking to me and then decide that you don't want to be part of the research then you can change your mind. Any information you have already provided will be destroyed without being used.

Karamat Iqbal

Educational achievement of Pakistani boys in Birmingham
Consent form for students

Name of interviewee:_____

I have received a letter giving me details of the above research project and asking me to take part. I understand what it means for me. I agree to take part in a single one-to-one interview.

I agree for my interview being recorded on the basis that my views will be reported anonymously. (*Please circle one option.*)   No   Yes

I understand that my views will be kept confidential and used anonymously to inform the research being undertaken.

I understand that taking part in the interviews is voluntary (up to me) and that I can withdraw at any time without having to explain why and without being penalised or disadvantaged in any way.

Signature of pupil participant in the research _____Date:_____

Appendix 3

Questionnaire

STUDENT QUESTIONNAIRE

School name:				
Gender:	Boy ☐	Girl ☐		
Ethnic Group:	White – British	☐	Indian	☐
	White – Other group	☐	Pakistani	☐
	Black – Caribbean	☐	Bangladeshi	☐
	Black – African	☐	Chinese	☐
	Black – Other group	☐	Asian – Other group	☐
Eligible for free school meals	Yes ☐	No ☐	Any other ethnic group	☐

On this sheet are some questions to find out what you think. This is not a test. There are no right or wrong answers. Answer each question saying truthfully what you think by putting a tick in the appropriate box.

PERSONAL

	Strongly Disagree	Disagree	Agree	Strongly Agree
I always attend school unless I'm ill				
Finishing school is important to achieve my career choice				
I think doing well at school is very important for my future				
It's important for me to have role models who are from my own ethnic background				
I work hard at school				
My family can afford to pay for my after-school activities and trips				

HOME AND FAMILY

	Strongly Disagree	Disagree	Agree	Strongly Agree
I have access to a computer at home				
Someone from my family usually comes to parents' evenings/reviews at school				
If I need help with my homework, there is someone in my family who I can turn to				
My community has strong links with my school				
I have a quiet place in which to do school work				
My family responsibilities interfere with my education				
My family think that school is very important for my future				
The school has staff who can speak to my family in our community language				

MY RELIGION

	Strongly Disagree	Disagree	Agree	Strongly Agree
My religion is very important in my life				
It is important for me that my teachers have a good understanding of my religion				
There are good links between my school and mosque/temple/church				
Teachers deal fairly with incidents involving religious abuse				

In the last 2 years, have you attended regular activities at a mosque/temple/church   Yes ☐   No ☐
If No, please skip to the next section – My Teachers

How often did you attend the above activities?
Once a week ☐   Twice a week ☐   Three or more times a week ☐

What did the above activities focus on? (please tick all that apply)
Religious education   ☐
Community language   ☐
School related work   ☐
Other   ☐ (please give details below)

MY RELIGION

	Strongly Disagree	Disagree	Agree	Strongly Agree
The religious classes I have attended were a waste of time				
I have to spend too much time in religious classes which interferes with my school work				
What I learnt in my religious classes should be taught at school				

MY TEACHERS

	Strongly Disagree	Disagree	Agree	Strongly Agree
Teachers show respect for my cultural heritage				
It is important for me to have teachers of the same sex as me				
Teachers in my school treat all pupils fairly				
It is important for me to have teachers from my ethnic group				
My teachers value different cultures				
It is important for me to have teachers from my religion				
Teachers deal fairly with racist incidents				

POST-16 OUTCOMES

I intend to stay in full-time education (either school or college) after year 11	Yes ☐	No ☐
What level of qualifications do you expect to achieve by the end of your education?	No GCSE/GNVQs ☐ Some GCSE/GNVQ passes ☐ 5 'good' GCSE/GNVQ passes ☐ 'A'/'AS' levels ☐ University Degree ☐	

What stops you achieving more at school?

What career do you think you will be following when you are 18?

Thank you very much for taking the time to complete this questionnaire.

Appendix 4

Interviewees

Academy pupils and parents

Pupils	Parents
Javed NFSM, 5GCSEs[4]	
Khalad FSM, 5 GCSEs	Nawaz Mirpur.[5] Been in UK 40 + years. Used to be CFC machine programmer
Ibrar FSM, 5 GCSEs	Zeinab & Afsar Lahore; Afsar born in Kenya, Zeinab born in Lahore. Been in UK 30+ years.
Wasim FSM, 5 GCSEs	Najeeb Mirpur. Been in UK 30 years. Used to work in business, restaurant, double glazing.
Imran NFSM, 5GCSEs	Ashraf Gurgushti. Carpet fitter.
Waheed NFSM, N5GCSEs	
Majid NFSM, 5GCSEs	

Academy teachers

Jean	Achievement Leader; used to be Head of RE. White, female
Mehboob	Science teacher. Pakistani. Male.
Zahida	SLE (Specialist Leader of Education). Pakistani. Female.

Community pupils and parents

Pupils	Parents
Razaq FSM, 5GCSEs	Tazeem Gujar Khan. Been in UK 18 years. Single mum.
Pervez NFSM, N5GCSEs	Sakina Gujrat. Been in Birmingham 6 years. Husband delivery man.
Saleem FSM, 5GCSEs	
Habibul NFSM, 5GCSEs	
Mazar NFSM, 5GCSEs	Zaman Lala Moosa, ex-Mirpur; moved because of Mangla Dam. Been in UK 40+ years. Electrician.
Faisal NFSM, N5GCSEs	Khalaq Mirpur. Been in UK 8 years. Manual labourer.
Israr NFSM, 5GCSEs	Faiz Mirpur. Been in Birmingham 37 years. Manual labourer.
Amir NFSM, 5GCSEs	Junaid Jehlum, ex-Mirpur; moved because of Mangla Dam. Born in Birmingham. Runs recruitment business.
Khadam NFSM, 5GCSEs	
Tahir NFSM, 5GCSEs	Jamil Gujar Khan. Been in Birmingham 45 years. works in health and safety

Community teachers

Linda	Head of Y11. White British. Female. Been at school for 6 years. Subject specialism: psychology.
Abid	Science teacher. Pakistani. Male. Been at the school three years Ex pupil.
Richards	Head teacher. White. Male.

Grammar pupils and parents

Pupils	Parents
Habib NFSM, 5GCSEs	Syed (father) Multan. Doctor. (Syeda, mother)
Aakif NFSM, 5GCSEs	
Bilal NFSM, 5GCSEs	
Hamzah NFSM, 5GCSEs	Wali Lahore. Been in UK for 5+ years. Hospital doctor.
Danyal NFSM, 5GCSEs	Hafza Faisalabad (husband from Mirpur). Been in Birmingham 18 years. Learning Support Assistant.
Hashmi NFSM, 5GCSEs	Daalat Mirpur. Born in Birmingham. Sales Assistant.
Iqbal NFSM, 5GCSEs	Shahida Mirpur. Service provider, care homes

Grammar teachers

Masood	Part-time cover teacher. Pakistani. Male.
Steve	Head of Years 10 and 11, also Head of Design and Technology. Been at school 20 + years. White. Male.

Head of Private Tuition Centre

Private tutor Yaqoob
Private tutor Afzal

Appendix 5

Interview schedules

Students

Research Question

Understanding Pakistani boys' achievement in Birmingham schools

Do teachers understand the distinctive cultural heritage of Pakistani boys and the impact this might have on the boys' achievement?

- Would you say your teachers understand your cultural background? – Understanding of your home life, community, religion
- How do you know? Can you give me some examples?
- Is it important that teachers have this understanding? – In what ways might this help you?
- What more could the school do about this? – Such as provide training?

Do the boys attend a mosque/madrassah after school?

- How many hours an evening do you spend at the mosque/madrassah?
- Do you think this has an impact on your school work? – Does it help? Does it hinder? In what ways?
- Would you like to attend more often /less often or is it about right? – Have you ever discussed the frequency of your attendance with your parents?
- What links are there between your school and mosque/madrassah? (If they don't attend a mosque now but did so in the past) what links were there then between the mosque and school?
- What links are there between you school and home? – What more needs to be done to improve these links?
- What other learning do you take part in after school? – Participation in leisure activities. Does this help with school work?

Does teacher race and gender matter in addressing educational achievement of Pakistani boys?

- Is it important for you to have teachers who are men? Is it important for you to have teachers who are Pakistani? What about teachers who are Asian or from other ethnic minority groups?

Do Pakistani boys have access to appropriate role models?

- Who do you look up? – Someone at school? In the family? In the wider community?
- *Do Pakistani boys experience low educational aspirations or low expectations from significant others? (Teachers/parents/peers etc.)*
- What are your plans after leaving school? – Such as going to college, university-away from home or in Birmingham.
- What do your teachers expect you to do? – ask for examples.
- What do your parents expect you to do? – ask for examples

Parents

Research Question

Understanding Pakistani boys' achievement in Birmingham schools

Do teachers understand the distinctive cultural heritage of Pakistani boys and the impact this might have on the boys' achievement?

- Would you say the teachers in your son's school understand your cultural background? – Understanding of your home life, community, religion.
- How do you know? Can you give me some examples?
- Is it important that teachers have this understanding? – In what ways might this help your son's education?
- What more could the school do about this? – Such as provide training?

Does your son attend a mosque/madrassah after school?

- How many hours an evening does he spend at the mosque/madrassah?
- Do you think this has an impact on his school work? – Does it help? Does it hinder? In what ways?
- What links are there between your son's school and the mosque/madrassah? – What more needs to be done to improve these links?
- What links are there between your school and home? – What more needs to be done to improve these links?
- Do you think your son's attendance at mosque has an impact on his school work? – Does it help? Does it hinder? In what ways?
- Would you like him to attend more often/less often or is it about right?
- What other learning does your son take part in after school? – Participation in leisure activities. Does this help with school work?
- Do you provide or have you in the past provided paid for tuition for your son? How much money did you invest on this? Was it worthwhile?

Does teacher race and gender matter in addressing educational achievement of Pakistani boys?

- Is it important for you to have teachers who are men? Is it important for you to have teachers who are Pakistani? What about teachers who are Asian or from other ethnic minority groups?

Do Pakistani boys have access to appropriate role models?

- Who does your son look up? – Someone at school? in the family?, in the wider community
- Does it matter if the person your son looks up to is not of Pakistani heritage?

Do Pakistani boys experience low educational aspirations or low expectations from significant others? (Teachers/parents/peers etc.)

- What are your son's plans after leaving school? – Such as going to college, university – away from home or in Birmingham.
- Is this in line with your plan?
- What do your teachers expect him to do? – ask for examples.

Teachers

Research Question

Understanding Pakistani boys' achievement in Birmingham schools

Do teachers understand the distinctive cultural heritage of Pakistani boys and the impact this might have on the boys' achievement?

- Would you say you understand your Pakistani pupils' cultural background? – Understanding of their home life, community, religion. Can you give me some examples?
- Is it important that you have this understanding? – In what ways does it help?
- What more should be done about this and by whom? – Such as provide training?

Do the boys attend a mosque/madrassah after school?

- Do your Pakistani pupils attend a mosque/madrassah after school? – How many hours an evening do they spend at the mosque/madrassah?
- What links are there between the school and mosque/madrassah? – What more needs to be done to improve the links?
- Do you think you Pakistani pupils' attendance at mosque has an impact on their school work? – Does it help? Does it hinder? In what ways?
- What other learning do your Pakistani pupils take part in after school? – Participation in leisure activities. Does this help with school work?

Does teacher race and gender matter in addressing educational achievement of Pakistani boys?

- Do you think it matters that there are male teachers in the school?
- Do you think it matters that there are Pakistani teachers in the school?

Do Pakistani boys have access to appropriate role models?

- Who do your Pakistani boys look up? – Someone at school? In their family? in the wider community

Do Pakistani boys experience low educational aspirations and expectations?

- What do you know about your Pakistani pupils' plans after leaving school? – College, university-away from home or in Birmingham.
- Are these plans appropriate to their ability? – ask for examples

Notes

1 This demonstrates the inseparability of religion and culture.
2 Ex-Mirpur parents had been displaced by the building of the Mangla Dam.
3 There were four schools involved. All were given pseudonyms.
4 Predicted grades.
5 This is the area within Pakistan where the parents came from.

Bibliography

Abbas, T. (2002). The home and the school in the educational achievements of South Asians. *Race Ethnicity and Education* 5(3) 291–316.

Abbas, T. (2003). The impact of religio-cultural norms and values on the education of young South Asian women. *British Journal of Sociology of Education* 24(4) 411–428.

Ali, N. & Holden, A. (2006). Post-colonial Pakistani Mobilities: The embodiment of the 'myth of return' in tourism. *Mobilities* 1(2) 217–242, July.

Archer, L. (2002). It's easier that you're a girl and that you're Asian: Interactions of 'race' and gender between researchers and participants. *Feminist Review* 72 108–132.

Atim, J. & Cantu, S. (2010). *Cultural Competence in Research*. The Harvard Clinical and Translational Science Centre. www.mfdp.med.harvard.edu/catalyst/publications/cultural_ competence_annotated_bibliography.pdf Accessed 4.10.2013.

Basit, T. (2003). Manual or electronic? The role of coding in qualitative data analysis. *Educational Research* 45(2) 143–154.

BCC. (2011). *Schools data*. BCC. Education Department.

Bondi, L. (2003). Empathy and identification: Conceptual resources for feminist fieldwork. *International E-Journal for Critical Geographies* 2(1).

Briscoe, R. (2003). Implementing culturally competent research practices: Identifying strengths of African-American communities, families, and children. *Focal Point* 17(1), Summer.

Cohen, L. & Manion, L. (1994). *Research methods in education*. London: Routledge.

Cohen, L., Manion, L. & Morrison, K. (2007). *Research methods in education* (6th edition). London: RoutledgeFalmer.

Colombo, M. (2005). Empathy and cultural competence-reflections from teachers of culturally diverse children. *Beyond the Journal: Young Children on the Web*, November.

Cox, G. (2001). *The causes of minority ethnic underrepresentation as school governors in East Birmingham*. East Birmingham *Plus* Parents Association.

Das, C. (2010). *Considering ethics and power relations in a qualitative study exploring experiences of divorce among British-Indian adult children*. COMCAD Arbeitspapiere, Working Papers No 76.

Dimmock, C. (2002). Research methods in educational leadership and management in Coleman, M. & Briggs, A. R. J. (eds.) *Research methods in educational leadership and management*. London: Paul Chapman.

Francis, B. & Archer, L. (2005). British–Chinese pupils' and parents' constructions of the value of education. *British Educational Research Journal* 31(1) 89–108.

Griffiths, M. (1998). *Educational research for social justice*. Buckingham: Oxford University Press.

Hall, S. (2017). *Familiar stranger*. London: Allen Lane.

Halstead, M. (2007). In place of a conclusion: The common school and the melting pot. *Journal of Philosophy of Education* 41(4) 829–842.

Hammersley, M. (1994). On feminist methodology: A response. *Sociology* 28(1) 293–300.

Henry, M. (2003). 'Where are you really from?': Representation, identity and power in the fieldwork experiences of a South Asian diasporic. *Qualitative Research* 3(2) 229–242.

Iqbal, K. (2013). *Dear Birmingham*. Bloomingdale: Xlibris.

Kanuha, V. (2000). 'Being native' versus 'going native': Conducting social work research as an insider. *Social Work* 45(5) 439–447.

Lofland, J., Snow, D., Anderson, L. & Lofland, L. (2006). *Analysing social settings: A guide to qualitative observation and analysis*. Belmont: Wadsworth.

McKinney, E. (2016). *Changing times: The future of education in Birmingham*. Birmingham: Birmingham Education Partnership.

Mellor, J., Ingram, N., Abrahams, J. & Beedell, P. (2013). Class matters in the interview setting? Positionality, situatedness and class. *British Education Research Journal*. DOI:10.1002/berj.3035.

Newby, P. (2010). *Research methods for education*. Harlow: Pearson Education.

Oppenheim, A. (1992). *Questionnaire design, interviewing and attitude measurement*. London: Continuum.

Peshkin, A. (1988). In search of subjectivity: One's own. *Educational Researcher* 17 17–21.

Ramazanoglu, C. (1992). On feminist methodology: Male reason versus female empowerment. *Sociology* 26 207–212.

Reay, D. (1996). Insider perspectives or stealing the words out of women's mouths: Interpretation in the research process. *Feminist Review* 53 57–73.

Rhodes, P. (1994). Race-of-interviewer effects: A brief comment. *Sociology* 28 547.

Ringeisen, H., Henderson, K. & Hoagwood, K. (2003). Context matters: Schools and the 'research to practice gap' in children's mental health. *School Psychology Review* 32(2) 153–168.

Robson, C. (2011). *Real world research: A resource for users of social research methods in applied settings* (3rd edition). Chichester: Wiley.

Shah, S. (2004). The researcher/interviewer in intercultural context: A social intruder! *British Educational Research Journal* 30(4) 549–575.

Shah, S. (2006). Sharing the world: The researcher and the researched. *Qualitative Research* 6(2) 207–220.

Song, M. & Parker, D. (1995). Commonality, difference and the dynamics of disclosure in in-depth interviewing. *Sociology* 29(2) 241–256.

Stuart, R. (2004). Twelve practical suggestions for achieving multicultural competence professional psychology: Research and practice. *American Psychological Association* 35(1) 3–9.

Watts, J. (2006). 'The outsider within': Dilemmas of qualitative feminist research within a culture of resistance. *Qualitative Research* 6(3) 385–402.

Woods, P. (1986). *Inside schools: Ethnography in educational research.* London: Routledge & Kegan Paul.

4 Meaning and importance of education for Pakistanis

Migrants and education

It is well known that education is often highly valued amongst immigrant groups due to what has been defined variously as the 'immigrant paradigm', 'immigrant mentality' and 'the immigrant bargain' (Caplan et al., 1991; Zhou & Bankston, 1994; Kao & Thompson, 2003; Winder, 2004; Francis & Archer, 2005; Luthra, 2010). This is where immigrant parents, who struggled for success in their new country, make sure that they do all they can to enable their children to succeed. Joly (1986), in her research amongst Birmingham Pakistanis, found that the parents had brought with them from Pakistan a value for education which they considered as the medium for social mobility and self-improvement. They did not want their children to follow in their footsteps into labouring jobs. Unsurprisingly, the parents expressed a high level of respect for education and teachers. They explained to her that, as Muslims, their religion had taught them to respect teachers, who were seen as 'spiritual parents'. Modood et al. (1994) pointed out that British Asians gave high priority to academic success, which they saw as a way of achieving economic success.

> This desire to see their children succeed was strongly influenced by their own lack of opportunities in education and their wish that their children should not have to suffer the discrimination, disadvantage and lack of job security they themselves had faced in employment in the 1960s and 1970s.
>
> (p. 53)

It could be argued that perhaps what helps Pakistani young people to succeed against the odds of being disadvantaged are such protective factors and attitudes and behaviours that are found in their community. The Pakistanis have been shown to have a unique heritage and strengths (Anwar, 1979). Bourdieu described such resources as capital (Anheier et al., 1995). He identified three general types of capital: economic, cultural and social. The first, economic, refers to monetary income as well as other financial resources. Cultural capital is said to exist in long-standing dispositions and habits acquired in the socialisation process. The third type of capital, social, is the sum of the actual and potential resources that can be mobilised through membership in social networks. Communities can differ in the amount of such capital they possess. Some may have all three while others may have more of one capital and less of another. While Pakistanis may be short on economic capital they may have plenty of cultural and social capital, including that which the wider society may not recognise nor indeed value.

Lareau and Horvat's (1999) spoke of 'White cultural capital' – where being White placed individuals at an advantage. In the same way, Werbner (1990) spoke of 'Pakistani capital', which they used to evade the impact of institutional racism. Modood (2004) pointed out that for the Pakistanis their ethnicity formed a resource which led to disadvantaged families producing graduates. For Yosso (2005), the concept of capital was something broader. She saw it in the plural which may help us to identify the resources of the Pakistani community. For example, she spoke of linguistic capital which Pakistani young people develop and learn to use from an early age (Robertson, 2006). They also have what Rex and Tomlinson (1979) described as the skill of being 'culturally bilingual', with an ability to operate in different cultural contexts, including in, at times, a hostile wider majority society. It is possible that Pakistani pupils' achievement is helped by such capital within the community in the form of its values and networks which promote particular educational goals (Dwyer et al., 2006).

Importance of religion for Pakistanis

Pakistanis are said to be a religious[1] community (Georgiadis & Manning, 2011), with a majority being Muslims.[2] Holmwood and O'Toole (2017) remind us that while there is a decline in religion in the population as a whole, there is an increase in religion amongst some ethnic minority groups, especially those in Birmingham. This can be seen from the most recent census data which showed that the two city wards – Washwood Heath and Bordesley Green where the fewest people said they had 'no religion' – were mainly populated by Pakistanis (Iqbal, 2013). According to the Muslim Council of Britain (MCB, 2007) Islam is an important reference point for Muslim children. They advised schools that they should, therefore, take a positive account of this dimension of Muslim young people. "The faith of Muslim pupils should be seen as an asset to addressing constructively many of the issues that young people face today, including educational failure" (p. 17). A number of studies have confirmed such importance of Islamic religion. The DFES (2006) reported nearly all the Pakistani pupils as Muslim, for whom their religion was very or fairly important. For Chattoo et al. (2004) the significance of religion amongst Pakistani young people and their families was 'beyond debate' (p. 24). "Indeed, passing on religious values to their children was defined as an important aspect of filial duty, a prerequisite for good parenting, by parents, grandparents as well as the young people themselves" (p. 24). Research in Peterborough

(Davies, 2016 email) showed that nearly all the students who stated that their religion was Islam were actively practising their faith. Basit (2009) reported that, for many Muslim young people, their religious identity was paramount. Francis and Robbins (2014) found a clear association between faith affiliation and purpose in life, especially for Muslim young people. Village et al. (2011) pointed out that young Muslims growing up in England embraced higher levels of positive religious affect than was the case amongst young Christians (which I am equating with being White). A similar conclusion had been arrived at by Lindsay and Muijs (2005). In their study of boys in the culturally diverse Northern English town of Oldham they found religion was more important for Muslim boys than the non-Muslims.

Research that was focused on Birmingham provided a similar picture. Abbas (2004) found that all Asian Muslim students in the city had viewed their religion with greater commitment, both inside of school hours and outside. Sahin (2005) similarly confirmed the importance of religion for the city's students he researched. He concluded that Islam remained an important factor structuring their lives and a majority of the students held very high positive attitudes towards it.

Dwyer et al. (2006) spoke of 'religion as social capital' which gave the young people strong impetus to perform well academically. They found that religion encouraged their subjects to both conform to parental norms and values and actively constructed their own values which saw education as an appropriate Islamic activity. Consequently, their religious commitment kept them engaged in their studies. For its young adherents Islam can act as a driver for educational achievement and shape their attitudes and values, orienting them towards normative patterns of study and work (Shah et al., 2010). Franceschelli and O'Brien (2014) spoke of 'Islamic capital', which they defined "as a body of convertible resources originating from Islam and used by parents as support for their children's upbringing". They found parents reporting that religion strengthened them as a family, such as through praying together.

Religion is said to provide young people standards to guide their life practices. It does so by providing them with moral direction, inter-generational role models, access to alternative sources of cultural capital and community links. The more the young people access religious influences and capitalise on this resource, the more it positively influences their life's outcomes (Smith, 2003). It has been argued that the community and leadership skills learnt by young people through religious participation enhanced their overall capital, which benefited them throughout life (Iannaccone, 1990). A number of researchers have pointed to the link between religious participation and educational achievement. Such participation led to higher self-esteem, which was an important predictor of higher attainment (Brown & Gary, 1991; Markstome, 1999; Erickson & Phillips, 2012). Byfield (2008) identified the positive impact of prayer for her subjects through the development of character and values and through the general pro-education culture of their church. She found that their Church gave her subjects access to a strong personal, social and community identity.

It has been pointed out that religion had the greatest impact on young people where they received the same messages from their school, the church and the wider community, what has been referred to as 'closure' (Coleman, 1988). I had experienced such 'closure' as a child, where the worlds of my family and school, in Kashmir, cohered with each other and which helped to 'join-up' my home and school lives. It points to a need for greater collaboration between school, home and the mosque for the Pakistani students.

It could be said that all humans have culture but only some have religion. For those in the latter category, such as the Pakistanis in this study, the distinction between the two is likely to be a non-issue; they are likely to conclude that religion is cultural and culture is religious. The separation of religion and culture in societies is often attempted but it is not easily achieved. The contested nature of the subject matter can be seen from Beaman (2012–2013). She referred to the decision by the European Court of Human Rights which decided that the crucifix, which is central to the Christian religion, was a cultural symbol, especially in countries such as Italy which had given rise to the case she discussed. She explored "the complex ways in which religion and culture are intertwined" (p. 73), by investigating whether the displaying of a crucifix in public buildings and saying prayers before political meetings were acts of religion or culture. In her keynote lecture at the Sociology of Religion conference 2016,[3] Beaman also offered a third case; exploring whether yoga was a cultural or religious activity in the context of Californian schools. My findings confirmed Abbas' (2003) research, amongst the same Pakistani community in Birmingham, that religion and culture not only go together, at times each concept is used as a synonym for the other, as shown by these responses:

> Our culture has got lots of religion in it. Some things are religious, some things are cultural and some are both. You can't always separate them.
>
> Grammar parent Shahida

> There is an inextricable link between religion and culture. You can't separate religion from Pakistani culture. The two are connected. Religion is a part of the culture.
>
> Academy teacher Mehboob

Students in my study were asked to state the importance of religion for them, using the survey question: "My religion is very important in my life". The responses (Table 4.1) indicated that Pakistani pupils had the highest level of agreement, 88.8%, in this matter, thus confirming previous research cited earlier. Religion was also important for other Asian pupils: 87% Bangladeshi and 85.7% Indian pupils agreed with the statement. What was particularly significant was the high percentage of Pakistani and Bangladeshi pupils

Table 4.1 My religion is very important in my life (%)

Ethnic group	N	Strongly disagree	Disagree	Agree	Strongly agree
White British	82	45.2	26.8	13.4	14.6
Pakistani	54	1.9	9.2	18.5	70.3
Indian	28	7.1	7.1	50.0	35.7
Bangladeshi	23	8.7	4.3	8.7	78.3

who strongly agreed with the statement – 70.3% and 78.3% respectively. These groups are generally known to be Muslim. As to White British young people, religion had relatively little importance, with only 28% agreeing with the statement.

The wider meaning of education for Pakistanis

While Pakistani parents value education and wish to exploit its fullest potential for their children it does not mean they desire exactly the same education on offer in the British context. Halstead (1986) pointed out that Muslim parents (such as the Pakistanis) had two aims for education of their children. First, they wanted to gain the maximum benefit from the education on offer in the state system and, second, they wished to preserve, maintain and transmit their distinctive Islamic beliefs and values, both through direct teaching and (ideally) through a school ethos informed by those values. He explained that some parents gave priority to the secular education leaving the Islamic education to be dealt with at home and in the mosque, while others wished for both aims to be integrated into one education. However, what the latter group of parents wished for was that the education offered in state schools should be "given a distinct religious flavour and brought into harmony with Muslim beliefs" (p. 367). Brighouse (2005), Chief Education Officer for Birmingham, pointed out that it was to be expected that elders in any society would seek to ensure their young learn those skills that will enable them and their society to survive and thrive. They hoped too that the young will carry on the beliefs that underpin their culture and acquire the learning that extends the knowledge which their society values. Khan-Cheema (1994) pointed out that while the education system in a pluralist society cannot provide a fully Islamic education, one can expect it to be in harmony with Islamic principles. Interestingly, government's own Swann Report (1985, p. 509) pointed out that if schools followed their advice and accommodated religious education needs of Muslim children then this would go a considerable way towards meeting the concerns of many ethnic minority parents about their children's education. It is also worth bearing in mind that Pakistanis, like other Muslims, aim for coherence and interdependency between 'Muslimness' and Britishness (Abbas, 2018). In her research amongst a mainly Pakistani community, Basit (1995) found that parents saw Islamic belief as a living legacy that had to be passed on to their children. This was something that was not just a priority for the fully practising Muslims; all Muslims felt it to be their duty to transfer Islam to their children (Franceschelli & O'Brien, 2014). Nelson (2006), in his research conducted in Pakistan (in and around Rawalpindi), found the parents wanting both *deeni* and *dunyavi*, 'religious' and 'of the world', education respectively. They were keen that both should be provided in an integrated manner within schools.

Education from an Islamic perspective is seen as multidimensional; it focuses on the Arabic concepts of *talim, tarbiya* and *tadib* (Hussain, 2004; Anderson et al., 2011; Yasin & Jani, 2013). All three dimensions are essential to the complete task of educating young people. *Talim* means to know and to learn. Knowledge is one of the basic covenants of Islam and acquiring knowledge is a religious priority for Muslims, a duty imposed by God (Hossain, 1979; Shah, 2012). *Tarbiya* is concerned with growth and development in order to reach the stage of maturity. It involves presenting to the students certain values – of goodness, truth and honesty – until they are woven into the fabric of their personality. The teacher is considered to be both one who has knowledge as well as one who trains the personality. The third term, *tadib*, focuses on becoming cultured, well mannered and disciplined. It describes good social behaviour. Shah et al. (2010) sum up the meaning of education for Muslims as follows (p. 1115):

> Education is not just to get a good job, education makes you a good citizen, a good person, part of the society, if you're educated ... you always try to do the better things, you communicate better, you speak better, this is good for society.

For Mabud (1992), belief in God was central to the Islamic notion of education. For him education was for the total growth and development of human beings and education which did not provide an awareness of God was incomplete. According to Ashraf (1986), "education should aim at the balanced growth of the total personality of Man. . . . (It) should cater therefore for the growth of Man in all its aspects: spiritual, intellectual, imaginative, physical, scientific, linguistic" (p. 4). Earlier he (Ashraf, 1979) distinguished education from instruction and explained that the former helped in the complete growth of an individual's personality whereas the latter merely trained him in the efficient performance of given tasks. A human being may be highly proficient in a number of tasks but may at the same time be cruel or who deliberately ignores his duty towards neighbours or family. For him such a person could be said to be a well-instructed individual but not truly educated. For Ashraf, central to being educated Islamically was what it means to be human in both this and the next world. Badawi (1979) similarly pointed out that formation of moral character and behaviour were central to Islamic education; not merely acquiring knowledge but being morally transformed by it.

Coles (2013) is a convert to Islam. He had been a Senior Adviser for multicultural education in Birmingham Education. He brought together a number of education experts with long-standing experience of working in Birmingham.

The list included Professor Mick Waters, Dr. John Lloyd, Gilroy Brown, Nargis Rashid and the Revd. Jackie Hughes, Diocesan Director of Education, in Birmingham. Between them they agreed that:

> an education service must have an overarching teleological vision, a sense of what an educated person should look like after ... years of compulsory schooling. This vision must be translated into a series of clear and explicit values which underpin the notion of an educated person.
>
> (p. 11)

Pakistani respect for education

Evidence of shared beliefs and values in the wider Pakistani community, especially as they relate to importance of education, has been reported. Like their parents, young Pakistanis were found to believe that education was very important to succeed in life. They had learnt this from their parents who, irrespective of their own education, were acutely aware of the status education would confer on the family. Basit (2013) found high aspirations amongst the parents and grandparents, including those who lacked full understanding of the educational process. According to the DFES (2006a, Table 13), Pakistani students were most likely, of all pupil groups, at 94.4%, to state that school work was worth doing; the figure for White British was 92.8%. They similarly were most likely to state, at 91.7%, that they worked as hard as they could at school; compared to 80.4% of White British. In my research Pakistani pupils were found to be positive about education. This was illustrated in their response to statements such as: "I work hard at school" (94%) and "I think doing well at school is very important for my future" (96%). This compared favourably with White British pupils.

Because of their religious and cultural socialisation many Pakistani young people are brought up to believe that the teacher is the most important actor in the teaching and learning process who does not merely function as a source of knowledge for the students but also as a model for good conduct (Kania et al., 2011). This quality is especially important given the teacher's role in delivering *tarbiya*, growth and development dimension of education. Consequently, teachers are generally respected by their Muslim pupils. In Berglund's (2012) research, teachers stood only behind parents and God in the eyes of Muslim pupils: 70% of those surveyed said they would confide in their parents, 58% in God and 50% in teachers. Only 5% of non-Muslim students claimed that they would confide in their teachers, placing them almost to the bottom of the list of possible responses. Arthur (2011) has drawn attention to the moral dimension of teaching and the moral role of the teacher. His research, involving 5,207 young people and 21 teachers in 25 Midland schools, suggests that, apart from parents, teachers are often regarded as the people most likely to have an influence on students' moral character. The teachers in his research agreed that the most powerful influence they have on their students is role modelling by exemplifying the behaviours they wished to see in their students and in society at large.

From the responses given by the Pakistani boys in my research it was clear that they did indeed have a high level of respect for education and for their teachers. They explained that this was what their parents had taught them. For some of them, the message was reinforced at their mosque too:

> The same level of respect; for teachers, for parents. That's the way I have been brought up. My parents have always told me that you've got to respect, whoever is older than you.... At the mosque there is the same teaching.
>
> Academy pupil Ibrar

> how you should treat your teachers, that's taught at the mosque. I've definitely tried to do that.
>
> Community pupil Mazar

Pakistani parents explained their high regard for education, which they had communicated to their children. They explained that they saw it as a vehicle for success for their children. The following comment reported by Academy pupil Javed provides an illustration of what has been previously described as the 'immigrant paradigm':

> My dad always gives me his own example. He worked in my Granddad's shop, then as a taxi driver before he bought the post-office. He says to me: "you should work hard when you are young and then it will be easy when you are old". He works long hours running his post office. He says: "if I worked hard when I was younger, I wouldn't be here now. I would have a good job, working 9–5". That's why he says education is important.

This quote confirms the findings of Joly's (1986) research about the community in Birmingham where parents had seen education as a way of avoiding their children following their parents in menial jobs.

The parents in my study expressed their commitment to education and explained the message they give to their children:

> At home, we stress the importance of education. We advise they should go to school on time, not to cause trouble with a teacher or any of the children. Not to fight. Not to be bud-tameez, (disrespectful). Whoever a teacher is, you should respect them and follow their instruction.
>
> Community parent Khalaq

> I always tell my children that you should respect your teacher. Whatever they say, follow it.
>
> Grammar parent Shahida

I have had no chance for education. I want a different future for our children.

Community parent Junaid

Community parent Zaman saw the role of teachers even higher. He elevated their status to that of *roohani waldain,* (spiritual parents):

We say to our children to treat the teachers as if they were your parents. So whatever the teachers tell you, you should do that ... basically be good at school.

Grammar parent Wali explained his family's tradition of valuing education:

My dad went out of his way for my education and that's what I feel I need to do for my kids as well.

The idea of respect was linked back to the parents' religion:

Our deen, religion, teaches respect; how you should treat your elders. It teaches about adab, manners. It's not just about namaz, prayer. Our deen teaches akhlaq.

Academy parent Ashraf

These findings were a confirmation of what had been acknowledged by the DCSF (2008), who had noted that religion can "contribute significantly to the moral climate of a school, encouraging high standards of respect and behaviour which are upheld by the religious belief systems of pupils' families and community groups" (p. 16). Academy parent Ashraf linked what they taught their children to their role as parents:

We teach the children about this (respect for teachers) at home too. In fact, our role at home is very important in that respect.

Community parent Tazeem described her son's behaviour and, in doing so, described what to her was the 'good student':

My son is theek, thaak (all–right), he is a good pupil. Teachers are happy with him. He does not misbehave. He attends every lesson. He has respect for time, he is never late. He does his work; homework too.

Between the 40 boys and parents interviewed, there were over 100 references to 'respect' in the interviews; around a half to respect for teachers and education, with the rest for elders, parents and adults in general.

Grammar Teacher Steve confirmed the commitment to education and high aspirations of Asian parents. He explained that the parents saw education as a route to success and aspired for their son to go to university, for sought-after courses:

> regardless of their background, a lot of the Asian parents are very keen for their child to succeed and they have high aspirations for their sons. They could be from the humblest background and still have that desire for their son.

Parents' investment in education

Pakistani parents are generally known for their willingness to invest in their children's education (Warren & Gillborn, 2003). In particular, they have been found to be willing to pay for private tuition for their children. Strand (2014) reported that they were more likely (than White British parents) to do so. He also reported that Asian parents were more likely to know where their children were when they were out, were less likely to quarrel with their child and less likely to be single parent households. Basit (2013) had similarly reported to Asian parents' investment into the education of their children. She found that almost all young people had their own room; all had a desk, books, a computer with internet and so forth. This was complemented by an expectation of hard work on a regular basis:

> It was strikingly clear that education was viewed as capital that would transform the lives of the younger generation. This educational capital was believed to be the most significant asset a young person could acquire and the families provided a range of support mechanisms to enable the young people to realise this aspiration.
>
> (p. 719)

Many of the parents in my study paid for extra tuition for their sons, such as coaching for the 11+ tests. In addition, the parents paid for the supplementary religious teaching of their children. The interview with Private tutor Yaqoob[4] shed light on their investment in their children's extra-education. He provided evidence from his perspective as a provider of such tuition. He explained that the Pakistani parents took education very seriously, including those who were poor. "They want their kids to do well. They are not just 'leave it up to the school', they want their children to have extra help. They really pay attention to their kids; they want them to do well".

Lareau (2003) has pointed out that parental strategies differed according to their socio-economic status. This was found to be true amongst the Pakistani community especially so for the Grammar parents. According to Grammar teacher Masood, "all pupils have tuition to get here, whatever their background". All seven of the Pakistani boys at Grammar reported having received such tuition. Much of the tuition was in core subjects such as English, maths and science. Some students had the tuition provided at home while others attended classes away from home. The parents interviewed verified the provision of such tuition:

> We arranged for our son to have private tuition. He went to a private tutor which gave him that extra something.
>
> Grammar parent Daalat

> We had a teacher come to the house to provide maths tuition. If we think he needs more help then we'll get the teacher back.
>
> Community parent Zaman

Of particular significance here was the investment by Grammar parents into their boys' Islamic religious education (IRE). Three of the five parents I interviewed reported that their children did not attend madrassah but had the benefit of the parents paying for a teacher to come to their house. This meant the children did not need to spend unnecessary time travelling to a madrassah and, furthermore, were able to benefit from more focused one-to-one tuition. The other Grammar parents reported that they had collectively organised supplementary religious education for their children:

> A few families get together and a couple of people deliver some sort of discussion about, you know, Islamic knowledge and life and all that. Self organised, a kind of study circle.
>
> Grammar parent Wali

> We hire a school building and provide Urdu, Arabic and Islamic Studies, up to GCSE level.
>
> Grammar parent Syed

Role of the Pakistani family

Pakistani young people generally grow up in a mainly collectivist culture where the distinction between the individual and the group is blurred (Bochner, 1994). Here they are able to benefit from their family's social capital (Khattab, 2003). The social capital acts as a channel for the transmission of parents' values, norms and expectations to their children. According to Basit (2013a), the social and cultural capitals amongst Asian families helped to propel their youngsters towards educational success where they were able to acquire educational capital. She found that education meant more to parents than its economic worth. It was seen as making the young people good human beings.

Thapar–Bjorkert and Sanghera (2010) found the parents using their own experiences of hardship, in the UK, to transmit the importance of education to their offspring. The older siblings "became important *role models*" (original italics) (p. 255), given that they, having been brought up in the same environment as the respondents, had become successful. They took on roles such as responding to school letters and reports and checking homework. Williams and Gregory (2001) presented siblings as a resource, who acted as a bridge between the school and home literacies and who interpreted the discourses, values and practices of the school and combined them with the practices within the home. Basit (1995, 2013) also saw siblings as a resource who helped the young people to make informed choices about education. Moreover, she pointed to the whole extended family as an important resource, who between them were able to stress on the young people the importance of education.

Ritchie et al. (2005) and Buchanan (2006) highlighted barriers to the take-up of educational opportunities due to the parents' lack of understanding of the education system. Here members of the extended family stepped in (Crozier & Davies, 2006). For example, older cousins might attend school events in place of parents. "Thus the social capital offered by the extended family ... compensated for parents' low educational and human capital" (Thaper & Sanghera, 2010, p. 19). I can add to this a personal example. When my nephew moved to Sixth Form College, neither of his parents felt confident to attend his Parents' Evenings. So I stepped in. For Crozier and Davies (2006), the Asian family was an untapped educational resource; "the extended family has the potential to be employed in the enhancing of the children's academic achievement if this resource were recognised and harnessed by the school, and inducted into educational knowledge" (p. 693).

In my research, as well as their positive role, the findings pointed to some negative impact of the family in relation to education. In response to the statement: "My family responsibilities interfere with my education", 31.4%, of the Pakistani pupils agreed, compared to 20.7% of the White pupils. The negative impact of the family was more of an issue for Pakistani boys; 37.8% of whom agreed with the statement, compared with only 17.6% Pakistani girls. This may be due to the patriarchal nature of the Pakistani family where more is expected of the boys, such as attending funerals. A number of parents offered a comment on this subject. Grammar parent Shahida spoke of the general demands of the Pakistani culture on its members. She pointed out that one consequence of this was that few Pakistani parents were able to participate in social activities at school with parents from other ethnic groups.

Some parents were found to prioritise their children's education and protect it from family activities. Community parent Junaid pointed out that if there was a wedding or a funeral they did not expect their children to become involved, unless it was a close relative. He also pointed out that in their wider family they arranged weddings in the summer holidays so that it did not disrupt children's education. He also explained their family provided a quiet space for the children to do their homework. When asked how important education was for them, he said:

> In our family we are very much (education) focused. If we are going somewhere over a weekend and they have exams to revise then that takes priority.

On the other hand, for Community parent Jamil, children's education was important but not any more important than weddings and funerals. He thought it was important for children to be present at such occasions, to pay their respect.

Deen and *dunya*: meaning of education

Parents were asked what education meant for them. It was clear that they placed an emphasis on both the religious and 'of this world'. Academy parent Ashraf's response was typical. Speaking in his mother tongue, Urdu-Punjabi, he explained that education had to include both *deen* and *dunya*, explaining what it meant:

> But for us it's both deen and dunya. We think both are important. Majority of people from our community believe that deen is very important; alongside (the rest of the education). Both deen and dunya are important. Without deen (the child) won't know where they have come from. We should have both deen and dunya. They have equal importance.

The evidence of this could be seen in his son, Academy pupil Imran, attending madrassah every day since primary school. He also spoke of what was expected of an educated person, that they should know about praying and how to treat people properly. He described it as 'naik tareeqa' (pious manner). Community parent Khalaq made the same point, explaining the reason why one should prepare for the after-life:

> It is my view that children should have deeni and dunyaavi education; both are important. Deeni education helps a person prepare for the next life. For that we need the Quran, prayer, fasting; we have to know about Allah Taala. Our dunyaavi education is necessary for this world.

Grammar parent Hafza elaborated on this by explaining what success meant:

> I tell the children: education is very important. Religion is very important. They have finished their Quran. They have to read their prayers.

Grammar parent Daalat similarly stressed the importance of religion in education; without this for him education was not complete:

> He needs to know what Islam is; it would make him a good human being. (Religion is) very, very important for us.

Community parent Zaman, when asked how important it was for his son to have religious/Islamic education, responded that their faith dictated that their son should learn the basic fundamentals of Islam, including reading the

Quran and the prayers. Grammar parent Shahida explained that there was a duty on the parents to provide religious education, as pointed out by Chattoo et al. (2004). Her interview was in fluent English. Nevertheless, she used the Urdu word for duty to explain their role as parents:

> As a parent, it's our farz, it's our duty, that your child knows the key parts of our religion, can read the Quran. Education, yes, it is important for life here. But we have to prepare for the life in the hereafter.

She then explained that religious education was not just 'other worldly'; it was important for this world too. Community parent Jamil similarly pointed out that it was not a matter of this world and the next but of leading a 'good' religious life in the face of the irreligious world. Like in earlier research conducted in the UK and in Pakistan, these Pakistanis had two aims for education: accessing the best of the education on offer in the British state education system and the preservation, maintenance and transmission of their Islamic beliefs and values, both through direct teaching and (ideally) through a school ethos informed by these values. In other words, the parents desired for their children to receive both educations; the 'dunyavi', worldly, and 'deeni', Islamically religious.

A number of the parents spoke of the meaning of education and outlined what being educated meant, confirming its multidimensional nature, i.e. *talim*, *tarbiya* and *tadib*. They spoke of the value of *adab* and *akhlaq*, manners and morals. For Community parent Faiz, *adab* was key for children. Grammar parent Wali spoke of *adab* being synonymous with 'being educated':

> his education to me is not just his academic performance, but, the overall personality that he develops. High grades are one aspect. You know, he needs to have good knowledge of things AND (original emphasis) overall development.

When asked to illustrate what this meant, he responded: "You know, for me if an elder comes in, you know, I would probably stand up". Community parent Sakina pointed out that *deeni* education helped to make the children better human beings. Grammar parent Syed similarly pointed out: "It's a vital part of his bringing up. Without religion, you're not a complete human being". For Grammar parent Daalat, being educated meant looking after one's parents, being good to the community, "your responsibility as a brother, to your relatives, as a neighbour, all things like that. As a good son, when the parents are old, you don't leave them, you look after them". The parents saw their task as being role models for their children and setting a good example for them:

> Our home atmosphere has influenced how he is. We have to set an example.
>
> Grammar parent Syed

You show by example. You are a role model yourself.

Grammar parent Daalat

Homework and study support

Homework has been reported as being beneficial in enabling students to become self-reliant, develop initiative and accustom them to the idea of working profitably out of school (Strand, 2008). It can reinforce and extend the school curriculum, develop skills of independent learning or help to link up home and school. It has been pointed out that spending two or more hours daily on homework was a strong predictor of better attainment as well as better social-behavioural outcomes (Sammons et al., 2011; Sylva et al., 2011). For Holmes and Croll (1989) there was a strong association between homework and performance in examinations while Cooper et al. (2006) concluded that positive effects of homework included immediate achievement and long-term academic and non-academic benefits. It increased the time students spent on academic tasks and made a positive impact to their achievement. For Sharp (2002), time spent on homework had a positive effect on the achievement of pupils, especially for pupils from disadvantaged backgrounds. For the DfEE (1998), learning at home is an essential part of good education to which children are entitled. They saw that homework played an important role in helping pupils to acquire skills and confidence and in raising their standards of achievement. It also encouraged them to engage in lifelong learning. The Teachers' Standards (DfE, 2011) asked teachers to set homework and plan other out-of-class activities in order "to consolidate and extend the knowledge and understanding pupils have acquired" (Part one, 4).

Ethnic minority parents have been found to be supportive of homework (Hughes & Greenhough, 2002; Hughes, 2005). However, it has been acknowledged that children from deprived backgrounds may find it harder than their peers to complete their homework, which may compound the gap between the more and the less advantaged (DCSF, 2009). Lack of appropriate space in which to do homework, lack of resources, not being able to turn to someone when needing help were some of the problems faced by children from disadvantaged families. Sallee and Rigler (2008) spoke of the 'weighted scales' of homework, when contrasting the situation of the differing socio-economic status students. Some go home to well-educated parents and well-resourced environments while others may have family responsibilities, parents who are not able to help with homework due to a range of factors and few educational resources in their homes. They signal how this can further disadvantage some students while helping others do even better. "To not take these differences into account when assigning homework is to contribute to the widening of the gap teachers are committed to closing" (p. 49). MacBeth et al. (2001) pointed out that the more formal education the parents themselves had the longer their children spent on homework.

In the US, teachers in the KIP (Knowledge Is Power) schools (Lack, 2009), recognising that their disadvantaged parents were unable to help their children with homework, gave the children their mobile phone numbers so they could call them at night for homework help (Tough, 2006). The Education Select Committee spoke of poorer children not having space to complete their homework (House of Commons, 2014):

> the evidence shows us that it is much harder for those youngsters we are talking about to do their homework ... in a room where nobody was eating, watching television or doing anything except their homework.

For the Select Committee, one possible response to this situation was to provide time for these children at the end of the school day so they could complete their homework. Earlier, the DFEE (1998) had pointed to the possibilities of offering homework opportunities "at places other than home. These may include opportunities at school, for example during lunch time or before or after school, as well as opportunities away from school premises, at libraries or community centres" (para 35). As a response, study support was recognised as an alternative to traditional way of doing homework and was adopted as a policy initiative by the New Labour Government (Elliott et al., 2004; DFES, 2006b). It was recognised that such provision can be particularly beneficial in raising the achievement of underachieving students. MacBeth et al. (2001) pointed out that study support was particularly beneficial for minority ethnic students and its impact on their attainment was over twice the size of that on the White students. *Playing for Success* was one example of study support provision, made available – through the Football Association – at a number of football clubs. The provision was managed by experienced teachers who used the medium and environment of sport to support work in literacy, numeracy and ICT. The initiative was found to have wide-ranging benefits (Sharp et al., 2003). Train and Elkin (2000) also pointed to the effective role of public libraries in delivering homework clubs.

In my study I explored the situation of Pakistani boys in relation to this issue; whether they had a quiet place in which to do their school work and whether they were able to turn to someone in the family if they needed help in completion of the work. The findings showed that 83% had a quiet place for this purpose; similar to the situation of their White peers. However, of those from poorer families, only 73% reported having such a facility. There was an additional problem the Pakistani boys faced: nearly a third of them reported that, if they needed help with their homework, there was no one in their family to turn to. This was a particular problem for those from poorer families where nearly a half of them reported to have such a problem, confirming previous research. Basit (1995) had pointed out the inability of her Pakistani parents to help their daughters with academic matters such as homework and subject option choices.

Notes

1 Howarth and Lees (2010) define religion in three ways: as a meaning system, to do with the visible signs of religious beliefs and practices or both combined. They also note the practice, by researchers, of allowing self-definition of religion, which is the approach I have taken.
2 According to the 2011 Census, 92% of the Pakistanis in England identified themselves as Muslim (Costu, 2013; Hussain & Sherif, 2014). As to what 'Muslim' means, Lewis (2003) points out that, for some, their Muslimness is mainly cultural, for others it is about religious rituals. There are also some for whom it may be little more than an attribute of ethnic identity. These perspectives are worth bearing in mind in interpreting what follows.
3 I was a delegate at the conference.
4 Private Tutor Yaqoob ran a tuition centre after school and on weekends. I was told the children came for extra support in their core subjects.

Bibliography

Abbas, T. (2003). The impact of religio-cultural norms and values on the education of young South Asian women. *British Journal of Sociology of Education* 24(4) 411–428.

Abbas, T. (2004). *The education of British South Asians.* Basingstoke: Palgrave Macmillan.

Abbas, T. (2018). Reconfiguering religious identities. *British Journal of Sociology of Education* 39(2) 161–165.

Anderson, P., Tan, C. & Suleiman, Y. (2011). *Reforms in Islamic education: Report of a conference held at the Prince Alwaleed Bin Talal Centre of Islamic Studies.* University of Cambridge.

Anheier, H., Gerhards, J. & Romo, F. (1995). Forms of capital and social structure in cultural fields: Examining Bourdieu's social topography. *American Journal of Sociology* 100(4) 859–903.

Anwar, M. (1979). *The myth of return.* London: Heinemann.

Arthur, J. (2011). Personal character and tomorrow's citizens: Student expectations of their teachers. *International Journal of Educational Research* 50 184–189.

Ashraf, S. A. (1979). Preface in al-Attas, S. M. (ed.) *Aims and objectives of Islamic education.* Jeddah: Hodder and Stoughton/King Abdulaziz University.

Ashraf, S. A. (1986). *New horizons in Muslim education.* Cambridge: Hodder & Stoughton/ The Islamic Academy.

Badawi, Z. (1979). Traditional Islamic education: Its aims and purpose in the present day in al-Attas, S. M. (ed.) *Aims and objectives of Islamic education.* Jeddah: Hodder and Stoughton/ King Abdulaziz University.

Basit, T. (1995). *Educational, social and career aspirations of teenage Muslim girls in Britain: An ethnographic case study.* Department of Education University of Cambridge: Ph.D. dissertation.

Basit, T. (2009). White British; dual heritage; British Muslims: Young Britons' conceptualisation of identity and citizenship. *British Educational Research Journal* 35(5) 723–743.

Basit, T. (2013). Ethic, reflexivity and access in educational research: Issues in intergenerational investigation. *Research Papers in Education* 28(4) 506–517.

Basit, T. (2013a). Educational capital as a catalyst for upward social mobility amongst British Asians: A three-generational analysis. *British Educational Research Journal* 39(4) 714–732.

Beaman, L. (2012–2013). Battles over symbols: The 'religion' of the minority versus the 'culture' of the majority. *Journal of Law and Religion* 28(1) 67–104.

Berglund, J. (2012). Teachers only stand behind parents and God in the eyes of Muslim pupils. *Journal of Beliefs & Values: Studies in Religion & Education* 33(3) 357–367.

Bochner, S. (1994). Cross-cultural difference in the self concept. *Journal of Cross-Cultural Psychology* 25(2) 273–283.

Brighouse, T. (2005). Towards a more just society. *Times Educational Supplement*, 21 January.

Brown, D. & Gary, L. (1991). Religious socialization and educational attainment among African Americans: An empirical assessment. *The Journal of Negro Education* 60(3) 411–426.

Buchanan, A. (2006). Children aged 0–13 at risk of social exclusion: Impact of government policy in England and Wales. *Children and Youth Services Review* 28 1135–1151.

Byfield, C. (2008). The impact of religion on the educational achievement of Black boys: A UK and USA study. *British Journal of Sociology of Education* 29(2) 189–199.

Caplan, N., Choy, M. & Whitmore, J. (1991). *Children of the boat people*. MI: University of Michigan Press.

Chattoo, S., Atkin, K. & McNeish, D. (2004). *Young people of Pakistani origin and their families: Implications for providing support to young people and their families*. London: Barnardo's.

Coleman, J. (1988). Social capital in the creation of human capital. *The American Journal of Sociology* 94 95–120.

Coles, M. I. (2013). *Reform of the national curriculum in England: Consultation response*. www.cstg.org.uk/wordpress/wp-content/uploads/2013/04/CoEd-Foundation-NC-Reform-Statement.pdf Accessed 11.6.2014.

Cooper, H., Robinson, J. & Patall, E. (2006). Does homework improve academic achievement? A synthesis of research, 1987–2003. *Review of Educational Research* 76(1) 1–62.

Costu, Y. (2013). Turkish and Pakistani Muslim communities in Britain; A comparative approach. *The Journal of International Social Research* 27(6) 178–184.

Crozier, G. & Davies, J. (2006). Family matters: A discussion of the Bangladeshi and Pakistani extended family and community supporting the children's education. *The Sociological Review* 54(4) 678–695.

Davies, A. (2016). Personal email, 23 July.

DCSF. (2008). *Raising the attainment of Pakistani, Bangladeshi, Somali, and Turkish heritage pupils: The national strategies: Secondary*. London: Department for Children Schools and Families.

DCSF. (2009). *Deprivation and education*. London: Department for Children Schools and Families.

DfE. (2011). *Teachers' Standards: Guidance for school leaders, school staff and governing bodies*. www.gov.uk/government/uploads/system/uploads/attachment_data/file/301107/Teachers__Standards.pdf Accessed 10.3.2016.

DFEE (Department for Education and Employment). (1998). *Homework: Guidelines for primary and secondary schools*. London: DfEE.

DFES. (2006). *Ethnicity and education: The evidence on minority ethnic pupils aged 5–16*. London: DFES.

DFES. (2006a). *Study support: A national framework for extending learning opportunities*. London: DFES.

Dwyer, C., Modood, T., Sanghera, G. & Thapar-Bjorkert, S. (2006). *Ethnicity as social capital? Explaining the differential educational achievements of young British Pakistani men and women*. Paper presented at the 'Ethnicity, Mobility and Society' Conference at University of Bristol, 16–17 March.

Elliott, J., Harker, E. & Oglethorpe, B. (2004). *Lessons from study support for compulsory learning*. London: DFES.

Erickson, L. & Phillips, J. (2012). The effect of religious-based mentoring on educational attainment: More than just a spiritual high. *Journal for the Scientific Study of Religion* 51(3) 568–587.

Franceschelli, M. & O'Brien, M. (2014). Islamic capital and family life: The role of Islam in parenting. *Sociology* 48(6) 1190–1206.

Francis, B. & Archer, L. (2005). British-Chinese pupils' and parents' constructions of the value of education. *British Educational Research Journal* 31(1) 89–108.

Francis, L. & Robbins, M. (2014). The religious and social significance of self-assigned religious affiliation in England and Wales: Comparing Christian, Muslim and religiously-unaffiliated adolescent males. *Research in Education* 92, November.

Georgiadis, A. & Manning, A. (2011). Change and continuity among minority communities in Britain. *Journal of Population Economics* 24 541–568.

Halstead, M. (1986). *The case for Muslim voluntary-aided schools: Some philosophical reflections.* Cambridge: Islamic Academy.

Holmes, M. & Croll, P. (1989). Time spent on homework and academic achievement. *Educational Research* 31(1) 36–45.

Holmwood, J. & O'Toole, T. (2017). *Countering extremism in British schools? The truth about the Birmingham Trojan Horse affair.* Bristol: Policy Press.

Hossain, S. (1979). A plea for a modern Islamic university: Resolution of dichotomy in al-Attas, S. (ed.) *Aims and objectives of Islamic education.* Jeddah: Hodder and Stoughton/King Abdulaziz University.

House of Commons. (2014). *Underachievement in education by White working class children.* London: The Stationary Office.

Howarth, J. & Lees, J. (2010). Assessing the influence of religious beliefs and practices on parenting capacity: The challenges for social work practitioners. *British Journal of Social Work* 40 82–99.

Hughes, M. (2005). *Homework and its contribution to learning.* Swindon: ESRC.

Hughes, M. & Greenhough, P. (2002). *Homework and its contribution to learning.* A report presented at an invitational DFES verification seminar. Bristol: University of Bristol.

Hussain, A. (2004). Islamic education: Why is there a need for it? *Journal of Beliefs and Values: Studies in Religion & Education* 25(3) 317–323.

Hussain, S. & Sherif, J. (2014). Minority religions in the census: The case of British Muslims. *Religion* 44(3) 414–433.

Iannaccone, L. (1990). Religious practice: A human capital approach. *Journal for the Scientific Study of Religion* 29(3) 297–314.

Iqbal, K. (2013). *Dear Birmingham.* Bloomingdale: Xlibris.

Joly, D. (1986). *The opinions of Mirpuri parents in Saltley, Birmingham about their children's schooling.* Warwick: CRER.

Kania, D., Romly, T. & Zarman, W. (2011). *Value education in the perspective of western and Islamic knowledge: International seminar on Islamic Education.* Ibn Khaldun University Bogor.

Kao, G. & Thompson, J. (2003). Racial and ethnic stratification in educational achievement and attainment. *Annual Review of Sociology* 29(1) 417–442.

Khan-Cheema, A. (1994). British Muslims and the maintained schools in Ashraf, S. A. & Hirst, P. H. (eds.) *Religion and education: Islamic and Christian approaches.* Cambridge: The Islamic Academy.

Khattab, N. (2003). Explaining educational aspirations of minority students: The role of social capital and students' perceptions. *Social Psychology of Education* 6 283–302.

Lack, B. (2009). No excuses: A critique of the Knowledge Is Power Program (KIPP) within charter schools in the USA. *Journal for Critical Education Policy Studies* 7(2) 126–153.

Lareau, A. (2003). *Unequal childhood*. London: University of California Press.

Lareau, A. & Horvat, E. (1999). Moments of social inclusion and exclusion; race, class and cultural capital in family-school relationships. *Sociology of Education* 72 37–53.

Lewis, P. (2003). Christians and Muslims in the West: From isolation to shared citizenship? *International Journal for the Study of the Christian Church* 3(2) 77–100.

Lindsay, G. & Muijs, D. (2005). *Challenging underachievement of boys in Years 8 and 10: A study for the Oldham Leading Edge Partnership*. Coventry: University of Warwick.

Luthra, R. (2010). *Assimilation in a new context: Educational attainment of the immigrant second generation in Germany*. ESRC. Institute for Social & Economic Research. Working Papers Series.

Mabud, S. (1992). A Muslim response to the Education Reform Act 1988. *British Journal of Religious Education* 14(2) 74–98.

Macbeth, J., Kirwan, T., Myers, K., McCall, J., Smith, I., McKay, E., Sharp, C., Bhabra, S., Weindling, D. & Pocklington, K. (2001). *The impact of study support*. London: DFES.

Markstome, C. (1999). Religious involvement and adolescent psychosocial development. *Journal of Adolescence* 22 205–221.

MCB (Muslim Council of Britain). (2007). *Meeting the needs of Muslim pupils in state schools*. www.religionlaw.co.uk/MCBschoolsreport07.pdf Accessed 10.3.2016.

Modood, T. (2004). Capitals, ethnic identity and educational qualifications. *Cultural Trends* 13(2) 87–105.

Modood, T., Beishon, S. & Virdee, S. (1994). *Changing ethnic identities*. London: Policy Studies Institute.

Nelson, M. (2006). Muslims, markets and the meaning of a 'good' education in Pakistan. *Asian Survey* 46(5) 699–720.

Rex, J. & Tomlinson, S. (1979). *Colonial immigrants in a British city*. London: Routledge & Kegan Paul.

Ritchie, C., Flouri, E. & Buchanan, A. (2005). *Aspirations and expectations*. Oxford: Family and Parenting Institute.

Robertson, L. (2006). Learning to read 'properly' by moving between parallel literacy classes. *Language and Education* 20(1) 44–61.

Sahin, A. (2005). Exploring the religious life-world and attitudes toward Islam among British Muslim adolescents in Francis, L., Robbins, M. & Astley, J. (eds.) *Religion, education and adolescence: International empirical perspectives*. Cardiff: University of Wales Press.

Sallee, B. & Rigler, N. (2008). Doing our homework on homework: How does homework help? *The English Journal* 98(2) 46–51.

Sammons, P., Sylva, K., Melhuish, E., Siraj-Blatchford, I., Taggart, B., Toth, K., Draghici, D. & Smees, R. (2011). *Influences on students' attainment and progress in key stage 3: Academic outcomes in English, maths and science in year 9*. London: Department for Education.

Shah, B., Dwyer, C. & Modood, T. (2010). Explaining educational achievement and career aspirations among young British Pakistanis. *Sociology* 44(6) 1109–1127.

Shah, S. (2012). Muslim schools in secular societies: Persistence or resistance! *British Journal of Religious Education* 34(1) 51–65.

Sharp, C. (2002). *Should schools set homework?* Slough: NFER.

Sharp, C., Blackmore, J., Kendall, L., Green, K., Keys, W., Macauley, A., Schagen, I. & Yeshanew, T. (2003). *Playing for success: An evaluation of the fourth year*. Nottingham: DFES.

Smith, C. (2003). Theorizing religious effects among American adolescents. *Journal for the Scientific Study of Religion* 42(1) 17–30.

Strand, S. (2008). *Minority ethnic pupils in the longitudinal study of young people in England, extension report on performance in public examinations at Age 16*. Institute of Education, University of Warwick.

Strand, S. (2014). Ethnicity, gender, social class and achievement gaps at age 16: Intersectionality and 'getting it' for the White working class. *Research Papers in Education* 29(2) 131–171.

Sylva, K., Melhuish, E., Sammons, P., Siraj-Blatchford, I., Taggart, B., Toth, K., Smees, R., Draghici, D., Mayo, A. & Welcomme, W. (2011). *Effective pre-school, primary and secondary education 3–14 project (EPPSE 3–14) final report from the key stage 3 phase: Influences on students' development from age 11–14.* London: Department for Education.

Swann Report. (1985). *Education for all.* London: HMSO.

Thaper, S. & Sanghera, G. (2010). Building social capital and education: The experiences of Pakistani Muslims in the UK. *International Journal of Social Inquiry* 3(2) 3–24.

Thapar-Bjorkert, S. & Sanghera, G. (2010). Social capital, educational aspirations and young Pakistani Muslim men and women in Bradford, West Yorkshire. *The Sociological Review* 58 (2) 244–264.

Tough, P. (2006). What it will really take to close the education gap. *The New York Times*, 27 November.

Train, B. & Elkin, J. (2000). Homework clubs: A model for the qualitative evaluation of public library initiatives. *New Review of Children's Literature and Librarianship* 6(1) 177–192.

Village, A., Francis, L. & Brockett, A. (2011). Religious affect among adolescents in a multifaith society: The role of personality and religious identity. *Journal of Beliefs and Values* 32(3) 295–301.

Warren, S. & Gillborn, D. (2003). *Race equality and education in Birmingham.* Birmingham City Council and Birmingham Race Action Partnership.

Werbner, P. (1990). *The migration process.* Oxford: Berg.

Williams, A. & Gregory, E. (2001). Siblings bridging literacies in multilingual contexts. *Journal of Research in Reading* 24(3) 248–265.

Winder, R. (2004). *Bloody foreigners.* London: Abacus.

Yasin, R. & Jani, M. (2013). Islamic education: The philosophy, aim and main features. *International Journal of Education and Research* 1(10) 1–18.

Yosso, T. (2005). Whose culture has capital: A critical race theory discussion of community culture wealth. *Race Ethnicity and Education* 8(1) 69–91.

Zhou, M. & Bankston, C. (1994). Social capital and the adaptation of the second generation: The case of Vietnamese youth in New Orleans. *International Migration Review* 28(3) 821–845.

5 The gaps in education

The role of madrassahs

Amongst most immigrant groups it is common to see additional provision of education in order to fill certain gaps in the provision on offer in the state system (Maylor et al., 2010). The response of Pakistanis in this respect was the development of madrassahs, which Rashid et al. (2006) characterised as supplementary schools for the Muslim community, set up to deliver Islamic education in order to preserve religious, cultural and linguistic identities. These places of learning are said to have a particular focus on learning the Quran. They operate either from local mosques, community centres or in people's homes. Such madrassahs have been in existence since the early days of post-war Pakistani migration to the UK (Hiro, 1991; Dahya, 1973; Khan, 1977; Anwar, 1979; Taylor & Hegarty, 1985).

From the perspective of British Pakistanis the key gap in the state education system was in relation to teaching of their religion. This had resulted from the secularist nature of state education (Felderhof et al., 2007; Arthur, 2015). Another shortcoming involved the teaching of mother tongue(s). Education policy was focused on the teaching of English, which was predicated on 'subtractive' bilingualism and 'subtractive schooling' (Fillmore, 1991; Garza & Crawford, 2005). This is where children start school with knowledge of, and competence in, more than one language and culture but the school system steers the children towards a monolingual and monocultural mindset. This has been referred to as the 'monolingualising' role of the education (Conteh & Brock, 2011; Safford & Drury, 2013; Sharples, 2014). Teachers with a 'monolingual mindset' play a critical role in the process within the context of a majority community that is generally hostile to bilingualism (Ellis, 2004; Rosowsky, 2010). Here it is worth referring to the exceptional message of the government-commissioned Bullock Report (1975). This encouraged schools to support minority languages, which influenced practice of some schools (Ofsted, 2008). An example from Birmingham was Moseley School, which offered Urdu in its languages curriculum. Some schools also offered Arabic, which is valued by Pakistani children given that it is the language of the Quran. Belle Vue School in Bradford was reported to have notable minority languages provision. This may provide a model for others. The school had well-qualified Urdu and Arabic teachers who used modern, language-teaching methods and drew on contemporary issues in order to ensure the relevance of the curriculum. Their provision was described by the students as 'fun' and 'excellent' (Ofsted, 2012, p. 2). The curriculum was enhanced by trips abroad, such as to Egypt, where students had the opportunity to speak Arabic in everyday situations. The Arabic provision at a number of other schools was reported by Tinsley (2015). Within Birmingham, Oldknow Academy was praised for its Arabic provision, including for its trip to Saudi Arabia (Ofsted, 2013): 60% of the cost of the trip had been met by the parents (YouTube, 2014).

As elsewhere, Pakistanis in Birmingham developed a cultural and religious infrastructure which included madrassahs (Chishti, 2008). Rex and Moore (1967) had found the Pakistani parents' desire for their children to retain their home culture, their language and religion. Hashmi (1973), in his study of Pakistanis in the Saltley area of the city, pointed out that parallel with starting school Pakistani children would also be sent to the local mosque, where they "spend one to two hours learning the Islamic way of prayer, the basics of Islam and also reading and writing in Urdu" (p. 6). Joly (1986) was one of the earliest academic researchers amongst Pakistani parents in Birmingham. She reported the community wishing for their heritage to be maintained through such supplementary provision. The parents had high regard for state education. However, they were also intent on preserving their culture and religion and were eager for its continuity through the generations. "The overwhelming majority of families had arranged for their children to study Urdu either in the mosque, or in a house taught by a relative or friend" (p. 13). The parents reported that all the children were learning the Quran (in Arabic). They also pointed out that the supplementary education was inadequate and placed a burden on the children, and a large majority, 66%, were in favour of the children being taught to read the Quran at school. Those who were opposed to this explained that they were "wary of initiatives which would entrust the teaching of Qur'an to a non-Muslim teacher. In their eyes, the Qur'an must only be taught by a well-qualified bona fide Muslim" (p. 23). An even higher number, 97%, were in favour of Urdu being taught at school. The parents wished for their heritage to be respected by the education system and for it to be included in the curriculum. In their view this would remove some of the ignorance and prejudice amongst the White pupils. "They should be taught (Pakistani culture), so there would be a better understanding; if they know our culture and our ways, there wouldn't be as much hatred as there is now" (p. 22). Cherti and Bradley (2011) provided the most recent picture of madrassah provision and reported that there were around 2,000 madrassahs attended by around 250,000 Muslim children across the UK. The focus of the madrassahs in their research was on the Quran and Islamic education, with a significant number also teaching languages such as Arabic and Urdu.

Supplementary schools are generally funded through fees from the children. However, within Birmingham, for a number of years the local authority provided funding for them. On one occasion 111 such schools were funded, the majority of which were Pakistani run. The then Chief Education Officer, Tim Brighouse, explained that the purpose of this support was to enhance the educational opportunities for children, to recognise the significance of community language and its relationship to educational achievement and to support the development of cultural awareness that can demonstrate a direct link with educational achievement (BCC, 2000). The funding support continued for a number of years (BCC, 2001, 2002, 2003). It has been reported that, in the financial year 2003–2004, Birmingham LA had spent £191,910 for this purpose (Maylor et al., 2010). This was to cover tutor fees, equipment, material costs and rent. The integral nature of supplementary schools in Birmingham was reported by Ofsted (2002, para 67) when they found the Key Stage 3 strategy being implemented with Advisers working with supplementary schools. A national example of funding of supplementary schools was through the establishment of the National Resource Centre for Supplementary Education.[1] Beyond the UK, Berglund (2015) has provided examples of funding support for Islamic Religious Education. In Finland it is argued that IRE helps students to become knowledgeable about their origins, with a strong sense of personal identity. This is said to create solid Finnish citizens that can contribute to social cohesion in unique and meaningful ways. They have published books about Muslims which are set in a Finnish environment. Within Sweden, a number of Muslim organisations receive financial support that can be used to sponsor their own Islamic instruction classes which have a focus on Quran Studies and Islamic history. In some schools, Quranic recitation is taught as part of IRE. The curriculum sets out to connect the 'macro' world of Islamic history to the 'micro' world of the pupils. Of particular interest are those narratives which help to reinforce the values of modern-day Swedish society, such as the importance of generosity and good neighbourliness.

Madrassah participation; the current picture in Birmingham

It is well known that Muslim children, such as the Pakistanis, in this study, participate in madrassah learning, a fact that has been acknowledged by Department for Education (DFES, 2006):

> most Muslim children attend classes in their local mosque where the primary purpose is to provide religious education. . . . The age at which most Muslim children start to attend . . . varies but is usually at about five years of age. Most continue to attend until they are 14.
>
> (p. 58)

They explained that children participating in such provision learn about their religion Islam, learn to read (without understanding) the Quran and learn languages such as Urdu and Arabic. My findings have confirmed this situation.

62.9% of Pakistani pupils were found to have participated in such activities or were currently doing so. For the majority, 67.6%, the focus of the activities was religious education; for 14.7% the focus was community language learning. The few White students (28%) who attended a church did so in order to participate in sport and leisure activities.

I explored Madrassah attendance during interviews with the students. They were asked whether they participated in religious activities after school or over the weekend. About a third of the students were currently participating in such activities while the rest had done so earlier in their life. Many of the pupils had been participating in such learning since primary school. I was able to verify this information through interviews with the parents.

Private tutor Yaqoob outlined the requirements for religious education, given his extensive knowledge of the subject matter. He confirmed that it was *farz*, obligatory, for the children to learn to read the Quran and *salaat*, prayer. He explained that it normally took three to four years for a child to *finish* their Quran, i.e. read it in Arabic from start to finish: "Memorising it off by heart takes a long time. But it depends on the child".

The amount of time the Pakistani students spent in madrassah activities varied between one and four hours, from three days a week to daily. During this time they were expected to learn to read the Quran in Arabic at least once. Some students went to a mosque or other location for such learning. A number of the parents hired the services of a religious teacher who would come to the house for a set amount of time.

I explored with the students their madrassah routine. The response from Academy pupil Imran was typical:

3.15: School finishes
3.30: Get home. Eat something, get changed, do *wudu*, ablution. Start reading the Quran at home, for about 30–40 minutes.
4.30: Walk to the mosque; sometimes get a lift.
6.00: Return home

Links between school and madrassahs

For the QCA (Qualifications Curriculum Agency), children's learning was a part of a bigger picture than school alone (Waters, 2007; Bartlet et al., 2008). It was the entire planned learning experience of a young person. This included the lessons that they had during the school day, but also recognised how much young people learnt from activities that take place out of school. They advised education practitioners and policymakers to 'join-up' the different elements of a child's learning life.

In my study, a key part of the 'big picture' are the madrassahs. However, based on my long-standing knowledge of Birmingham, generally there are few links between schools and madrassahs. Roach and Sondhi (1997) pointed out that the relationship between state and supplementary schools was patchy and transactional in nature. Moreover, a number of the supplementary schools regarded the relationship as being exploitative. The approach taken by Hornsby (2005), a head teacher of a mainly Pakistani-Birmingham school, was very much an exception but could offer a model of effective practice. He provided a list of questions for schools to use to help teachers gain a better understanding of madrassahs.

A number of writers and researchers have asked whether more could be done to integrate the madrassah provision into the mainstream education system. Richardson and Wood (2004) argued for greater integration of the different elements of Muslim young people's lives and suggested a joining-up of what they do at school with their lives at home and at the mosque. Gent (2011) asked whether a time will come when teachers from madrassahs and the state education sector would work together for mutual benefit. For him, a starting point might be the recognition of the legitimacy of the learning at madrassahs by the mainstream teachers, including the valuing of the achievements of Muslim students in areas like Quranic memorisation and recitation. Earlier, Gent (2006) made a case for collaboration between state schools and madrassahs. However, he warned against the dangers of the state education system setting out, with a 'colonial' mindset, to bring madrassahs 'up to scratch'. For him it was important to recognise that the two systems of education were different with their own distinct philosophies, strengths and weaknesses. He made a case for the state education sector to take a positive interest in the madrassah experiences of their Muslim pupils and suggested that structures be set up to facilitate cross-fertilisation of ideas and methods amongst madrassahs and between madrassahs and the state schools. Hewer (2001) asked whether the mainstream education sector could embrace "a religious ethos and an Islamic perspective as part of its strategy to raise the educational standards of children from disadvantaged minority communities (such as the Pakistanis)?" (p. 524). Lewis (2006) spoke of the potential of *imams*, mosque leaders, to act as providers of bridging capital between Muslim parents and local schools. Ipgrave et al. (2010) provide effective examples of state schools responding to the needs of Muslim communities. Halstead (2007) and Shah (2008) pointed out the potential of Islam in the teaching of moral education for Muslim majority schools. Robertson (2006) stressed the importance for schools to build on the wider cultural and linguistic heritage of their children. However, she accepted that, in order to build on pupils' strengths, interest and experiences, the teachers would need to know what they were. Cherti et al. (2011) reported that where links between schools and madrassahs existed it had significant advantages for children and improved relations with the local community. For example, one madrassah had suspended classes to support the local schools when key stage tests were being conducted, allowing children to spend time with revision. In turn, the schools closed at the Muslim festival of Eid so that families could celebrate together. Pupil attendance and behaviour had improved in the schools, leading to higher levels of attainment.

I explored whether there were any links between the two areas of Pakistani boys' education – school and madrassah. Students were asked to respond to the statement: "There are good links between my school and mosque/temple/church". Overall, less than one third, 31.4%, of the Pakistani pupils agreed. A number of respondents pointed out the potential benefits of links between the school and the madrassah. Academy pupil Khalad said such links would be a good idea through which the two systems of education could "collaborate, and combine their knowledge about the student". Discipline was likely to be one area of possible benefit, through a joined-up response from the school and the madrassah. Academy pupil Javed spoke of a fellow Pakistani student who disrespected the teachers. His school teacher spoke to the local imam who had a word with the boy and his behaviour improved. Therefore, he thought it a good idea for there to be such links:

> If the school had links with the madrassah, they could ring them up and say this student's done this and they are not happy with it. Then the madrassah can deal with it as well as the school.

Academy teacher Mehboob also supported such links, pointing out its more general benefits:

> There may be issues that the school is facing with the boys. They could be addressed by the Imam. It could be: the children smoking; it could be there's ethnic tension amongst pupils; many things. It would help us to sing from the same hymn sheet.

He also thought some of the teaching at the school would benefit from being reinforced at the mosque, such as on issues like sexuality. The students may not be sure where Islam stands on such matters so if the teaching came from the imam, they may pay more attention to it. Academy teacher Zahida also felt the links would be a good idea. She believed it would give the school teachers an insight into the world of the madrassah; they would learn about the type of education the boys were receiving there. She suggested a way forward could be for the school to set up a working party:

> And the Pakistani presence in the school is growing, yeah, its growing.[2] So, I think that's really important; to have credible working party or committee or someone who carries out some action research in that area.

The majority of the links between the schools and madrassahs were at Community. The boys and teacher interviewees explained that the links between their school and local mosques was due to the effort of their Head Teacher:

> Yes, the Headteacher knows the mosque leaders very well. He visits the mosque regularly. He has a good bond with the Imams.
>
> Community pupil Amir

Richards, the Head Teacher, confirmed the links:

> I have good links with the mosques. I know the imams well. We tackle issues together. There was a drug issue in the community, with certain boys. Imam phoned me up at home. "Mr Richards, can you help me out. Yeah, can you help me out". I said, yes, we'll work together. We got together, we shared information. He tackled it from his end, I tackled it from mine.

He pointed out that he had established meaningful and on-going relationships with imams from a number of the mosques in the school's vicinity. He explained that these religious leaders (as well as other faiths in the area) know that his door is always open to them. He went on to explain that on one occasion he had even been invited, as a neutral and trusted outsider, to help resolve some conflict between two of the mosques. He had been to a number of the mosques, to visit and *speak at* (his emphasis):

> There is the Khomeni mosque, then there's one down near the sports ground, Bengali mosques, Pakistani mosques, predominantly all Sunni based, with some exceptions. I've got links now with the one on Acacia Road,[3] that's just been built. So lots of links in there, constant dialogue and conversation with, you know the key thing is to keep the communication links open.

Richards explained that he went to the mosques about once every half term; after the Friday prayer, the busiest day for the mosques:

> They invite me in. I go in front of the congregation. There can be over a thousand men there. I'm able to do a short talk. Often, I have said I am a man of faith. I know you have faith. I am here to serve your community, serve the children. If you need to talk, you should come and see me. I say a little bit about the school, what we're doing.

He pointed out that, on a few occasions, the imams have come into the school, to discuss issues that face their congregations and which they think he as a Head Teacher might be able to help with:

> They come in my office and talk to me, about whatever they want to. I talk about my faith, they talk about theirs. We walk around the school, so they can see what's happening in our curriculum. You know the children see me walk around with the imams in the classrooms. There's a transparency about what we're doing.

Positive outcomes of madrassahs

We have seen from the survey responses that for the majority of Pakistani students the focus of the after-school classes was religious education. Much of this time appeared to have been spent on learning to read the Quran and the basics of Islam such meaning and practice of praying. Some students spoke of other learning too, such as *adab* and *akhlaq*, (manners and morals); how they should behave towards teachers, other elders and the wider community. Community pupil Mazar explained that the teaching at his madrassah, which was focused on manners and morals, had made a positive difference to his behaviour as a pupil. He said that, as a result of what he had been taught, he is better behaved at school. Academy pupil Javed agreed:

> I used to argue a lot with teachers. Now I don't. It's linked to the attendance at the mosque; they teach you to respect the teachers and not argue with them.

For Francis et al. (2009), there are diverse benefits of supplementary education, including a space to negotiate identities, a space for the transmission and celebration of aspects of 'culture' and a 'space' free from racism and additional education (in community language and/or other subjects and skills). Hall et al. (2002) reported that madrassahs provided the students opportunities to learn, to socialise and to belong. Students found that attendance at these schools was a way of reclaiming their cultural and social identity, something they felt they could not achieve at mainstream school. The authors concluded:

> The most striking message, then, from our evidence is that the supplementary school imbues its participants with a sense of belonging to a community that supports them practically, culturally, socially, emotionally and spiritually ... support through strong ethnic identity and community attachment.
>
> (p. 410)

From the Pakistani community's perspective, the long-term benefit of such supplementary education is the transmission of their religion to the younger generation. This has been reported to be of importance even to those parents who were not fully practising but who still felt the duty of transferring Islam to their children (Franceschelli & O'Brien, 2014). It would appear that such transmission of their religion is successful with reference to Islam when compared with other communities (Scourfield et al., 2012).

There appears to be a lack of published research on the impact of supplementary schools, such as on improvements in attainments (Strand, 2007). A Bristol project, aimed at Muslim children, was reported to have made significant impact on the attainment of pupils (Maylor et al., 2010). In addition to academic achievement, improved behaviour and a commitment by pupils to their studies was noted. Furthermore, staff attitudes, in terms of raised expectations of the pupils and improved relations with parents were also listed as an outcome of the supplementary provision. Strand (2007) had found that more than 80% of pupils reported that attending supplementary school helped them with their mainstream school work. In 2007, the DFES funded the Madrassah Literacy Project run by QED-UK, a community-based organisation serving the Pakistani community in Bradford (Cherti et al., 2011). Their project helped to create a dialogue between madrassahs and schools. It was initiated in order to foster understanding between different communities and to improve levels of literacy and overall educational attainment of ethnic minority pupils. In 2009, the Open Madrassah Network was developed by the Bradford Council. The programme paid local qualified teachers to teach booster classes for 'borderline' primary and GCSE students in four Muslim supplementary schools. It also gave pupils the opportunity to study for GCSEs in Arabic, Urdu and religious education. Shah et al. (2010) reported on the work of the Pakistani community in Slough which had set up a homework club. This had been started by middle class members of the community for their working class co-ethnics. It was staffed by volunteers including university and secondary school students. It was explained that the provision was set up "to provide children with supplementary education and to provide working class children with some of the extra educational tuition which more middle-class parents 'buy'" (p. 1118).

Here it is worth considering the matter of 'ethnic retention' and its likely benefits on education of young Pakistanis. The term was coined by researchers to refer to minorities embracing the characteristics of their group such as identifying as a Muslim, speaking one's mother tongue and observing religious practices. It has been shown that such ethnic retention was positively related to school performance. According to Akiba (2007), Vietnamese students tended to have "higher grades and were more likely to be college bound when they (a) actively participated in the Vietnamese community and (b) were fluent in both English and Vietnamese" (p. 223). Their counterparts, on the other hand, who were more distant from Vietnamese culture and language, were less likely to be academically successful. This was, in part, due to the former being able to draw on the resources of both cultures. Consequently, they are more resilient and have higher self-esteem (Phinney, 1991; LaFromboise et al., 2006). In the context of this study, it is likely that Pakistani students are able to derive some benefit from their active ethnic and religious identification. It is possible, however, that there is greater potential for such benefits to be realised through a more effective organisation of the practices and processes involved.

Problems with madrassahs

A number of researchers have identified problems with the madrassah system. Richardson and Wood (2004) quoted teachers saying that madrassah attendance had had a deleterious effect on work during school time, and consequently on levels of attainment. Cherti et al. (2011) found madrassah provision to compare unfavourably with the state system. Only 14% were found to require their teachers to have QTS (Qualified Teacher Status). The imams were "found to not be up to speed with current educational thinking and practices" (p. 12) as a majority had received their training outside the UK. "This is seen as problematic ... particularly because large numbers of UK congregants of mosques and madrassahs are now British-born and may not be responsive to the language and ideas of spiritual leaders hired from overseas" (p. 12). They reported some of their participants raising concerns about the role of madrassahs in reinforcing differences between British and Muslim identities.

Lewis (2006) reported the Institute of Islamic Scholars as saying:

> the student, after spending a good part of the day at (state) school, comes exhausted both mentally and physically to the madrassah. If the teacher then conducts his lesson without preparation, planning or using relevant methods, how would that then capture the imagination, attention and hearts of the students.
>
> (p. 174)

Lewis also referred to the poor pay and job security of the imams, the mosque leaders, who deliver madrassah teaching. Earlier Halstead (1986) had identified a number of shortcomings in the madrassah provision: additional financial burden on the community and academic burden on the pupils, their approach and methods and inadequate premises, unqualified teachers, corporal punishment and rote-learning. Elsewhere, he reported schools complaining that their Pakistani students spent far too much time at their 'mosque school' (Halstead, 2005). Taj (1996), commenting on the Pakistani community in Bradford, pointed out that while IRE had the potential for being a force for good, this would not be realised if teaching was not accompanied by guidance in a language which the children could understand. "It is equally important that supplementary religious education is provided with the interests of the child as paramount; all too often it is conducted at the convenience of the providers, during the school week, leaving pupils tired and unresponsive to their wider education" (p. 8). According to the Association of Muslim Social Scientists (AMSS, 2004), participation in supplementary education can be stressful for the children "some of whom spend seven days a week attending schools of various descriptions or who study in the evening when other children are relaxing at home with their parents. Parents too suffer, transporting their children between two schools and bearing various extra costs" (p. 35). In Birmingham, Rashid et al. (2005) pointed out that, while for Pakistani boys attending madrassah was seen as an integral part of their development as Muslims,

> several teachers expressed concern about the supplementary education both in terms of fatigue pupils suffered by attending school and then Madrassahs and the teaching and discipline within the Madrassah, which often contradicted the practices within schools.
>
> (p. 20)

A number of safeguarding issues have been identified in relation to the madrassah provision. Cherti et al. (2011) pointed out that madrassahs did not always carry out CRB checks on the teachers. Upon the publication of their report, there was a discussion on the Islam Channel (5 December 2011),[4] hosted by the Birmingham community activist, Salma Yaqoob. In her introduction, she stated that "teaching standards are not often of the best quality . . . and a teacher was recently imprisoned for 10 weeks for kicking and slapping boys" (0.40–0.55 minutes). Later in the programme (13.30–13.45 minutes) Yaqoob said: "I've witnessed this myself . . . in the mosques it was not unusual for sticks to be used, to hit the children". Also present on the programme was Mogra[5] who was running a madrassah, in Leicester (Bawden, 2011) which may have the potential to be a model for the rest of the community. He explained that his madrassah had a zero tolerance of abuse of children. All of the teachers were CRB-checked and received training in child protection. Teachers were expected to model compassion. Children were said to enjoy attending the madrassah.

Elsewhere, the madrassah system has come under criticism with reference to pedagogical problems, where some of its teaching methodology spilled into the school education. Rosowsky (2000, 2001) pointed out that when children read a text in their school teaching it is a given that they will understand its meaning; this is not so in the madrassah. Within the latter the children are enabled to *read* but not necessarily *comprehend*. They learn to decode the text orally and recite the words. This different approach to reading was said to have "significant effects on reading behaviour in general and can, and does, affect reading in the second, or additional, language, which is, in this case, English" (Rosowsky, 2000, p. 46). Mogra (2007) pointed out that within madrassahs "curriculum development has generally taken a back seat" (p. 390). He confirmed that the quality of education provided in the madrassahs was significantly inferior to that of state-funded schools:

> The premises and resources are often inadequate, the teachers often unqualified and the methods, which may include rote-learning and strict discipline, are often out of tune with contemporary western educational thinking and practice. . . . There may be little place for discussion and intellectual understanding.
>
> (p. 389)

In his research into the teaching of the Quran in Irish Muslim schools, Sai (2017) found that memorisation played a dominant role in the teaching where pupils were not exposed to understanding or explanation of what they recited or memorised. "Teacher and instruction-centred Qur'an education, with a mechanistic and ritualistic approach which aimed solely at memorisation, seemed to limit the potential of the pupils" (p. 8). For Sai, such an approach may encourage passivity; this is not ideal for young children who are likely to be accustomed to a more student-centred style in their normal schooling. He felt that professional development for Quran teachers on pedagogical practice ought to be a priority. In his view Quran teachers have the potential to have a very positive and influential role in the delivery of Islam to younger generations. Every effort should be made to realise the potential. Sahin (2005) also drew attention to the problems of pedagogy in the madrassah system. He asserted that "Muslim educators must face the difficult question of *what it means to be Islamically educated* (original emphasis) in a multicultural society" (p. 167). He concluded that the traditional IRE "with its teacher-text centred approach and memorizing-based methods" (p. 179) did not help young Muslims to develop a mature Islamic subjectivity. He found the overwhelming emphasis in IRE was on outward teaching of Islam rather than creating a dialogue. "A case in point is the way in which young Muslims are introduced to the Quran. Despite the fact that many British young Muslims speak and think in English, there is not a well worked-out Quranic pedagogy in English" (p. 179). He identified the implications of this. "Thus, many of these young people are left ignorant of this fundamental source of Islam or at the mercy of radical transnational Islamic groups, which try to indoctrinate them into a rigid ahistorical understanding of Islam" (p. 179). Such 'vulnerabilities' can be a particular issue for young Muslims with low educational achievement (Iacopini et al., 2011). The House of Commons (2012) also identified underdeveloped or confused religious under-standing as a vulnerability to young people holding extremist views.

Sahin (2005) made a case for a different approach in Islamic education, pointing out that, "according to the Quran, the educational process cannot be reduced to a mechanical process of training or indoctrinating, one-way transmission" (p. 180). He pointed out that the person–oriented developmental Quranic model of education, with its emphasis upon thinking, places the crit-ical dialogic process at the very heart of Islamic educational self-understanding. Elsewhere, he (Sahin, 2013) found the young Muslims "complained that the traditional Islamic education received at home and at the supplementary mosque schools was inadequate to help them respond Islamically to the rapid changes and challenges of secular multicultural polity" (p. 103). He stated that the young people "wanted to achieve a personal understanding and meaning in being a Muslim" (p. 103). In his view, this made it necessary to bring about a contemporary Islamic educational culture in order to facilitate a transformative process whereby young Muslims gain knowledge and under-standing of Islam and develop an intelligent Muslim faith. Elsewhere (Sahin, 2016) he saw it as necessary to challenge indoctrinatory practices and provide young Muslims with Islamic literacy that integrated reflective thinking skills and intercultural understanding. This would help the young people to engage intelligently and confidently with their faith heritage and wider society. Others have presented a similar argument. For Abbas (2017) "The answer to extremism is not moderation, but a highly critical and informed ide-alism" (p. 14). Coles (2008) pointed out that the pedagogical style which young Muslims experienced in the madrassahs was very different from that which they encountered in the schools. He pointed out that many of the madrassah teachers were not equipped to connect with the worlds of their students. Brohi (1979) stressed the importance of the development of critical thinking in Muslim children when it comes to learning about Islam. For Anderson et al. (2011): "No education could be successful and self-sustaining without encouraging critical thinking" (p. 21).They pointed out that the Muslim community had neglected this approach in favour of learning without understanding with its emphasis on *simply* transmitting rules and norms. For them, it was vital to use education to restore a sense of intellectual and political autonomy, enabling people the power to decide for themselves. They saw the objective for Islamic education to make Muslims autonomous human beings in their environment.

From time to time the shortcomings of the madrassah system are discussed amongst the Pakistani Muslim community. In one such discussion on Facebook (1.2.2018), Professor Tahir Abbas, an academic with a deep knowledge of Birmingham, pointed out that there was a problem of capacity amongst local madrassahs; it was beyond them to teach British-born Muslims: "hence, why a few at the margins go from there to dodgy fatwas online etc., and then we get extremism, etc. . . . There are genuine issues of capacity, based on resources and training".

The opportunity cost of madrassah participation

Extracurricular activities have been said to be beneficial, especially for poorer students (Broh, 2002; Everson & Millsap, 2005; Feldman & Matjasko, 2005). Hattie et al. (1997) pointed out that "physical activities can be used as an effective medium for participants to recognise and understand their own weaknesses, strengths and resources and thus find the wherewithal to master the difficult and unfamiliar in other environments" (p. 45). They demonstrated that there were marked increases as a consequence of the adventure programmes in the domains of social competence, interpersonal communication and educational achievement. Hirsch (1987) outlined the importance of cultural literacy[6] in education, especially for disadvantaged children. Participation in extracurricular activities is said to be one source of such literacy. According to Lareau (2003), the extracurricular activities enabled children to gain more than the skills of playing cricket, violin etc. In the process, "the children learn to think for themselves as special and as entitled to receive certain kinds of services from adults. They also acquire a valuable set of white-collar work skills, including how to set priorities, manage an itinerary, shake hands with strangers, and work on a team" (p. 39). Marsh and Kleitman (2002) concluded that students who participated in extracurricular activities did better academically than their peers. They found that such activities had numerous academic outcomes, particularly for poorer students. For Massoni (2011), "through extracurricular activities, students learnt skills in leadership, teamwork, organisation, analytical thinking, problem solving, time management, learning to juggle many tasks ..." (p. 86). According to Wikeley et al.

(2007) the activities enabled young people to develop self-control and confidence and learn about learning, while Collins et al. (2015) pointed out that by not getting involved in extracurricular activities a student's perception of the school might be solely as a place of work, rather than one where a wider range of interests are pursued.

Within the Scottish education system, there was recognition for the role played by extracurricular activities (Learning and Teaching Scotland, 2010). Such activities enabled "staff and students to see each other in a different light, building positive relationships and improving self-awareness and understanding of others" (p. 7). The activities enabled the students to contextualise their understanding within curriculum areas.

The English government and its agencies have recognised the important role played by extracurricular activities in children's education. For Ofsted (2008a), education outside the classroom leads to improved outcomes in achievement, motivation, personal development and behaviour. It also provides extra depth to pupils' learning and experience. In a White Paper (HMSO, 2005), it was seen as important

> that children and young people have a rich and exciting range of opportunities and activities, beyond the school day, that will allow them to follow their interests, broaden their horizons, remove barriers to learning and motivate them to greater achievements.
>
> (p. 58)

Elsewhere, the DCSF (2007) pointed out that participation in extracurricular activities can "help to improve attitudes to, and engagement with, school; build social and communication skills; help young people avoid taking risks such as experimenting with drugs or being involved in anti-social behaviour or crime; and improve their self-confidence and self-esteem" (p. 6). Chowdry et al. (2009) pointed out that "young people who participate in positive activities at age 14 tend to have higher test scores" (p. 50). The then Secretary of State Michael Gove pointed out that most schools that excelled academically had a programme of extracurricular activities (DfE, 2014). He saw the purpose of such activities to help to build character and give children's talents an opportunity to grow and to allow them to discover new talents they never knew they had.

Participation in extracurricular activities also has implications for community cohesion as it is an opportunity for pupils to interact with those outside of their own ethnic group. Those who participate in them meet many new people, who they otherwise would not encounter (Massoni, 2011). This facilitates encounters between young people from different ethnic and faith groups and leads to better understanding, thereby building community cohesion (DCSF, 2007). Elsewhere (CIC, 2007), it has been pointed out that such provision for young people was a critical starting point for tackling the tensions between different groups in the community. Here it is worth pointing out that Pakistanis have been identified as a segregated community (Burgess & Wilson, 2004), making it even more important for their young people to have the chance to mix with others from outside their ethnic group.

Young people benefit from extracurricular activities in other ways too. Research by World Challenge (2015) showed that extracurricular activities enabled young people to gain entry to university and lead successful lives in the workplace. They pointed out that whilst academic grades were the most important factor considered by university admissions teams,

> evidence of extra-curricular activities remains an important part of the application process for 97% of respondents. Universities most value evidence of extra-curricular activities when deciding between applicants with similar grades and for courses that have an interview stage.
>
> (p. 2)

Of the universities researched, 58.5% indicated that it was important for students to demonstrate experience beyond academic achievements in their university applications and that 20–30% of a student's personal statement should be focused on extracurricular experience. Sullivan (2001) linked the acquisition of cultural capital with educational attainment. This included familiarity with the dominant culture in society and ability to understand and use educated language. Cultural activities were seen to enable pupils to succeed at school. "Possession of cultural capital does have a significant effect on GCSE attainment" (p. 911). Zimdars et al. (2009) pointed out that for students who apply to Oxford, cultural knowledge played a significant role, alongside academic attainment, "perhaps because it allows the applicant to persuade the admissions tutors that they have the right sort of intellectual breadth and potential, which may not be adequately assessed by examination results" (p. 660). They concluded that in such a situation students from lower SES and South Asians scored significantly lower than their White higher SES peers. In their report for the DfE, Thornton et al. (2014) recommended to state schools, serving disadvantaged communities, to provide extracurricular activities so the pupils could draw on them in an interview and compete with their more advantaged peers from the independent schools. In 2008, Education Scotland expanded the focus of its inspection process to include the learning available to young people outside schools. This could be a model for the inclusion of madrassah learning within the Ofsted framework.

Herein lies the problem for Pakistani youngsters. Their participation in madrassah classes comes with a cost. While there, they miss out on extracurricular activities being participated in by their peers. It also leads them to do less homework. Strand (2007a) spoke of the overall negative impact if religious activities competed with or reduced time that might otherwise be spent on curriculum-related activities. "Pakistani, Bangladeshi and Indian pupils attending religious classes more than once a week report doing *less* (original italics) evenings homework than those who do not attend classes" (p. 78). Regular participation in religious activities had been found to impact on homework in the Oldham study (Lindsay and Muijs, 2005, p. 20).

> Muslim boys confirmed the importance of religion but also gave details of the time they spent on associated activities, especially attendance at the mosque. This factor has many positive aspects, but it is also important to acknowledge the impact on the boys' time. This varied with different estimates given among the boys, partly a reflection of different mosques' practices. In all cases it was significant with, for example, one school's boys estimating 2 hours per night. This is the same as the average time spent on homework by the boys in this sample.

So, if Pakistani young people are spending their time at the madrassah, at the expense of doing their homework and participating in educationally useful activities, it is worth considering the implications of this.

A number of the teachers pointed out to me that by attending madrassah classes Pakistani students were missing out on extracurricular activities at the school. They explained the benefits of such activities and their likely implications for those who do not participate in them. A few of the student interviewees also shed light on the subject. Academy teacher Zahida pointed out the negative implications of madrassah attendance by her Pakistani students for their relationships with their fellow pupils and for community cohesion:

> I have after school classes and they say: "well, I have to go to the mosque, miss". So really, they're missing out on that social cohesion and that interaction and widening their circles which is really imperative in a multicultural society. Because they're then almost cocooned within, missing out on all the other things that perhaps would widen their horizons as well. They're missing out on valuable extra-curricular, social, emotional development.

She pointed out that students should mix with everyone else and expand their understanding and their friendship groups. They could also tap into the wealth of the arts, drama and music through extracurricular activities. She explained how this would impact on the students' later life:

> If I'm looking at someone's CV and I think they're a well rounded individual, participated in group activities, I would certainly think there is more to that person. A lot of them 'its, its school and then straight to the mosque'.

Academy teacher Jean was also concerned how the Pakistani boys were missing out:

The other thing they don't realise is the importance of out of school activities. And that is something we have to get across.

She explained that lack of participation in extracurricular activities would have implications for the pupils when they wish to obtain a place in the sixth form, where it's a competitive process requiring a broad CV. According to her, pupils who have not participated in extracurricular activities could be seen as too narrow in focus and too limited in outlook. Community teacher Linda pointed out the other consequences of after-school participation in mosque activities:

> If they've been at school all day and then they go to the mosque, they have very little time to do their homework. And also, they have very little down time. It impacts on their behaviour when they are at school.

Grammar pupil Hamzah recognised the importance of extracurricular activities and saw the importance of having a broader CV "because it enabled you to become more interesting as a person as well as appearing so to employers". He said his participation in such activities made a positive difference to his relationships with the other boys. Grammar pupil Bilal pointed out the benefits of 'meaningful contact' (Ramalingham, 2013) with fellow students: "by spending time together, informally, you see a different side of people. That helps you to get to know them".

Rummidge: case study of one school

During my supplementary research, Alex, an RE teacher, confirmed that there were children in his school who attended madrassah five days each week. He pointed out that:

> They spend too much time at the mosque after school and this interferes with after school 'intervention lessons'. They say they cannot take part in such lessons because they have to go to the mosque. It is a recurring issue. Many parents will also say that their child needs to leave school at the end of the day so he can attend the mosque. The whole school is usually deserted of Muslim students, from about 4pm.

He explained that the Muslim students could be missing out on extracurricular activities, homework catch-up and intervention classes. The latter provision is made available for those who maybe behind some learning or need additional explanation of some concept. He explained that a number of the subjects have 'drop-in' sessions where students can attend for additional help on something they did not grasp in lessons. He also said that the Pakistani involvement in sport was low. A lot of the sporting activities happened after school – when most of them would be at the mosque. There was a similar problem in creative arts. He pointed out that there was almost zero participation from Pakistani students in creative arts. "Because many families would rather their child went to the mosque, instead of being involved in art and music" (Rummidge is a school that specialises in performing arts). And he explained that conservative families would be opposed to music in any case. He explained there was a cultural divide. Many of the Muslim parents think that it is only core subjects that matter, that arts was not important. He spoke of ghettoisation and a negative impact on community cohesion; at the end of school the Pakistani students or Muslim students going off to the mosque while others may be doing football or some other activity. He said it was divisive.

Furthermore Alex spoke of behaviour problems involving Pakistani boys. He said he was used to being told by the boys' parents that their sons were well behaved at the mosque but not so at the school. In his view this was to do with the boys being used to very strict rules at the mosque and at home too. School was the only space they could "let loose a little bit". He explained the outcome of this:

> We had Eid last week. We had no Muslims in the school. There were three, maybe four incidents of behaviour in the whole school. Normally there are ... forty, fifty incidents. We have about 60% Muslims in the school. It is interesting; wouldn't you say?

This comment points to a conflict between what the boys are used to in different domains of their lives, which then causes them to behave badly at school. It also calls for greater communication and coherence between the teachers at school, at the madrassah and the parents.

Improving madrassah provision

The madrassah provision has been said to have certain weaknesses which require attention. Amongst them is the general burden on the child and a financial demand on the parents, many of whom are on low income. As the children are not able to participate in extracurricular activities they lose out on general benefits, academic benefits, confidence-building, relationship-building and cohesion through 'meaningful contact' between pupils of different ethnic groups. In the light of this, it is necessary to explore alternative ways for the students to receive their IRE.

A few of the boys and parent interviewees were critical of madrassahs. They said madrassahs placed a great deal of time pressure on the children and possibly impacted on their school work. Academy parent Nawaz said, after the child had been to school all day, to then go to the madrassah for two to three hours was a big demand on the child:

> I think that's a bit too much for a child. The child probably falls behind because he doesn't have time to devote to his other study. Because too much time is taken in the evening by the mosque.

Table 5.1 I have to spend too much time in religious classes which interferes with my school work

Ethnic group	N	Strongly disagree	Disagree	Agree	Strongly agree
White British	17	58.8	29.4	5.9	5.9
Indian	12	41.7	58.3	0	0
Pakistani	26	46.2	30.8	15.4	7.7
Bangladeshi	14	42.9	57.1	0	0

Academy parent Najeeb pointed out that the mosque system for children was 'quite flimsy'. There were many problems with it. "(Those who run the teaching in the mosque) want to earn some money". He also spoke of the time burden placed on the children:

> After having been at the madrassah for two hours, he has to do his homework. He has no time to watch TV. I have noticed how hard such a situation can be on the child.

Academy pupil Wasim also pointed out that going to the madrassah meant "there was not enough time to do homework, projects, that kind of stuff". Confirming Cherti et al. (2011), Academy parents Afsar-Zeinab referred to the problem of madrassah teachers being brought in from Pakistan who were not familiar with the language and educational context of the children which can be a barrier to effective communication. They suggested that schools and the Pakistani community could work together, to recruit suitable teachers for such provision "just as they have chaplains in the prison service. We could do something similar at school". They also felt this would help to 'join-up' the two worlds for the children: the school and the mosque/madrassah.

Education continues to be highly valued by Pakistani young people. Their families invest both time and money to ensure that their children are able to receive the maximum benefit from it. Religion also continues to be of high importance to Pakistani young people, confirming previous research (Halstead, 1986; Nelson, 2006). As the state system only provides *dunyavi*, worldly, education, this leaves a gap, in the eyes of the Muslim parents, for *deeni*, religious, education. This they set out to fill through madrassah classes. The students were asked for their response to the statement: "I have to spend too much time in religious classes which interferes with my school work". Of those Pakistani students who responded to the question (n = 26), nearly a quarter agreed. While this was only a small number of students, they were the largest group to respond in this way (Table 5.1). In the light of this it is necessary for the madrassah system to be reconsidered.

Religious accommodation by schools

In the context of the increasing Muslim presence in society, the accommodation of their religion has become a key challenge for multicultural Europe

(Hewer, 2001; Fetzer & Soper, 2003; Meer and Modood, 2007; Modood, 2013). This is clearly the case for education, especially in places such as Birmingham where Muslims have been the largest religious group for a number of years. The significance of the issue is even greater in the light of my research which has shown that, of all the main ethnic groups, their religion was the most important for Pakistanis. Here, the concept 'transformative accommodation' appears to be relevant (Shachar, 2004). It relates to statutory authorities and minority communities (such as Pakistani Muslims) working together, to resolve their different values and expectations. With reference to education, the concept relies on a US ruling at the request of the Amish community. The Supreme Court had approved an accommodation measure to allow Amish children to be withdrawn from state school at the age of fourteen (after they had received eight years of state education), so that they could be educated for two more years according to the wishes of the Old Amish Order community.

All three schools in my study were found to be 'accommodating' – providing 'religious space' (Ameli et al., 2005) – the needs of Pakistani Muslim students. A good illustration of religious 'accommodation' was provided by Community pupil Pervez. He had recently joined the school, having previously attended an Islamic boarding school. When asked to compare Community with his Islamic school, he responded that there was little difference between the two. In a number of ways he had found Community to be a better school:

> There are more facilities at this school; that's the main difference. I think this school is quite better than that; the education it provides. The teaching is quite better and the facilities.

Later, I spoke to his mother, Community parent Sakina. She confirmed that "he has made a good transition. He is now settled".

I explored the matter of prayer at the schools, from a student perspective. I asked them whether they were able to pray at the school. Were facilities provided for them to fulfil the requirements of *wudu*? Students at all three schools spoke about the facility they had for congregational prayers. This was at lunchtimes, especially on Fridays. None of the schools had 'proper' *wudu* facilities, though Community came close to it. Community Head Teacher Richards detailed the practice of prayer at his school and how it had developed:

> When I took over my post, in 2008, there was, maybe 20 students on a Friday. Now we have up to 300–400 students. Normally we use the hall. We've got a photograph of virtually half the school (500–600) praying on the Astroturf.

The other two schools appeared to be 'reactively accommodating' of Muslim pupils whereas at Community faith was positively valued, as Head Teacher Richards pointed out: "(For us), faith is valued at the school, it is seen to be linked to education; that reflection is a good thing. So, therefore, it's been encouraged". He said that he had, on occasions, talked to the boys, after they'd been praying and found them quite receptive to his message:

> So, it's a useful way of addressing students as well and respecting their culture and standing there and talking to them after they've been praying.... They've been quiet and focused. So, they tend to be quite receptive. I talk to them just a few minutes. The boys have been kneeling, they're sitting there, they've been praying. They're attentive looking. Quiet, interested in what you've got to say. There is a heightened, a heightened spiritual awareness.

The Harrow SACRE (2013) supports the aforementioned view when it comes to impact of prayer. It reminds schools that, in secular communities, such as many schools, children who are religiously committed can feel they cannot be themselves and, therefore, keep silent about this central part of their identity. In such a situation, space for prayer and reflection may enable such pupils to bring their 'whole self' to the school. This may help to increase pupils' self-esteem and self-confidence and, possibly, contribute to their learning and achievement. They provide the following examples from pupils talking about what prayer means for them:

- *"When I pray in the morning, I feel refreshed. Now I feel refreshed at lunchtime!";*
- *"Being quiet helps me not to feel distracted. It helps me not to be distracted in the afternoon";*
- *"It helps me to reflect on what I've done and what I could change to be better";*
- *"Praying helps me to forget bad things that have happened and make a fresh start".*

Gent (2011) has pointed out the impact of religious activity on Muslim children, in his case the devotional act of becoming a *hafiz*, memorising the Quran. He had categorised the benefits as religious, social, educational and personal. He spoke of one boy who had pointed out how it had made him feel clean inside and gave him a sense of peace. Gent also quoted a child saying that prayer was energy-generating.

Grammar Teacher Steve pointed out that, at their school, they have a room set aside for the Muslim pupils to pray; it was in the part of school where they would not be disturbed. According to him, it was well used, especially on a Friday. As to ablution, the students used the toilets. This was also confirmed by his colleague, Grammar Teacher Masood:

> When you say 'facilities' there are toilets where they can go and do *wudu*. There are not facilities like you have in a mosque, for example. They have toilets where they can do *wudu*. It's *acceptable* (he stresses the word). It's acceptable.

It would appear that at both Academy and Grammar, the accommodation of Muslim pupils' prayer needs is at a most basic level. Neither provided proper *wudu* facilities, which was a problem for Grammar pupil Hashmi: "We should have proper *wudu* facilities. It's not good that we have to do it in the sink".

Academy teacher Mehboob – an advocate for the Muslim children in the school, in matters such as prayer – pointed out that some of the boys did not participate in prayers due to there being no ablution facilities:

> If the school provided *wudu* facilities, I reckon you'd get 500 kids lined up. A lot of the boys complain that they don't pray because they can't make *wudu*. Because, they say, the toilets are too dirty. So, that seems to be a barrier for them. Without proper *wudu* facilities, you get water everywhere.

Academy had the opportunity to change the facilities. However, instead of improvements, it made the situation worse. During work carried out as a part of its Building Schools for the Future programme, it installed unisex toilets, whereas previously there were separate toilets for boys and girls. "I can't see pupils making *wudu* in there; cos they're very exposed". In Mehboob's opinion, facilitating prayer would lead to improvement in the pupils' behaviour:

> And, I think prayer could be used to encourage students to seek knowledge, improve their manners and respect the community. I think prayer can be used as a mechanism to get kids a little bit focused.

Madrassah at school?

The education system continually strives to improve the curriculum within the school system. However, the madrassah provision appears to have escaped such efforts. Given the importance attached to religion by Pakistani parents, it is to be expected that they will continue to want their children to participate in such supplementary education. This calls for improving the education provided, which may contribute to raising educational standards for Pakistani boys. Could one option be to bring madrassah provision within the school system? This was explored with the students through the questionnaire (Table 5.2). Given the Pakistani students' response – that they had to spend too much time in religious classes which interfered with their school work – it was not a surprise that a significant number – nearly two-thirds of those who responded

Table 5.2 What I learnt in my religious classes should be taught at school

Ethnic group	N	Strongly disagree (%)	Disagree (%)	Agree (%)	Strongly agree (%)
White British	17	29.4	29.4	23.5	17.7
Indian	11	18.2	45.5	36.4	0
Pakistani	25	0	36.0	32.0	32.0
Bangladeshi	14	28.6	21.4	42.9	7.1

to the statement – agreed that IRE, which they learnt in the madrassah classes, should be taught at the school.

The Pakistani parents interviewed were keenly supportive of the idea of bringing IRE into the wider education system. Their responses indicated that this was an innovative way to approach the matter; something that had not been explored before. Academy parent Nawaz thought it a good idea for IRE to have the same level of quality as the rest of the school curriculum:

> Yes and you are right. And it's one of the good ideas. I will be the first to agree, to say that this is a good thing that Mr Karamat has suggested.

He was treating my open-ended question as an idea. This has been referred to as an 'arousal effect', (Brown & Tandon, 1978) where the researcher's questions affect the subject's perceptions of, and feelings about, the topics of discussion and questions posed by the researcher lead respondents to think afresh about issues and possibilities, in this case, for providing IRE. Academy parent Najeeb was definite in his support for the idea:

> We desperately need to attend to this matter. Making religious provision at the school would be best. It would save a lot of hassle and time. The children can then study other things. They may even have spare time, to do things they want to, such as watch TV.

He said the current system of providing IRE was "not solid; quite flimsy", with the quality being low. "There can be as many as 60 children per teacher. The facilities and the general learning environment can be poor too". Community parent Junaid thought it was a 'fantastic' idea, using the school buildings for such provision:

> That would be very good, forward thinking and also very responsive; something that will get a good response from the local community, from the local parents.

Community parent Zaman pointed out that if IRE was provided by the school then it would free up his son and enable him to participate in extracurricular activities.

As to how IRE could be offered 'within' the education system, parents explained that such provision could be made available "after normal school finished or over the weekend". Community parent Khalaq, like others, was keen for his son's school to provide IRE and suggested how it could be provided:

> They could do it in the morning. If they were to start their day with Quran, then they would have barkat, they would be blessed, for the rest of the day. It would bless the child and the school. We know if a person starts their day with prayer in the house, they have rehmat, blessing,

all day. The other (non Muslim) children could benefit too; they might become interested in our religion. The teachers will also be blessed.

For Grammar parent Shahida, the school providing such religious education would help to create consistency and regularity. Community parent Zaman was similarly keen on the grounds of safeguarding: an area which has been said to require attention. He thought it would be a good idea for madrassah teachers to be CRB–checked, and even better if the religious teaching was provided at the school. For him, the current system of unregulated IRE had the potential of children being taught the wrong (extremist) ideas:

> But we could have something after school. So religious teaching could be done at the school. They could hire a Muslim teacher. That way, you would know your kids are learning in a safe environment. In this day and age, it's very easy to manipulate a child, like put hatreds towards certain races. So it would be better if the religious teaching was in the school environment.

Academy Teacher Jean also spoke about the possible anti-Christian influence of some madrassahs. "One group did not want to write about Jesus because they said that was what they had been taught at the madrassah". Her Pakistani colleague, Academy Teacher Zahida, supported this with her own example:

> There was an instance where a student had been told . . . listening to music was against Islam. It troubled me. So, I spoke to the imam at the mosque. He was quite rigid and actually his views were quite retrograde, in a Wahabi-like Islam, saying, no, no, you can't have that. It's corrupting; it's western influence. Well, it's not really, when you think of Sufism and everything like that; that is inherent within Islam as well. But, they saw that as western corruption. So, there, there was the misconception but that's what they were feeding the students.

Cherti et al. (2011) had drawn attention to the poor quality of the madrassah system and the curriculum provided. Academy teacher Mehboob agreed that improvements could be made, with better teaching and modern resources, students could be taught much more in the time they spent at the mosque.

I asked whether the schools providing IRE would raise any questions of authenticity. A number of the parents suggested that as long as qualified and competent teachers were employed to deliver IRE then this would have the confidence of the Muslim parents. Community parent Junaid said:

> as long as it is an imam who understands and he is a good quality teacher then I don't think there's an issue. A mosque is there for prayer; to learn Arabic or to learn the Quran doesn't have to be in a mosque. I personally was taught in a house.

A few of the parents suggested that some of the teaching usually provided through the madrassahs could be integrated into the schools' curriculum. For them, Urdu and Arabic should be provided, alongside other non-English languages. Some also mentioned that Islamic Studies should be provided as a GCSE subject. I shall return to this in the final chapter.

Notes

1 (www.supplementaryeducation.org.uk).
2 As of 18.07.2013, the Pakistani pupils in Academy made up 29.3%. Through my ongoing wider work with the school I have learnt that, as of May 2016, this figure had gone up to 40.7%.
3 Not the real name
4 https://ibrahimmogra.com/2012/08/07/madresa-and-the-united-kingdom/ Downloaded 21.03.2018.
5 Mogra has been the Assistant Secretary General of the one of the main Muslim representative organisations, Muslim Council of Britain.
6 "[T]he network of information that all competent readers possess. It is the background information, stored in their minds, that enables them to take up a newspaper and read it with an adequate level of comprehension, getting the point, grasping the implications, relating what they read to the unstated context which alone gives meaning to what they read" (p. 2).

Bibliography

Abbas, T. (2017). The 'Trojan Horse' plot and the fear of Muslim power in British schools. *Journal of Muslim Minority Affairs*.

Akiba, D. (2007). Ethnic retention as a predictor of academic success: Lessons from the children of immigrant families and black children. *The Clearing House: A Journal of Educational Strategies, Issues and Ideas* 80(5) 223–226.

Ameli, S., Azam, A. & Merali, A. (2005). *Secular or Islamic? What Schools do British Muslims want for their Children?* Volume 3 of the British Muslims' Expectations Series, Summary of a report by for the Islamic Human Rights Commission.

AMSS (Association of Muslim Social Scientists). (2004). *Muslims on education*. Surrey: AMSS.

Anderson, P., Tan, C. & Suleiman, Y. (2011). *Reforms in Islamic education: Report of a conference held at the Prince Alwaleed Bin Talal Centre of Islamic studies*. University of Cambridge.

Anwar, M. (1979). *The myth of return*. London: Heinemann.

Arthur, J. (2015). Extremism and neo-liberal education policy: A contextual critique of the Trojan Horse affair in Birmingham schools. *British Journal of Educational Studies* 63(3) 311–328.

Bartlet, S., Devlin, B., Hadfield, M., Jopling, M., McGregor, D. & Worrall, N. (2008). *QCA big picture of the curriculum: Component playlists*. Wolverhampton: University of Wolverhampton.

Bawden, A. (2011). Thinktank issues new report on madrasas. *The Guardian*, 28 November.

BCC. (2000). *Submission to the Stephen Lawrence inquiry public policy review panel Birmingham by the Chief Education Officer*. BCC. Education Service.

BCC. (2001). *The third annual report on raising the achievement of pupils most at risk of underachieving (Education Development Plan Priority 4)*. BCC. Education and Lifelong Learning Scrutiny Committee, 30 January.

BCC. (2002). *The fourth annual report on raising the achievement of pupils most at risk of under-achieving (Education Development Plan Priority 4)*. BCC. Education Department.

BCC. (2003). *Annual report on raising the achievement of pupils most at risk of underachieving*. BCC. Education and Arts Overview and Scrutiny Committee, 29 January.

Berglund, J. (2015). *Publicly funded Islamic education in Europe and the United States*. Washington: Centre for Middle East Policy.

Broh, B. (2002). Linking extracurricular programming to academic achievement: Who benefits and why? *Sociology of Education* 75(1) 69–95.

Brohi, A. K. (1979). Education in an ideological state in al-Attas, S. M. (ed.) *Aims and objectives of Islamic education*. Jeddah: Hodder and Stoughton/King Abdulaziz University.

Brown, L. & Tandon, R. (1978). Interviews as catalysts in a community setting. *Journal of Applied Psychology* 63(2) 197–205.

Bullock Report. (1975). *A language for life*. www.educationengland.org.uk/documents/bullock/bullock1975.html Accessed 10.3.2016.

Burgess, S. & Wilson, D. (2004). *Ethnic segregation in England's schools*. London: Centre for Analysis of Social Exclusion; London School of Economics.

Cherti, M. & Bradley, L. (2011). *Inside Madrassas*. London: IPPR.

Cherti, M., Glennie, A. & Bradley, L. (2011). *'Madrassas' in the British media*. London: IPPR.

Chishti, M. (2008). *Lok virsa: Exploring the Muslim heritage*. Studley: Brewin.

Chowdry, H., Crawford, C. & Goodman, A. (2009). *Drivers and barriers to educational success: Evidence from the longitudinal study of young people in England*. London: Department for Children Schools and Families.

CIC (Commission on Integration and Cohesion) (2007). *Our shared future*. West Yorkshire: Crown Copyright.

Coles, M. (2008). *Every Muslim child matters*. Stoke-on-Trent: Trentham Books.

Collins, M., Collins, G. & Butt, G. (2015). Social mobility or social reproduction? A case study of the attainment patterns of students according to their social background and ethnicity. *Educational Review* 67(2) 196–217.

Conteh, J. & Brock, A. (2011). 'Safe spaces?' Sites of bilingualism for young learners in home, school and community. *International Journal of Bilingual Education and Bilingualism* 14(3) 347–360.

Dahya, B. (1973). Pakistanis in Britain: Transients or settlers? *Race and Class* 14 241–277.

DCSF. (2007). *Aiming high for young people: A ten year strategy for positive activities*. London: DCSF.

DfE. (2014). *Michael Gove speaks about securing our children's future*. www.gov.uk/government/speeches/michael-gove-speaks-about-securing-our-childrens-future Accessed 17.4.2018.

DFES. (2006). *Ethnicity and education: The evidence on minority ethnic pupils aged 5–16*. London: DFES.

Ellis, E. (2004). The invisible multilingual teacher: The contribution of language background to Australian ESL teachers' professional knowledge and beliefs. *International Journal of Multilingualism* 1(2) 90–108.

Everson, H. & Millsap, R. (2005). *Everyone gains: Extracurricular activities in high school and higher SAT scores*. New York: College Entrance Examination Board.

Felderhof, M., Thompson, P. & Torevell, D. (eds.). (2007). *Inspiring faith in schools: Studies in religious education*. Aldershot: Ashgate.

Feldman, A. & Matjasko, J. (2005). The role of school-based extracurricular activities in adolescent development: A comprehensive review and future directions. *Review of Educational Research* 75(2) 159–210.

Fetzer, J. & Soper, C. (2003). The roots of public attitudes towards state accommodation of European Muslims' religious practices before and after September 11. *Journal for the Scientific Study of Religion* 42(2) 247–258.

Fillmore, L. (1991). When learning a second language means losing the first. *Early Childhood Research Quarterly* 6 323–346.

Franceschelli, M. & O'Brien, M. (2014). Islamic capital' and family life: the role of Islam in parenting. *Sociology* 48(6) 1190–1206.

Francis, B., Archer, L. & Mau, A. (2009). Language as capital, or language as identity? Chinese complementary school pupils' perspectives on the purposes and benefits of complementary schools. *British Educational Research Journal* 35(4) 519–538.

Garza, A. & Crawford, L. (2005). Hegemonic multiculturalism: English immersion, ideology and subtractive schooling. *Bilingual Research Journal* 29(3) 599–619.

Gent, W. (2006). *Muslim supplementary classes and their place within the wider learning community: A Redbridge-based study.* University of Warwick: Doctor of Education thesis.

Gent, W. (2011). The world of the British hifz class student: Observations, findings and implications for education and further research. *British Journal of Religious Education* 33(1) 3–15.

Hall, K., Ozerk, K., Zulfiqar, M. & Tan, J. (2002). This is our school: Provision, purpose and pedagogy of supplementary schooling in Leeds and Oslo. *British Educational Research Journal* 28(3) 399–418.

Halstead, M. (1986). *The case for Muslim voluntary-aided schools: Some philosophical reflections.* Cambridge: Islamic Academy.

Halstead, M. (2005). British Muslims and education in *Muslims in the UK: Policies for Engaged Citizens.* Hungary: Open Society Institute.

Halstead, M. (2007). Islamic values: A distinctive framework for moral education? *Journal of Moral Education* 36(3) 283–296.

Harrow SACRE. (2013). *Guidance on offering space for prayer and reflection in school.* www. harrow.gov.uk/www2/documents/s108380/sacre Accessed 22.3.2018.

Hashmi, S. (1973). *A spotlight on Asian affairs.* Birmingham Community Development Project.

Hattie, J., Marsh, H., Neill, J. & Richards, G. (1997). Adventure education and outward bound: Out-of-class experiences that make a lasting difference. *Review of Educational Research* 67(1) 43–87.

Hewer, C. (2001). Schools for Muslims. *Oxford Review of Education* 27(4) 515–527.

Hiro, D. (1991). *Black British, White British.* London: Grafton books.

Hirsch, E. D. (1987). *Cultural literacy.* Boston: Houghton Mifflin Company.

HMSO. (2005). *Higher standards, better schools for all.* White Paper.

Hornsby, R. (2005). The weltanschauung approach to inclusion. *Race Equality Teaching* 23(3), Summer. Stoke-on-Trent: Trentham Books.

House of Commons. (2012). *Roots of violent radicalization: Nineteenth Report of Session 2010–12.* London: The Stationery Office.

Iacopini, G., Stock, L. & Junge, K. (2011). *Evaluation of Tower Hamlets prevent projects.* London: The Tavistock Institute.

Ipgrave, J., Miller, J. & Hopkins, P. (2010). Responses of three Muslim majority primary schools in England to the Islamic faith of their pupils. *International Journal of Migration and Integration* 11 73–89.

Joly, D. (1986). *The opinions of Mirpuri parents in Saltley, Birmingham about their children's schooling.* Warwick: CRER.

Khan, V. (1977). The Pakistanis: Mirpuri villagers at home and in Bradford in Watsòn, J. (ed.) *Between two cultures: Migrants and minorities in Britain.* Oxford: Basil Blackwell.

LaFromboise, T., Hoyt, D., Oliver, L. & Whitbeck, L. (2006). Family, community, and school influences on resilience among American Indian adolescents in the Upper Midwest. *Journal of Community Psychology* 34(2) 193–209.

Lareau, A. (2003). *Unequal childhood.* London: University of California Press.

Learning and Teaching Scotland. (2010). *Curriculum for excellence through outdoor learning.* https://education.gov.scot/Documents/cfe-through-outdoor-learning.pdf Accessed 22.3.2018.

Lewis, P. (2006). Imams, Ulema, and Sufis: Providers of bridging social capital for British Pakistanis? *Contemporary South Asia* 15(3) 273–287.

Lindsay, G. & Muijs, D. (2005). *Challenging underachievement of boys in Years 8 and 10: A study for the Oldham Leading Edge Partnership.* Coventry: University of Warwick.

Marsh, H. & Kleitman, S. (2002). Extracurricular school activities: The good, the bad, and the nonlinear. *Harvard Educational Review* 72(4) 464–514.

Massoni, E. (2011). Positive effects of extra curricular activities on students. *ESSAI* 9(27). http://dc.cod.edu/cgi/viewcontent.cgi?article=1370&context=essai Accessed 10.3.2016.

Maylor, U., Glass, K., Issa, T., Kuyok, K., Minty, S., Rose, A., Ross, A., Tanner, E., Finch, S., Low, N., Taylor, E., Tipping, S. & Purdon, S. (2010). *Impact of supplementary schools on pupils' achievement.* DCSF.

Meer, N. & Modood, T. (2007). *The political and policy responses to migration related diversity in Britain's education system: A European approach to multicultural citizenship: Legal political and educational challenges.* EMILIE.

Modood, T. (2013). *Multiculturalism and Muslims in Britain and France.* www.publicspirit.org.uk/multiculturalism-and-muslims-in-britain-and-france/

Mogra, I. (2007). Moral education in the makātib of Britain: A review of curriculum materials. *Journal of Moral Education* 36(3) 387–398.

Nelson, M. (2006). Muslims, markets and the meaning of a 'good' education in Pakistan. *Asian Survey* 46(5) 699–720.

Ofsted. (2002). *Inspection of Birmingham local education authority.* https://reports.ofsted.gov.uk/sites/default/files/documents/local_authority_reports/birmingham/012_Local%20Authority%20Inspection%20as%20pdf.pdf Accessed 22.3.2018.

Ofsted. (2008). *Every language matters.* London: Ofsted.

Ofsted. (2008a). *Education outside the classroom.* London: Ofsted.

Ofsted. (2012). *Bell Vue girls' school: Inspection report.* London: Ofsted.

Ofsted. (2013). *Oldknow academy: School report.* London: Ofsted.

Phinney, J. (1991). Ethnic identity and self-esteem: A review and integration. *Hispanic Journal of Behavioural Sciences* 13(2) 193–208.

Ramalingham, V. (2013). *Integration: What works?* London: Institute for Strategic Dialogue.

Rashid, N., Lattif, R. & Begum, S. (2006). *Supporting safe and effective education in madrassas (Supplementary schools).* Birmingham City Council.

Rashid, N., Naz, I. & Hussain, M. (2005). *Raising achievement of Pakistani and Bangladeshi boys.* Birmingham City Council.

Rex, J. & Moore, R. (1967). *Race community and conflict.* London: Oxford University Press.

Richardson, R. & Wood, A. (2004). *The achievement of British Pakistani learners.* Stoke-on-Trent: Trentham Books.

Roach, P. & Sondhi, R. (1997). *Education interventions: Local measures to improve the educational attainment of ethnic minority school pupils.* Birmingham: Westhill College of Higher Education.

Robertson, L. (2006). Learning to read 'properly' by moving between parallel literacy classes. *Language and Education* 20(1) 44–61.

Rosowsky, A. (2000). Reading and culture: The experience of some of our bilingual pupils. *English in Education* 34(2) 45–53.

Rosowsky, A. (2001). Decoding as a cultural practice and its effects on the reading process of bilingual pupils. *Language and Education* 15(1) 56–70.

Rosowsky, A. (2010). 'Writing it in English': Script choices among young multilingual Muslims in the UK. *Journal of Multilingual and Multicultural Development* 31(2) 163–179.

Safford, K. & Drury, R. (2013). The 'problem' of bilingual children in educational settings: Policy and research in England. *Language and Education* 27(1) 70–81.

Sahin, A. (2005). Exploring the religious life-world and attitudes toward Islam among British Muslim adolescents in Francis, L., Robbins, M. & Astley, J. (eds.) *Religion, education and adolescence: International empirical perspectives.* Cardiff: University of Wales Press.

Sahin, A. (2013). *New directions in Islamic education.* Leicestershire: Kube Publishing.

Sahin, A. (2016). Let's tap into Islam's heritage of critical education to defeat extremism in schools. *The Guardian,* 12 January.

Sai, Y. (2017). Teaching Qur'an in Irish Muslim schools-curriculum, approaches, perspectives and implications. *British Journal of Religious Education* 40(2) 148–157.

Scourfield, J., Taylor, C., Moore, G. & Gilliat-Ray, S. (2012). The intergenerational transmission of Islam in England and Wales: Evidence from the citizenship survey. *Sociology* 46(1) 91–108.

Shachar, A (2004). *Multicultural jurisdictions.* Cambridge: Cambridge University Press.

Shah, B., Dwyer, C. & Modood, T. (2010). Explaining educational achievement and career aspirations among young British Pakistanis. *Sociology* 44(6) 1109–1127.

Shah, S. (2008). Leading multi-ethnic schools: Adjustments in concepts and practices for engaging with diversity. *British Journal of Sociology of Education* 29(5) 523–536.

Sharples, R. (2014). Constructing and contesting the 'ideal learner': Multilingual children in the UK school system in Angouri, J., Harrison, T., Schnurr, S. & Wharton, S. (eds.) *Learning, working and communicating in a global context-proceedings of the 47th annual meeting of the British association for applied linguistics.* London: Scitsiugnil Press.

Strand, S. (2007). Surveying the views of pupils attending supplementary schools in England. *Educational Research* 49(1) 1–19.

Strand, S. (2007a). *Minority ethnic pupils in the longitudinal study of young people in England.* London: DFES.

Sullivan, A. (2001). Cultural capital and educational attainment. *Sociology* 35(4) 893–912.

Taj, M. (1996). *A 'can do' city: Supplementary report to the Bradford Commission on community relations.* Bradford: Taj.

Taylor, M. & Hegarty, S. (1985). *The best of both worlds . . .?* Berkshire: NFER-Nelson.

Thornton, A., Pickering, E., Peters, M., Leathwood, C., Hollingworth, S. & Mansaray, A. (2014). *School and college-level strategies to raise aspirations of high-achieving disadvantaged pupils to pursue higher education investigation.* London: Department for Education.

Tinsley, T. (2015). *The teaching of Arabic language and culture in UK schools.* Alcantara Communications.

Waters, M. (2007). *The big picture of the curriculum.* London: QCA.

Wikeley, F., Bullock, K., Muschamp, Y. & Ridge, T. (2007). *Educational relationships outside school.* York: Joseph Rowntree Foundation.

World Challenge. (2015). *Giving you the edge: What is the real value of extra-curricular experience in the university application process?* Buckinghamshire: World Challenge.

YouTube. (2014). *Islam in British schools: The Trojan Horse letter.* TV debate, 6 September. www.bing.com/videos/search?q=trojan+youtube+islamic+schools&view=detail&mid=9 B71A2288922533A702F9B71A2288922533A702F&FORM=VIRE Accessed 10.7.2016.

Zimdars, A., Sullivan, A. & Heath, A. (2009). Elite higher education admissions in the Arts and Sciences: Is cultural capital the key? *Sociology* 43(4) 648–666.

6   A diverse teaching workforce

Representative diversity

It is suggested that a workforce that is representative of the people it serves is more likely to help ensure that the interests of all groups are considered in the decision-making and the policymaking process becomes more inclusive. This is based on the theory of 'representative bureaucracy' (Bradbury & Kellough, 2011). According to the theory, the beneficiaries benefit from the discretionary efforts of bureaucrats, given that such efforts are a function, in part, of the attitudes, values and beliefs that result from the bureaucrats' social background. It has been argued that representative bureaucracies are beneficial to ethnic and racial minorities and in educational contexts (Selden, 1997; Sowa & Selden, 2003; Pitts, 2005; Eckhard, 2014).

The key role of minority teachers

Within the field of education, researchers and policymakers have accepted that the workforce should be diverse and should reflect the ethnic diversity of society. Minority teachers are said to provide role models (Quiocho & Rios, 2000; Egalite et al., 2015), provide cultural expertise (Ross, 2001; Basit & Santoro, 2012), act as a 'bridge' between, and 'translators' of, minority and dominant cultures and act as cultural brokers (Irvine, 1989). For Howard (2010), minority teachers fulfilled the role of advocate for minority students. Abbas (2004), in his Birmingham-based research, had found working class Asian parents particularly in favour of having Asian teachers.

Minority teachers are said to have the potential to bridge the ever-widening divide between minority pupils and their mainly White teachers (Magaldi et al., 2016). They can, if given the space and opportunity, bring a more authentic perspective based on their own lived experience and first-hand knowledge. Through their counterstorying they can interrupt majoritarian narratives, "defined as a mindset of positions, perceived wisdoms, and shared cultural understandings brought to the discussion of race" (Fránquiz, 2011, p. 282). While such narratives position the norms of the White majority as standard and shape the school curriculum they are said to be inaccurate constructions of the knowledge and lived experiences of minority children, families and communities. "We contend that if teachers are not given opportunities to deconstruct majoritarian tales in educational practice, then racist norms will continue to define how teachers view themselves, schooling, families and students" (p. 282).

Kohli and Pizarro (2016) pointed out that minority teachers are likely to have a heightened awareness of educational injustice and racism. For Ross (2001), minority teachers were better at challenging racism and, given that they might have been its victim, they are more likely to understand some of its subtleties. He and Howard (2010) have supported the concept of 'inclusive diversity', where it is not so much important for, say, Pakistani students to be taught *directly* by Pakistani teachers but more an indirect benefit; by having them on the staff, to see them around the school and have occasional contact with them. Teachers are said to do much more than teach content; they also personify content (Kennedy, 1991; Howard, 2010). They provide a model of what it is like to be an educated person; something for the young people to aspire to:

> If we want students to believe that they themselves might one day be … mentors, guides and educated people, then we need them to see diverse examples of such people, including at least one who looks like they, the students, look.
>
> (Kennedy, 1991, p. 660)

Stewart et al. (1989) supported the 'role model' argument. "Black teachers can have a special impact on Black students simply by being in the classroom. A Black teacher serves as a role model for Black students, thereby exposing Black students to other Black individuals who have been successful" (p. 143). For Steele and Aronson (1995), the presence of same-race teachers may reduce 'stereotype threats' and boost minority students' confidence, esteem and enthusiasm. Such a threat is said to occur when a student perceives that she/he could be viewed through the lens of a negative stereotype and lowers academic engagement and performance as a result. For example, a Pakistani student might perceive to be treated stereotypically by a White teacher on racial, cultural or religious grounds.

Roch and Pitts (2012) pointed out that where schools' workforce was representative of their communities there was a positive influence on minority students' performance. Similarly, Eckhard (2014) pointed out that where there is a bureaucratic *drift*, i.e. there is a lack of bureaucratic representation, policies are not effective. The problem here can be even more profound where the majority-background bureaucrats are prejudiced against minorities. Arshad et al. (2004) reported that minority students appreciated having teachers from their own ethnic group, expecting them to better understand the students and assist them to feel more comfortable. Warikoo (2004) pointed to there being a better connection between teachers and pupils from the same ethnic background arising out of their common cultural background and the teachers' heightened understanding of the students' family and cultural context as well as parental interactions with the school.

The attainment level of minority students is said to be helped by the presence of teachers from their own background (Weiher, 2000). Egalite et al. (2015) asserted that an absence of teachers from their own ethnic group can lead to a lack of shared values, dispositions and symbols which might undermine classroom learning and teacher–student interactions. They also supported the idea of ethnic minority teachers serving as role models and being uniquely positioned to act as advocates and cultural translators for ethnic minority students. They concluded that same-race teachers made a particular difference for their students' attainment. Basit and Santoro (2012) also supported the employment of minority teachers in schools serving multicultural populations. They found these teachers fulfilled important roles related to the heritage of the minority ethnic students. Many of the teachers in their research were appointed because of their ethnicity and knowledge about languages and their potential to develop sound home–school relationships. The teachers found that their particular expertise was often drawn upon by their colleagues who lacked the necessary cultural understanding. The minority teachers were able to foster home–school relationships for minority parents who otherwise had little contact with their children's schools. The researchers concluded that minority ethnic teachers had significant contributions to make to the schooling of minority ethnic students because of their knowledge about their students' cultural practices, religions and home lives.

It is argued that the likelihood of discontinuity between minority children and their schools is lessened where the school employs teachers from minority background (Klopfenstein, 2005). These teachers are more able to provide the 'cultural congruence' for the students and match their home and school environments. For Howard (2010), minority teachers helped minority students to adjust to the lack of synchrony between home and school culture and made "connections between their own backgrounds and school systems, which are commonly founded on the values and norms of the dominant culture" (p. 4). According to Carrington (2002) teachers who share the ethnic and cultural backgrounds of the increasingly diverse student bodies may serve "to provide insights that might otherwise remain hidden" (p. 181). For Delpit (1995) the argument was not so much that teachers must be of the students' ethnic group but that efforts should be made for the teaching workforce to be diverse.

A word of caution needs to be stated here, so to not present minority teachers as the perfect solution. They may have the potential to make a certain specialist contribution but their limitations need to be acknowledged, one of which refers to the concept 'internalised racism' (Padilla, 2001). This is where minorities adopt majority White perspectives such as by accepting their own communities as inferior. For Speight (2007), such a process "refers to the acceptance, by marginalized racial populations, of the negative societal beliefs and stereotypes about themselves" (p. 129). As a solution to this problem, Kohli (2014) has suggested that there should be opportunities, through ITT and CPD, for minority teachers to unpack their internalised racism.

Local teachers can also play an important role in schools. Most schools have a small number of such teachers and support staff who are from the local community. Even if they no longer live there, they will have been raised there and will maintain contact with friends, former neighbours and relatives in the area. They may have a unique understanding of the school's cultural and social context and may be able to act as a bridge between the school and its wider community. Such staff usually share common ethnic, religious and cultural identities which provide a foundation on which school community partnerships can be constructed. Reed (2009), a proponent of local teachers, also spoke of 'commuter teachers', who only come into the neighbourhood to work and as soon as they finish, they get into their cars and leave the area. They may be at the school for many years but may never go outside its gate. They, therefore, may be unlikely to understand what it is like to live in the locality, let alone understand the community's resources. Local teachers may be better equipped for the task of delivering what Flynn et al. (2009) defined as 'place-based' education. For them, "using the place as content is a viable means for increasing student achievement, increasing community involvement" (p. 137). Here Murrell's (2000) concept of 'community teachers' is relevant. Such teachers are said to have the contextualised knowledge of culture, community and identity of children and their families as the core of their teaching practice. They are said to possess the 'multicultural competence' needed for effective service in such contexts. These teachers are usually individuals who typically live and work in the same neighbourhoods and communities where students from diverse backgrounds live and go to school. They are said to have a positive and hopeful outlook on education, seeing it as the key to success for the young people whom they serve. Most are said to articulate a sense of commitment to their community.

Government support for diversity in the teaching workforce

For many years the idea of a diverse teaching profession had government support. Swann Report (1985) had argued that ethnic minority teachers would be a source of cultural expertise within schools and would help to challenge racism and contribute towards meeting the particular needs of ethnic minority pupils, acting as role models for them. Furthermore, presence of minority staff would provide reassurance for ethnic minority parents that their needs would be understood and would help to counter "the inherent incongruity of all White teaching staffs, often living well away from the catchment areas of their schools" (p. 604). Therefore, Swann recommended that "far more consideration should be given, in making appointments, to the extent to which a particular ethnic, cultural, linguistic or religious background is an *additional and desirable* feature for a job in *any* (my emphasis) school – whether multi-racial or 'all-White'" (p. 605). In recognising that much of a teacher's influence on the pupils was indirect, i.e. who they are rather than just what they do, Swann argued that "an education which seeks to prepare all pupils for life in a pluralist society can surely best be provided by a teaching force which is itself pluralist in character" (p. 605).

Blair and Bourne, in their report for the DFEE (2000), supported the need for a diverse teaching workforce. "All participants in the study thought that it was necessary to have more minority ethnic group teachers ... more needed to be done to attract 'minority' teachers into the profession" (p. 162). In their view such teachers would help to "affirm a positive sense of identity among ethnic minority children", would enable schools to better understand the issues faced by minority group children, would be "a positive influence on their colleagues and the culture of the school", would be "able to communicate with minority children in their first language" and would be better "able to encourage and motivate them" (p. 162). In response, the DFES (2003) made it clear that the "school workforce should reflect the diversity of the school population" (p. 19). Elsewhere, they (HMSO, 2005) broadened the reach of such workforce diversity to ensure that schools had Black and minority ethnic school leaders in order for the workforce to be "more reflective of the pupils in our classrooms" (p. 86). In their report for the DFES, Cline et al. (2002) stated that teachers as well as children and parents had argued that there would be many advantages to their school if it had teachers from a wider range of cultural backgrounds on the staff. The diversity case was spelt out by the National Audit Office (2004) who argued that service users such as children, parents and the wider community are likely to have their needs met better by a workforce that matches their own background. Furthermore such service users are more likely to have confidence in the organisations and those who work within them. Those responsible for teacher recruitment were advised to take workforce diversity into account and work towards achieving a workforce whose composition reflects that of the local community. The DCSF (2009) has also encouraged schools to recruit from their local communities, and, in particular, those who were ex-pupils at the school.

National steps towards diversity in teaching

In order to achieve diversity within the teaching workforce, a number of measures have been employed at the national level, including the setting of recruitment targets, targeted advertising, mentoring schemes, taster courses and training bursaries (Carrington, 2002). In 1997, Estelle Morris, the then Junior Minister for Education, launched a campaign to attract more ethnic minority teachers. She said it was "absolutely right that ethnic-minority children should be taught by teachers from their own communities ... (but she added that) *all children* (my emphasis) would benefit from a diverse teaching force" (Ghouri, 1997). The WRECC report (1999) had also made the point that it was "essential for White pupils and their parents to interact with Black professionals if we are to overcome racism" (p. 4). Soon after (DFES,

2001) it was reported that the TTA had "set targets to increase the proportion of entrants to training from ethnic minority groups to 9% by 2005/06" (p. 24). Later (HM Government, 2005) efforts were made to build on the aforementioned target "to ensure we have a workforce including head teachers and school leaders which is more reflective of the pupils in our classrooms" (para 8.14). They also committed to providing support to ensure that all teachers had the skills and confidence to teach in diverse classrooms. TTA enlisted the support of community organisations in order to achieve a diverse teaching workforce. Wolverhampton Race Equality Council Consortium (WRECC, 1999) was commissioned to undertake an action research project on the recruitment and retention of ethnic minority teachers. The Consortium included Bilston Community College, the institution where I was the Deputy Director: Equal Rights and Opportunities Management Unit. One of the ways I directly contributed to this work was by setting up the Black Access into Teaching Advisory Group. The final report of the project stated that, in order to achieve a diverse teaching workforce, it needed statutory authorities, educational institutions and communities working in equal partnership.

There has been support for diversity from within the teaching profession. The head teachers in the research by Walker et al. (2005) were of the view that it was important that the staff profile should parallel the ethnic profile of the pupils. They placed a high priority on both the recruitment and development of suitable staff, with the idea that they would provide positive role models for the students and bring cultural knowledge that comes only from living within a culture. They recruited ethnic minorities into non-teaching roles and then nurtured them towards qualified teacher status. They took Positive Action, within the equality legislation, in order to develop the careers of their minority staff. Achieving a balanced staff profile was also seen as a means of openly expressing the school's dedication to its students and community. Recently, the government has supported diversity initiatives within school leadership through the Leadership Equality and Diversity Fund (NCTL, 2015). The purpose of the fund was to help address under-representation of particular groups in school leadership positions "in particular there are significant leadership gaps for Black and Minority Ethnic and female leaders" (p. 4).

According to the available data for the teaching workforce, there continues to be an under-representation of ethnic minorities, especially of Pakistanis, when the percentage of teachers is compared with that of the Pakistani pupils. According to the DfE (2013, Table 8), in November 2012, there were 93.3% White and 0.8% Pakistani teachers. At the same time, 78% of the pupils were White and 3.8% of Pakistani heritage (Table 6.1).

Birmingham efforts to improve teacher diversity

Historically, Birmingham Council has had a strong commitment to achieving a diverse workforce so that it reflected the local population (CRE, 1987;

Table 6.1 National proportions of the Pakistani and White teachers and pupil population, 2013

Ethnicity	School workforce (%)	School workforce (No)	Pupils (%)	Pupils (No)
White	93.3	836,070	78.0	5,195,778
Pakistani	0.8	7,192	3.8	253,127

Solomos & Back, 1995). In order to achieve this aim, the council had set a 20% target for the recruitment of ethnic minority employees and put in place a Positive Action programme. While at the time the council was successful in achieving its general workforce aim, it did not have the same level of success with reference to its teaching workforce (BCC, 1994). Here, it was accepted that the proportion of teachers from Black and minority ethnic groups "still falls far short of the proportion of Black and minority ethnic adults in the City's population (20%) and Black and minority ethnic children in the Committee's schools (38%)" (p. 26). In a communication to head teachers, it was stated that "the percentage of Black and minority ethnic children within our schools needs to be reflected in the ethnic composition of staff in school and Education Department as a whole" (BCC, 1997, p. 4). Elsewhere, it was acknowledged that there was "a huge mismatch between pupils and teachers, in that the pupil population is made up of *39%* (original emphasis) Black and minority ethnic pupils. Conversely the number of Black (meaning minority) teachers stands at *only 6.7%* (original emphasis)" (BCC, 1998, section 4).

There are two examples of local effort, in Birmingham, directed at achieving greater diversity in the teaching workforce. The MERITT (Minority ethnic recruitment in initial teacher training) scheme ran for many years, during which time it helped to train 150 teachers from Pakistani and other minority ethnic groups, including some who had progressed to leadership level (BCC, 2004, 2008). The other example involves a specially designed ITT course (Campbell & Felderhof, 2007). This had been designed by Westhill College, a local provider of teacher training. The outcome was the successful launch of a concurrent B.Ed. degree in which the main subject element was Islamic Studies. Structurally, it reflected the Religious and Theological Studies course largely rooted in the Christian tradition. On completion, the students qualified for the award of the Muslim Teacher's Certificate which the Birmingham Muslim Coordinating Committee had agreed should be awarded; this was on the model of the Catholic Teacher's Certificate. Campbell and Felderhof explained that Westhill had established the training course as a part of its Christian duty to support the Muslim community and recognise the integrity of its faith. It was also seen as important for the Muslim community to speak for itself and be given space in the world of Higher Education on terms negotiated with the Muslim community. The course was terminated when the college was taken over by Birmingham University in 2001. However, the problem of ethnic minority under-representation in the school workforce persisted,

Table 6.2 Birmingham: proportions of the Pakistani and White school workforce (2009) and pupil population (2011)

Ethnicity	Pupils (%)	Teachers (%)	Pupils (No)	Teachers (No)
White	37.9	55.0	65,835	4785
Pakistani/Kashmiri	24.5	3.8	42,558	335

especially with reference to Pakistanis (Table 6.2). In 2009, Birmingham employed 3.8% Pakistani teachers, compared to a Pakistani pupil population of 24.5%. The LA recognised the importance of ethnic make-up of teachers to be similar to that of the pupils. They produced a strategy whose purpose was to address the imbalance between the demographics in the teaching workforce and pupil population (BCC, 2006).

Teacher diversity: the views of Pakistani boys, their parents and teachers

With the above backdrop we now find out whether teacher diversity is considered important for Pakistani boys, their parents and their teachers. In my research students were asked whether it was important for them to have teachers of their ethnic and religious heritage. Over one third, 35.2%, of Pakistani students agreed that it was important to have teachers of their ethnicity, while slightly more, 42.6%, agreed that it was important to have teachers from their own religion. Lindsay and Muijs (2005) had found a majority of boys in Oldham supporting the importance of having teachers from their own ethnic group.

In my study, interviews with pupils, parents and teachers were used to shed greater light on the importance of teacher diversity. There was a mixture of views across the three school communities. While some thought it a good idea to have Pakistani teachers and/or a diverse school workforce, others said it made no difference who the teachers were. About a half of the pupils and parents, across the three school communities thought it was a good idea to have Pakistani teachers and/or a diverse school workforce and a similar number said it made no difference whether there were any Pakistani teachers in the school. Respondents gave a number of reasons for having Pakistani teachers:

• It would help to generate a better rapport between teachers and their Pakistani pupils:

> You relate to them a bit more. Because, you know, they're from the same background as you. You do feel more at ease with them. But in terms of teaching, what matters is they are good at their job and help you learn.
>
> Grammar pupil Habib

- It would be a way to link home-school lives of the pupils:

    Teachers from your own background have a better understanding of the issues you might be facing. They will know what it's like, what you are going through. To have a teacher from your own background, you can talk more about the cultural things; about weddings, stuff like that. We might also have a joke; speak in our mother tongue. It helps to build relationship too.

    Academy pupil Ibrar

- It would help for the teaching workforce to reflect the pupil population:

    It's nice to see a Pakistani teaching. It shows they are not outsiders. There should be different races of teachers. There's a lot of Pakistanis in England so that should reflect (in) the amount of teachers you see. The amount of teachers you see should reflect the amount of students.

    Academy pupil Waheed

Academy teacher Mehboob supported the idea of a diverse teaching workforce, including in leadership roles. In his view, this would make a difference; seeing people of their own ethnicity in senior roles would help to raise the boys' aspirations. For Academy teacher Zahida, this would provide role models and bring a diversity of perspectives:

Pakistani teachers; yes, absolutely. I think it's important because of that connection isn't it? I think we need those role models. I think having, if you have a richness of staff, you're enriching everyone else.

Academy teacher Jean also thought it a good idea to have diversity in the staff:

I think it would be good to see one or two of them on the senior leadership role, which there isn't.

Grammar Teacher Masood was the only Pakistani teacher the school employed – on a part-time contract. He emphasised the role model potential of Pakistani teachers:

Just by me being here, they can see that a Pakistani can be successful, can be a teacher. Whereas before me there were only English, White teachers. I am the first Pakistani teacher in this school.

He explained the Pakistani boys responded differently to him, compared with other teachers:

Yes they do. They come and shake my hand and say "Salaam-alaikum, how are you?" I say "fine". They might make small talk; they might ask me, "what time is juma (Friday prayer) or whatever". You know it, having me as a Pakistani teacher just eases their way into the school.

Community parent Junaid pointed out that it was good to have a diverse teaching team that reflected the demographics of the school: "You know, in a school such as this, if it had all White teachers then there might be an issue". For him, what mattered even more was that they had a "good understanding about Islam, that Muslim culture is different". For him it was important for teachers to understand where the pupil is coming from: "You know, they can't just treat everyone the same".

The following comments were made by pupils and parents in whose view a teacher's ethnic background was not important; what mattered was their understanding of the children's needs and their heritage and the quality of their teaching:

I'd say, no it's not important. As long as they're doing their job properly, teaching the kids properly, that's the important thing. I don't think they've got an Asian teacher at the school.

Grammar parent Shahida

I don't think its *important* (original emphasis). Any teacher, as long as it's a good teacher and he understands the child's needs, you know a teacher's a teacher. As long as they have a good teaching ability and at the same time have a good understanding, of Islam.

Community parent Junaid

Not really. As long as they understand where you are coming from.

Academy pupil Majid

No. I'd rather have.... If it was a case of a Pakistani teacher and another teacher who wasn't Pakistani but was better, I'd rather have the better teacher.

Grammar pupil Danyal

What matters is the way they teach. It doesn't matter what race or colour they are.

Community pupil Tahir

There were isolated comments from parents where they expressed opposition to having teachers from their own community. This was due to their worries about confidentiality, as shown in this quote from Academy Parent Najeeb:

next time there is a wedding, funeral or some other community gathering, the teacher may talk about our child with others in the community.

Whereas parents may freely discuss things with an English teacher because their two paths are unlikely to cross.

Pakistani boys and female teachers

In the survey the students were asked whether it was important for them to have teachers of the same sex. Very few of them, 16.6%, felt this to be important. This was explored further through interviews with the pupils and their parents. A large majority of them, 89.5%, said it made no difference, while the remainder stated that teachers of the same sex would be a good idea but it was not essential; what mattered to them was 'good quality' teachers.

From time to time one hears education practitioners and others point out that Pakistani boys have a problem with female teachers. This common-sense based perspective may have been what led Academy teacher Jean to, without any invitation, comment on the subject:

> I sometimes feel that the boys, some of them, are quite disrespectful to women. And I would put that down to their cultural background.

I was able to seek views of other teachers on the subject. Her colleague, Academy teacher Mehboob, thought this was too simplistic. He thought Pakistani boys were no different from other boys; in that they would:

> try their luck with any teacher. I don't think this is something that's pushed in the culture, definitely not in the religion.... So, I think some people do jump to the conclusion that sometimes boys, Pakistani boys, may, you know, disrespect female teachers a little bit.

His female Pakistani colleague, Academy teacher Zahida, also expressed a similar view:

> Quite a few times I've heard some teachers say: "oh well, you know Pakistani boys don't like women, especially women in authority and they don't respond well to women because it's a cultural thing". I've heard it quite a few times at this school and other schools as well.

I asked whether she herself had experienced any such behaviour, given that she was a woman:

> I have never experienced anything of that sort to say that they're not taking me serious because of my gender.

In my interview with Community teacher Linda. I did not ask about female teachers and Pakistani boys' attitudes towards them. I simply posed the standard question: "Is it a good idea to have male teachers?" to which she responded:

> There is a perception that Asian boys respond better to men. I am head of Y11. I am White, female, below average height, and I've had no problems.

She elaborated on the subject:

> I think it comes from people's perceptions. And I think it's their behaviour; if they assume there is going to be an issue, then there *is* (original emphasis) an issue. But, I think it's a myth. I've heard it, people say it in the school but I absolutely disagree.

She was asked whether during her time she had ever had any issues with Pakistani boys:

> I've never had an issue. I've never, never experienced any sort of discrimination from the boys. I've never felt that they've treated me like anything other than a person in-charge of a classroom, as a teacher. I've never felt like my gender or ethnicity has had any effect at all.

Her colleague, Community teacher Abid, offered a similar view:

> I think, it rather depends on the teacher. There may be some issue occasionally but it's a minority of them (the boys). We make it clear to them right at the beginning when they start school, what we expect from them. But there is this perception out there that Pakistani boys struggle with female teachers but I don't think that is true. I've not seen any evidence of that here.

For him the solution lay in the schools providing good teachers who could deliver good lessons, to keep all the pupils engaged, regardless of whether they were male or female. He also felt it was important for schools to make clear to the pupils their (the school's) equal opportunities expectations. Academy teacher Mehboob suggested that schools could seek the support of the imams, who would be well placed to remind the boys of the religious position.

Pakistani boys' role models

It has been recognised that young people need support and encouragement from adults in the community beyond the school (Phillip & Hendry, 2000; Bricheno & Thornton, 2007). More widely, the DFEE (2000) spoke of 'community learning champions' who "would be from within the community rather than being 'parachuted in' and have an enabling and co-ordinating role – talking to parents and the wider community and encouraging them into the school" (p. 40). Here it is worth noting the reservations expressed by Maylor

(2009) that young people do not always relate to people of their own ethnicity. This may equally apply to Pakistani pupils in relation to Pakistani teachers.

I asked the students in my research whether they considered it important to have role models from their own ethnic group. Around a half, 49.9%, of Pakistani pupils agreed that this was important. This was broadly similar to the response from White pupils, 51.1%. During the interviews, the boys informed me that they had role models from within the family in line with research on this subject (Crozier & Davies, 2006; Thapar-Bjorkert & Sanghera, 2010; Berglund, 2012; Basit, 2013).

> I look up to my mum. I respect her for what she's done.
>
> Community pupil Razaq

> My dad. He worked his way up; he was from a village in Pakistan. I admire how hard he has worked to get to where he is.
>
> Grammar pupil Habib

> One of my uncles. He is a doctor. He's done really well. He went out to India and Pakistan to help people. So him, he would be my role model.
>
> Grammar pupil Bilal

> My brother, he has just graduated with law. He would be my role model. He told me it's better to go to university.
>
> Community pupil Mazar

> My cousins who've done degrees, like doctors, technicians. You look at them, you see yourself doing that.
>
> Community pupil Tahir

> I also look up to my sister. She was always into her books.
>
> Academy pupil Ibrar

Religious role models

Religious involvement is said to make it easier for young people to access role models who act as the pathways to their success (Brown & Gary, 1991; Byfield, 2008). Also, that religious organisations provide an amiable and cross-generational environment which was conducive to the development of meaningful and influential adolescent–adult relationships. Such relationships are known to provide an increased sense of moral order. Erickson and Phillips (2012) pointed out that as parental relationships and influence waned for young people, they needed others whose example could be followed. This was where adults in religious organisations were able to step in.

> When adolescents participate in organized religion, they gain access to older attendants who may offer care, attention, counsel, or otherwise positive encouragement. The relationships youth form with these religious adults

offer opportunities for role modelling and interpersonal ties that can have important implications for educational attainment.

(p. 570)

For them ties with religious-based mentorships are important for educational attainment because they represent a connection to a formal organisation that has similar constraints to the education system.

A number of the boys were found to draw support from their religious beliefs, mentioning specifically the Prophet Mohammed (Davies, 2016), as their role model:

> Religious leaders; like our Prophet Mohammed (peace be upon him) like how he lived his life in terms of like, he encouraged knowledge. He said: you should travel the world just to seek knowledge. Because of that, I would probably choose him as one of my role models. It makes me work harder. It definitely does.
>
> Community pupil Mazar

> I studied the prophets' lives, especially Prophet Mohammed (peace be upon him). I study it every Sunday. So I try to emulate that as a part of my religious experience.
>
> Grammar pupil Aakif

A few mentioned their teachers, both at school and the mosque, as the people they looked up to:

> I want to have a beard and have respect; like my ustaadji, my mosque teacher. He prays five times a day and everything. (He) gives respect and gets respect, that kind of thing; I want to be like that.
>
> Community pupil Faisal

> My school teachers and those at the mosque. The way they support people, the way they live their life.
>
> Community pupil Pervez

> The school teachers I look up to. The mosque teachers; they tell you how they've changed, what they've been through themselves.
>
> Community pupil Israr

I asked the teachers whether there were people in their community or history that the Pakistani students would emulate. Academy teacher Zahida responded that most of the students would lack knowledge of such people, as it was not something taught in the school.

> I'd be surprised if most of them knew when Pakistan became independent. They wouldn't know about Muhammed Ali Jinnah. I doubt it if they'll

know about Allama Iqbal, I doubt it. They'll probably know very little about Pakistani history.

She pointed out that the real problem was that her teacher colleagues had little or no knowledge of such key figures from the Pakistani community and history. Consequently, Pakistani boys would not be provided such knowledge, unless they had middle class, educated parents ("but if you're coming, your family are from a rural background, farming people, they won't have that kind of education"). During the interviews with the parents, I came across one parent mentioning that in their family they made sure the children had some understanding of key people from the Pakistani community and history.

The current Pakistani representation in Birmingham schools

In order to understand the current level of Pakistani representation, selected schools were asked for data on their pupils, teachers, Senior Leadership Team (SLT) and governors. This was through the Freedom of Information site, www.whatdotheyknow, where all the data are published. The responses are summarised in Table 6.3.[1] In relation to Pakistanis, it indicates a colonial model of governance – mainly White people managing brown people. With the exception of one school, Kings Norton Girls, all schools who supplied the data have an under-representation[2] of Pakistani teachers and governors. Two schools – King Edward Camp Hill Boys and King Edward Camp Hill Girls – have no Pakistani teachers at all. In all schools there is further under-representation of Pakistanis in their governing bodies. Two schools – Holyhead and Queensbridge – have no Pakistani governors at all. One school, Bishop Vesey, has neither any Pakistani teachers nor any Pakistani governors. It is likely that in these schools, where there are no Pakistani teachers or governors or both, there exists an environment that discourages the Pakistani children to express their Pakistaniness, as pointed out by Tim Boyes, CEO of Birmingham Education Partnership. Furthermore, the question that needs to be asked is whether the Pakistanis are to remain as passive recipients of educational provision or are allowed by the system to become active participants in making key decisions. While there has always been such Pakistani under-representation, the current situation is the worse yet. There appears to be poor equality literacy amongst school leaders, a number of whom did not understand what is meant by under-representation nor how to measure it. According to Holmwood and O'Toole (2017), at the heart of this situation is the government academisation programme which has taken schools out of the local authority control. Whereas previously there was a 'hierarchical' system of governance through local education authorities there is now 'heterarchical' governance of schools, where the system is composed of a network of bodies including schools, trusts, consultancies and for-profit companies.

Table 6.3 Pakistani representation (pupils, teachers, support staff, senior leaders, governors) in selected Birmingham schools

School	Pupils %	Teachers %	Support staff %	Senior Leaders %	Governors %
Bishop Vesey	8	0	0	0	0
Broadway	46	8	7	8	14
Fairfax	3	1	0	0	1
George Dixon	26	16	15	0	17
Heartlands	33	21	8	17	
Holyhead	23	3	1	0	0
King Edward Camp Hill Girls	19	0	0	0	
King Edward Camp Hill Boys	16	0	10	0	8
King Edward Handsworth	38	3	9	0	
King Edward Handsworth – Girls	19	3	10		
Kings Heath Boys	34	6	3	1	2
Kings Norton Girls	3	4	7	0	8
North Birmingham	14	3	0	0	
Queensbridge	27	8	8	0	0
Saltley	66	37	20	22	63
Shenley	1	0	0	0	
Waverley	67	21	21		
Wheelers Lane	33	12	10	10	9
Yardleys	64	10	13	0	17

It is based on a corporate model of governance which has little or no place for parents and communities being served by the schools, leading to the particular exclusion of the Pakistani community. Many of the schools are operating as islands, isolated from others or are part of a small group within a multi-academy trust. Given that this is a broader problem it is unlikely that any one school will address it. The one body that could do something about this, but is unlikely to, is the Birmingham Education Partnership (BEP) (McKinney, 2016). While they have assumed some of the local authority functions, such as school improvement, they do not appear to see a problem such as Pakistani under-representation in education their priority. According to Holmwood (2018), the Birmingham governance of education is the whitest it has ever been. The example he cited to illustrate this was that of BEP. This was backed up by the data they provided on their own situation of Pakistani representation. This offers a poor lead to the schools in their sphere of influence. According to the data they supplied, they currently have one employee, in an admin role (11%), and one board member (10%) who are Pakistani. They have indicated that there is no strategy to address the Pakistani under-representation within their organisation. Therefore, the situation is likely to stay the same or become worse.

Notes

1   The following Birmingham secondary schools failed to supply the data requested, in spite of numerous reminders: Holy Trinity, Great Barr, Kings Norton Boys, Lordswood Girls, King Edward Five Ways, Rockwood, Ormiston, St Albans, Harborne, Holte, Aston, King Edward Sheldon Heath.
2   Where there were fewer Pakistani teachers when compared with the proportion of Pakistani pupils.

Bibliography

Abbas, T. (2004). *The education of British South Asians*. Basingstoke: Palgrave Macmillan.

Arshad, R., Diniz, F., Kelly, E., O'Hara, P., Sharp, S. & Syed, R. (2004). *Minority ethnic pupils' experiences of school in Scotland*. Scottish Executive, Education Department.

Basit, T. (2013). Educational capital as a catalyst for upward social mobility amongst British Asians: A three-generational analysis. *British Educational Research Journal* 39(4) 714–732.

Basit, T. & Santoro, N. (2012). Playing the role of 'cultural expert': Teachers of ethnic difference in Britain and Australia. *Oxford Review of Education* 37(1) 37–52.

BCC. (1994). *Statistical report 1993/94*. BCC. Education committee.

BCC. (1997). *Equal opportunities: Circular no. S285*. BCC. Education Department.

BCC. (1998). *Education department: Asian Achievement Group*. BCC. Education Department, 9 March.

BCC. (2004). *Minutes of recruitment and retention task group*. BCC. Education Department, 15 March.

BCC. (2006). *Recruitment, support and retention of teachers*. BCC. Overview and Scrutiny, 10 October.

BCC. (2008). *A guide to MERITT trainees and participating schools*. BCC. Education Department.

Berglund, J. (2012). Teachers only stand behind parents and God in the eyes of Muslim pupils. *Journal of Beliefs & Values: Studies in Religion & Education* 33(3) 357–367.

Blair, M. & Bourne, J. (2000). *Making the difference: Teaching and learning strategies in successful multi-ethnic schools*. London: DFEE.

Bradbury, M. & Kellough, J. (2011). Representative bureaucracy: Assessing the evidence on active representation. *The American Review of Public Administration* 4(2) 157–167.

Bricheno, P. & Thornton, M. (2007). Role model, hero or champion? Children's views concerning role models. *Educational Research* 49(4) 383–396.

Brown, D. & Gary, L. (1991). Religious socialization and educational attainment among African Americans: An empirical assessment. *The Journal of Negro Education* 60(3) 411–426.

Byfield, C. (2008). The impact of religion on the educational achievement of Black boys: A UK and USA study. *British Journal of Sociology of Education* 29(2) 189–199.

Campbell, W. & Felderhof, M. (2007). A pioneering experiment: A report on Islamic studies within a teaching qualification. *Journal of Beliefs & Values* 28(3) 297–308.

Carrington, B. (2002). Ethnicity, 'role models' and teaching. *Journal of Research in Education* 12(1) 40–49.

Cline, T., Abreu, G., Fihosy, C., Gray, H., Lambert, H. & Neale, J. (2002). *Minority ethnic pupils in mainly white schools*. Norwich: Department for Education and Skills.

CRE (Commission for Racial Equality). (1987). 1:5 target for Birmingham Council. *Employment Report* 8(1), March.

Crozier, G. & Davies, J. (2006). Family matters: A discussion of the Bangladeshi and Pakistani extended family and community supporting the children's education. *The Sociological Review* 54(4) 678–695.

Davies, A. (2016). Personal email, 23 July.

DCSF. (2009). *The Extra Mile (Secondary): Achieving success with pupils from deprived communities.* London: DCSF.

Delpit, Lisa. (1995). *Other people's children: Cultural conflict in the classroom.* New York: The New Press.

DFE. (2013). *SFR15/2013: School workforce in England: November 2012.* London: DfE.

DFEE. (2000). *Removing the barriers: Raising achievement levels for minority ethnic pupils.* London: DfEE.

DFES. (2001). *Schools achieving success.* London: DFES.

DFES. (2003). *Aiming high: Raising the achievement of minority ethnic pupils.* London: DFES.

Eckhard, S. (2014). Bureaucratic representation and ethnic bureaucratic drift: A case study of United Nations minority policy implementation in Kosovo. *American Review of Public Administration* 44(5) 600–621.

Egalite, A., Kisida, B. & Winters, M. (2015). Representation in the classroom: The effect of own-race teachers on student achievement. *Economics of Education Review* 45 44–52.

Erickson, L. & Phillips, J. (2012). The effect of religious-based mentoring on educational attainment: More than just a spiritual high. *Journal for the Scientific Study of Religion* 51(3) 568–587.

Flynn, J., Kemp, A. & Perez, D. (2009). You can't teach where you don't know. *Curriculum and Teaching Dialogue* 12(1&2) 137–151.

Franquiz, M. (2011). Challenging majoritarian tales: Portraits of bilingual teachers deconstructing deficit views of bilingual learners. *Bilingual Research Journal: The Journal of the National Association for Bilingual Education* 34(3) 279–300.

Ghouri, N. (1997). Wanted: The best minority teachers, *Times Educational Supplement,* 7 November.

HM Government. (2005). *Higher Standards, Better Schools for All.* Norwich: HMSO.

HMSO. (2005). *Higher Standards, Better Schools for All.* White Paper.

Holmwood, J. & O'Toole, T. (2017). *Countering extremisim in British schools? The truth about the Birmingham Trojan Horse affair.* Bristol: Policy Press.

Howard, J. (2010). The value of ethnic diversity in the teaching profession: A New Zealand case study. *International Journal of Education* 2(1) 1–22.

Irvine, J. (1989). Beyond role models: An examination of cultural influences on the pedagogical perspectives of Black teachers. *Peabody Journal of Education* 66(4) 51–63.

Kennedy, M. (1991). Policy issues in teacher education. *National Centre for Research on Teacher Education.* 2–12.

Klopfenstein, K. (2005). Beyond test scores: The impact of Black teacher role models on rigorous math taking. *Contemporary Economic Policy* 23(3) 416–428.

Kohli, R. (2014). Unpacking internalized racism: Teachers of colour striving for racially just classrooms. *Race Ethnicity and Education* 17(3) 367–387.

Kohli, R. & Pizarro, M. (2016). Fighting to educate our own: Teachers of color, relational accountability, and the struggle for social justice. *Equity & Excellence in Education* 49(1) 72–84.

Lindsay, G. & Muijs, D. (2005). *Challenging underachievement of boys in years 8 and 10: A study for the Oldham Leading Edge Partnership.* Coventry: University of Warwick.

Magaldi, D., Conway, T. & Trub, L. (2016). 'I am here for a reason': Minority teachers bridging many divides in urban education. *Race Ethnicity and Education*.

Maylor, U. (2009). 'They do not relate to Black people like us': Black teachers as role models for Black pupils. *Journal of Educational Policy* 24(1) 1–21.

McKinney, E. (2016). *Changing times: The future of education in Birmingham*. Birmingham: Birmingham Education Partnership.

Murrell, P. (2000). Community teachers: A conceptual framework for preparing exemplary urban teachers. *The Journal of Negro Education* 69(4) 338–348.

National Audit Office report. (2004). *Delivering public services to a diverse society*. London: The Stationery Office.

NCTL (National College for Teaching and Leadership). (2015). *Leadership equality and diversity fund*. Nottingham: NCTL.

Padilla, L. (2001). But you're not a dirty Mexican: Internalized oppression, Latinos & law. *Texas Hispanic Journal of Law and Policy* 7 59–133.

Phillip, K. & Hendry, L. (2000). Making sense of mentoring or mentoring making sense? Reflections on the mentoring process by adult mentors with young people. *Journal of Community & Applied Social Psychology* 10 211–223.

Pitts, D. (2005). Diversity, representation, and performance: Evidence about race and ethnicity in public organizations. *Journal of Public Administration Research and Theory* 15 615–631.

Quiocho, A. & Rios, F. (2000). The power of their presence: Minority group teachers and schooling. *Review of Educational Research* 70(4) 485–528.

Reed, W. (2009). The bridge is built: The role of local teachers in an urban elementary school. *The School Community Journal* 19(1) 59–75.

Roch, C. & Pitts, D. (2012). Differing effects of representative bureaucracy in Charter Schools and traditional public schools. *The American Review of Public Administration* 42(3) 282–302.

Ross, A. (2001). *Towards a representative profession: Teachers from the ethnic minorities*. Conference paper London Metropolitan University.

Selden, S. (1997). Representative bureaucracy: Examining the linkage between passive and active representation in the farmers home administration. *American Review of Public Administration* 27(1) 22–42.

Solomos, J. & Back, L. (1995). *Race, politics and social change*. London: Routledge.

Sowa, J. & Selden, S. (2003). Administrative discretion and active representation: An expansion of the theory of representative bureaucracy. *Public Administration Review* 63(6) 700–710.

Speight, S. (2007). Internalized racism. *The Counseling Psychologist* 35(1) 126–134.

Steele, C. & Aronson, J. (1995). Stereotype threat and the intellectual test performance of African Americans. *Journal of Personality and Social Psychology* 69(5) 797–811.

Stewart, J., Meier, K. & England, R. (1989). In quest of role models: Change in Black teacher representation in urban school districts, 1968–1986. *The Journal of Negro Education* 58(2) 140–152.

Swann Report. (1985). *Education for all*. London: HMSO.

Thapar-Bjorkert, S. & Sanghera, G. (2010). Social capital, educational aspirations and young Pakistani Muslim men and women in Bradford, West Yorkshire. *The Sociological Review* 58(2) 244–264.

Walker, A., Dimmock, C., Stevenson, H., Bignold, B., Shah, S. & Middlewood, D. (2005). *Effective leadership in multi-ethnic schools*. Nottingham: NCSL.

Warikoo, N. (2004). Race and the teacher–student relationship: Interpersonal connections between West Indian students and their teachers in a New York City high school. *Race Ethnicity and Education* 7(2) 135–147.

Weiher, G. (2000). Minority student achievement: Passive representation and social context in schools. *The Journal of Politics* 62(3) 886–895.

WRECC (Wolverhampton Race Equality Council Consortium). (1999). *Recruitment and retention of teachers from the ethnic minority communities.* Wolverhampton: WRECC.

7 Teacher understanding of Pakistani pupils

Linking up the pupils' worlds

Some groups of pupils are said to do well in school because their cultures are congruent with the culture of the school while others perform badly because of the discontinuities between their wider lives and their time at the school (Ogbu, 1982; Tyler et al., 2008). Here minority communities and their children can experience discontinuities because what counts as education in the dominant society may be different from how they see education and their often disadvantaged context can be a major determinant of home–school relations (Lareau & Horvat, 1999; Markose, 2008). Parents in deprived families have been known to lack the ability and the resources necessary to provide their children a stimulating home learning environment. Middle class parents on the other hand are said to have the know-how needed to take advantage of the education system, and, given they are from a similar background as many of the teachers, school is likely to be a friendlier place for them (Whitty, 2001; Byrne, 2009). Brighouse (2007) stressed the same happening with White middle class boys whose lives at home and at school have continuity, they are able to encounter a 'home-from-home' and a familiar place where they can feel settled and enjoy the resources on offer. This, for him, results from the design of the curriculum, its staffing comprising of White middle class teachers and the general ethos of the school; all of these value the culture of the White middle class. Working class parents, on the other hand, are prone to defer to the superior knowledge and status of teachers and are inclined to leave the child's education to the school (Evans, 2007; Demie & Lewis, 2011). For Goodall (2012), when working with parents, schools' expectations are those of the dominant, (White) middle class culture, while for Crozier (1999), working class parents tend to be more distant from the school due to its own culture and discourses. For minority parents, the deracialisation of parental involvement compounded the exclusion they faced from schools. While the majority of Pakistanis are from lower SES, a growing number are described as middle class. Archer (2010) has pointed out that such parents echo White middle class parents in their active involvement in the school and in their potential to be 'angry parents' (Ranson et al., 2004) 'storming' into schools to challenge teachers and head teachers.

The government-commissioned Bullock Report (1975, para 20.5) had made a case for connecting children's school lives with those lived outside:

> No child should be expected to cast off the language and culture of the home as he crosses the school threshold, nor to live and act as though school and home represent two totally separate and different cultures which have to be kept firmly apart. The curriculum should reflect many elements of that part of his life which a child lives outside school.

And yet, for Coles (2004), this is exactly what happens for Muslim children. He pointed out that Muslim pupils are required to leave their religion at home because so often the school is simply unaware of the centrality of Islam in the life of its Muslim pupils. Many teachers do not feel equipped to help steer their pupils through the complicated Islamic minefield.

Richardson and Wood (2004) spoke of disjointed lives of Pakistani young people; there was little or no link between their home, school and their learning at the mosque. They illustrated the situation as a triangle whose three corner points were not joined-up. Sahin (2013) similarly spoke of the conflicting demands and expectations of the culture of the Muslim child's home, mosque, secular multicultural life and peer group. Rhamie and Hallam (2002) stressed the importance of joining pupils' worlds in order to create a common purpose, culture and values. Damon and Colby (1996) similarly pointed out the importance of all the people and institutions in a child's life to collaborate. Merry (2005) found it important to create cultural coherence in young people's lives, which can aid children by "minimizing unnecessary cognitive dissonance in their early years" (p. 479). Ogbu (1982) spoke of the cultural discontinuity hypothesis, according to which some groups do well in school because their cultures are congruent with school culture while others do less well because of the distance between their school and home lives. One exception to this appears to be the practice within Harrow SACRE (2013). In their guidance on meeting the needs of children's religious needs they acknowledged that in a secular community those who have a religious commitment sometimes feel that they can never be totally themselves. They keep silent about a central part of their identity. Leading a 'bi-cultural' life can be stressful for the children. They recommend to schools that they provide for the children a space for prayer and reflection in the possibility that it may allow pupils to bring their 'whole self' to school. It may help the pupils to feel that they wholly belong to their school community. Such practices may lead to pupils developing increased self-esteem and self-confidence which may indirectly lead to their greater engagement with learning and achievement.

It is commonly accepted that parents will need to support their children if the latter are to succeed at school (Strand, 2007). According to Desforges and Abouchaar (2003), pupils' achievement is influenced by many people, including parents. For them, parental involvement takes many forms including good parenting in the home and provision of a stable environment and has a significant positive effect on children's achievement. Melhuish et al. (2008) pointed out that what parents do at home is learnable. Michael et al. (2007) pointed out that family and community involvement in schools leads to improvements in academic achievement of students.

Effective home–school relationships have been cited as a protective factor (Callanan et al., 2009). For Deslandes (2001), home and school were spheres of influence for a child and interaction between the two was at an optimum when both functioned as genuine partners. For Wilson (2009), young people who perceived their parents to be monitoring their activities had higher levels of achievement. Caplan et al. (1991), based on their research with Vietnamese community, concluded that family had a clear and unambiguous effect on children's achievement. They suggested that such effect acted as a protective factor in the face of formidable obstacles the students might face. They pointed out that this had implications for schools: "there has to be an understanding that education is a reciprocal process and that the home should be (fully) involved" (p. 168). However, to do so schools would need to provide an

> education that is culturally responsive, whereby attempts must be made to identify and incorporate into its philosophy and pedagogy those aspects of the students' cultures that are central and conducive to learning and conventional achievement.
>
> (pp. 168–169)

Later, the authors reiterate their position. They pose the question: how can schools enable children to feel at home in school and with their learning. They advise that schools cannot go it alone in this endeavour, independent of the diverse social and cultural systems of their students. They also point out that to achieve this aim would require schools to become "more aware of the backgrounds of their students and employing those values and other cultural aspects that promote learning" (p. 173). In my view it is conceivable that, for bridges to be built between them and the Pakistani community, schools and their staff would need to understand their Pakistani communities. Furthermore, they would benefit from having more Pakistani teachers, especially those who are deeply rooted within the local community and Pakistani governors.

Teacher–pupil relationships

The school is a relational environment, given the amount of time young people and teachers spend with each other. Teachers' capacity to imbue productive values about school work, motivate students to engage in the learning, to listen to, respect and to understand their students; all of these rely on the effectiveness of teacher–student relationships (Murray-Harvey, 2010). In relation to minority and disadvantaged young people, Alexander and Entwisle (1987) pointed out that teachers who had a sense of commitment to them and had high expectations of them were more successful in working with them. They pointed out that good teaching was not simply a matter of using time wisely or delivering the right lesson plan; it involved teachers having the right relationships with the children. According to Pigott and Cowen (2000), positive teacher–pupil relationships support a pupil's feeling of security in the school setting and help to facilitate academic achievement. Additionally, when teachers have a close relationship with their pupils, they report having communication that is more open with those children. In turn, children who have greater open communication with the teachers feel more comfortable asking clarifying questions and volunteering to participate in classroom activities. Birch and Ladd (1997) pointed out that children were better able to utilise as a source of support the teachers with whom they had close relationships. Children in such situations also saw the school as a supportive environment.

Significant associations have been reported between quality of teacher–child relationships and achievement as children "with higher quality relationships participate more and are more engaged in the classroom than those with lower quality relationships" (O'Connor & McCartney, 2007, p. 345). In particular, the right teacher–student relationships help establish an environment that leads to improved pupil learning outcomes (Haertel et al., 1981; Leadbeater, 2008; OECD, 2011); effective teaching (Delpit, 1995); greater enjoyment (Gorard & See, 2011); social/emotional competence (Murray-Harvey, 2010) and success in teaching interactions and increased student achievement (Warikoo, 2004). According to the DFES (2006), teacher–pupil relationships are part of ethos and the single most important factor affecting students' achievement in school. Good relationships enabled students to overcome many barriers they faced in their education:

> Students thought relationships were good when learning and teaching approaches allowed them to express and share their own experiences. These approaches had the effect of affirming or validating their identities and made them feel good about themselves.
>
> (p. 12)

They reported the opposite outcome on their achievement "when students did not feel adequately respected, cared for, affirmed or understood" (p. 12). A similar message was reported in Department for Education publications. Chowdry et al. (2009) pointed out that "good teacher-pupil relations at age 14 are positively associated with progress between Key Stage 3 and Key Stage 4 and are consistently negatively associated with engagement in a range of risky behaviours (including truancy) at ages 14 and 16" (p. 49). Callanan et al. (2009) identified a number of 'within the school system' causes of disengagement and underachievement, one of which was relationship with teachers. "Young people particularly valued teachers who they felt talked to them with respect, listened to their views, showed an active interest in their attainment and treated them more like an adult. ... Where there was a strong positive relationship with a teacher, young people would describe working harder and attending those lessons more regularly" (p. 33). In Pomeroy's (1999) research in a secondary school context, the ability of the teachers to establish positive relationships was seen as very important for the students and a consistently described feature of their experience of school. They equated this with being a good teacher.

It is likely that teacher–pupil relationships are affected by commonality of background. According to the DFES (2006), "teachers are likely to interact more with children from a background similar to their own and tend to interact less with children from backgrounds they know little about" (p. 13). Warikoo (2004), based on interviews with teachers, supported this view but only in part. She found that West Indian teachers had strong points of connection with their West Indian students and teachers served as advocates for the students when cultural differences were an issue. However, she found that non–West Indian teachers also connected with West Indian students. For example, White teachers had drawn upon common experiences of immigration and African American teachers had drawn upon common experiences of race prejudice. This provides evidence that while teachers maybe more likely to make connections with and hence successfully teach children who share their background such as ethnicity, many a good teacher, without necessarily coming from the same ethnic background as their students, can find points of connection with them.

Teacher understanding of pupil background

Central to the teacher–pupil relationship is the understanding teachers have of their pupils and the world they inhabit. Before I began my current study, I encountered a newsletter from Antidote (2010), an education consultancy, who spoke of Muslim students complaining that teachers did not know them as individuals.

> The students reported that they were not spoken to by name. They weren't recognised by staff outside classrooms in the corridors and canteen. They found that staff mixed up their names and regularly exchanged the names of girls that were friends and tended to be found together or, worse in their opinion, addressed them as 'Hey you!'

The students wanted staff to invest more time in getting to know them as people, their likes, dislikes, tastes and opinions.

It has been pointed out that teachers cannot teach children well if they lack an understanding of their students' cultures and lives, and if they lack meaningful relationships with their families (Warren, 2005). This had been acknowledged by the government-commissioned Swann Report (1985) which considered it important for teachers to have "respect for and understanding of the cultural heritage which belongs to the children growing up in our society [and] sensitivity to the diversity of cultural background in today's school population" (p. 560). With particular reference to Muslim children, the DCSF (2008) stressed the importance for teachers to understand the pupils' religious and cultural identities. They placed this within the wider frame of "the rich Islamic heritage and culture" (p. 15). Elsewhere, the DCSF (2009) advised schools to respect local people, their culture and values and suggested that teachers should get to know the local community and become involved in its activities. To be effective and successful in doing so, "staff need to: understand the nature of the locality the children live in; empathise with the local community and its values; and be aware of the barriers to achievement but not to allow these to lower expectations" (p. 28). Robertson (2006) pointed out the importance for teachers to have an understanding of their pupils' background and on-going cultural lives. This was based on her in-depth study of five Pahari-speaking Pakistani-Kashmiri children in both mainstream school and madrassah classes. For Murrell (2000), appropriately trained teachers who are able to show cultural sensitivity to their pupils are able to produce strong achievement results from their minority students. For Pomeroy (1999), central to being a good teacher was understanding one's pupils: knowing their name, their hobbies and interests, what is going on in their lives, and knowledge of the pupils' culture and religion, their linguistic experiences and abilities and their general cultural context.

Here the work of Moll et al. (1992) is relevant. They coined the phrase 'funds of knowledge', which were historically accumulated and culturally developed within communities, and for them the knowledge of such funds can enable teachers to connect with their pupils as whole beings and at a deeper level. Otherwise, the teacher–pupil relationship is likely to be 'thin' and 'single stranded' where the teacher only knows the pupil from his or her performance within the rather limited classroom context, not necessarily what pupils may bring to the school from their wider lives. The teachers are, therefore, unable to build on what the minority children already know. They also spoke of the dynamic nature of the cultural context of the students and their families; to become aware of them is never a one-off exercise but requires on-going learning by teachers. They suggested that teachers should go into the community, gain a deep understanding of its context and then draw out relevant learning which can be linked to the formal curriculum of the school. Teachers can then help to bridge the students' lives inside of school with the world they experience outside. This was similar to what Walker et al. (2005) had reported. The head teachers they studied recognised that their schools could not be successful if they operated in a vacuum and, therefore, stressed the importance of understanding and connecting with the broader community. They saw it as essential for teachers to have a presence in the wider community as a way of helping their students to achieve. They worked hard to understand their students' beliefs and value structures and to appreciate reality through their eyes. Head teachers constantly reiterated to staff the need to locate their leadership and work within the unique context of their school.

Lee's (2001) concept of 'cultural modeling' is relevant here. According to this, students bring to school a rich array of knowledge from their wider cultural lives, which offers a fertile bridge for scaffolding school-based learning. For such work to succeed it was seen as necessary for there to be trusted relationships between the school and its wider community. According to the National Council of Teachers of English (NCTE),[1] students do not enter school as empty vessels to be filled with knowledge. Rather, they bring with them rich and varied language and cultural experiences which need to be recognised and valued. In their view teachers and teacher educators should actively acknowledge, celebrate and incorporate the funds of knowledge as pedagogical strategies that are culturally and linguistically responsive. For the NCTE, teachers need spaces to learn about the communities in which they will teach and opportunities to explore and experience the contexts in which students live and form their cultural identities. According to the DFES (2004, p. 10) schools have much to gain from the experiences and understandings of pupils, their families and communities. In their view, drawing on the students' funds of knowledge would enrich a school in a range of valuable ways.

There have been a number of projects which have used the 'funds of knowledge' approach in the education of minority children, which may provide models of practice. Conteh (2012) reported teachers' efforts to understand the pupils' wider lives by visiting the children's homes and madrassahs. This enabled them to take account of the 'context' in their teaching (Noordhoff & Kleinfeld, 1993). The Home-School Knowledge Exchange (HSKE) was an action research programme in which parents, teachers and children exchanged knowledge between home and school (Hughes & Pollard, 2006). Andrews and Yee (2006) provided two case studies from the HSKE project, involving Muslim children's lives and learning out of school. They considered the implications for educational practice of drawing on such funds of knowledge. Sadly, there are times when children's funds of knowledge 'leak' into the classroom but without its learning potential being fully utilised (Thomson & Hall, 2008). Marshall and Toohey (2010), in their focus on Punjabi Sikh children in a Canadian context, drew attention to 'funds of knowledge' which challenged school notions of secularity, gender, equity and cultural authenticity. For them such knowledge had the potential for becoming a resource for children, teachers and the wider community. Shalabi and Taylor (2011) pointed out that the most fundamental funds of knowledge in Muslim households are the Islamic culture and contributions of cultural institutions such as mosques. For them, students' academic performance is enhanced when they receive teaching that utilises aspects of their home culture, pointing out that the role of parents, as representatives and reinforcing agents of funds of knowledge, was the most significant factor in shaping minority students' identities and social experiences.

As to what particular knowledge teachers should have of their minority students, the DFES (2006) advised that they should "know something of the languages and literacy practices of families, their cultural and religious traditions.

They should find out about any supplementary schooling or religious education the child receives" (p. 16). As well as books and websites they suggest that such understanding can be acquired from community organisations, the children, their parents and minority teachers. They also point out that children are more likely to provide the teachers information about their personal lives when they know the teachers respect them and value their culture and want to understand the complexities of their lives. Hoque (2018), with reference to Bangladeshi Muslims in Tower Hamlets, provides a list of questions to guide teachers' understanding of their Muslim pupils. The list is equally relevant to understanding Pakistani children:

- *Do we really know who our students are?*
- *Are we aware of the wider social, community and cultural issues that many of our pupils are living through?*
- *Do we know why faith and religion (Islam) is important to many of our pupils?*
- *How do our pupils understand and negotiate complex notions of culture, community, nation, faith, religion and spirituality?*
- *Why is it important that our curriculum is relevant to the lives of our pupils, reflecting their social world?*
- *Why do some girls wear the hijab and some boys grow beards and others do not?*

At a fundamental level, Kohli and Solorzano (2012) pointed out that it is important for teachers to know their pupils' names as this is a central part of children's identity and often carries cultural and family significance. For them it is also important that teachers learn to pronounce the children's names properly, especially in relation to minority children who are often subjected to their names being mispronounced by their teachers. Sue et al. (2007) defined such mispronunciations as an example of racial microaggression and explained that these "are brief and commonplace daily verbal, behavioural or environmental indignities, whether intentional or unintentional that communicate hostile, derogatory or negative racial slights and insults towards people of color" (p. 271). Such experiences are also said to be what has been described as 'everyday racism' (Essed, 1990). Having lived in England as a minority and with a name which was often 'different' my own experience can support this argument as can the experience of many other minority background people I know. I have often had my name mispronounced or worse, not called out when it was required. On one occasion when the latter happened at the hands of a government education agency, it was the subject of a formal complaint.

Role of teacher training

Gay and Howard (2000) set out the agenda for ITT. With an increasing racial, cultural and linguistic gap between teachers (predominantly White) and students (increasingly diverse), they made the case that all trainee and practising teachers need to develop multicultural knowledge and pedagogical skills. They stated that such education should be mandatory and thorough. "No students should graduate from any teacher education programme and be certified or hired to teach without being thoroughly trained in multicultural education" (p. 7). Furthermore, they made a case for ITT courses to require, of trainees, a certain pre-entry multicultural knowledge and competence. This would then give them appropriate foundations to build on the relevant pedagogical knowledge. Although this case was made 16 years ago, as an idea, it may still be relevant to the current situation in ITT. According to Sleeter (2001), White pre-service teachers still come to teacher preparation with little experience in culturally, linguistically and racially diverse contexts, with very little understanding of structural inequality and institutional racism, and with serious cultural and racial biases. She made the case for increasing the number of 'community teachers' – teachers (particularly from minority backgrounds) whose teaching practice was effective with students in culturally, linguistically and ethnically diverse urban communities. She stressed the importance of producing appropriately situated and contextualised knowledge for trainee teachers and recommended that they immerse themselves into their schools' wider communities.

During the early part of the New Labour government, equality and diversity training was recognised as being important for teachers and those entering the profession in order to enable them to think about and reassess their assumptions about, and understand the points of similarity they might share with, students from diverse backgrounds. The Teacher Training Agenda (TTA, 2000) saw it as the responsibility of teachers to prepare all pupils for a life in a culturally diverse society. In order to help ITT providers to train new teachers accordingly, they provided guidance and resources. Providers were asked to make sure that trainees were equipped with "the knowledge, understanding and skills they need to raise the attainment of minority ethnic pupils and improve the quality of their education" (p. 9). This was reiterated through the professional teacher standards (TTA, 2003) where it was made clear that teachers have "high expectations of all pupils; respect their social, cultural, linguistic, religious and ethnic backgrounds; and are committed to raising their educational achievement" (S1.1, p. 7). However, during the latter phase of New Labour, equality and diversity training had been de-prioritised and consequently education policy had moved away from a focus on 'particular' needs and circumstances of minority children. Klein (2007) reported that the majority of newly qualified teachers had not been prepared to teach in culturally diverse schools. "Most training institutions deal with equality in a day, or just one session, or not at all" (p. 119). She was of the view that the body of knowledge created in the wake of government reports (Swann Report, 1985; Eggleston Report, 1986) had disappeared from the late 1980s onwards. Meer and Modood (2007) also pointed out that diversity was something that had been covered during the 1980s but then had gone off the agenda. According to Gillborn (1997), there was a "largely deracialised discourse such that a concern with ethnic inequalities of achievement and opportunity has been effectively removed from the policy agenda" (p. 345). According to Crozier (1999a) such deracialising of ITT and related educational discourses had led to teachers becoming technicians or applied scientists. This has placed even greater responsibility on the school-based CPD (continuing professional development) on diversity (Blair, 2002). According to Walker et al. (2005), ethnic minority students considered it important for the schools to have staff who had an understanding of their cultural background as well as diverse staff who could be their role models. "They argued that the ethnicity profile of the staff was a visible and genuine indication of the school's commitment to equality issues" (p. 32). They listed examples of effective practice, which called on schools to respect and be inclusive of all cultures and "institute strategies that are consistent with the cultural characteristics of the students" (p. 7). The head teachers in the schools studied demanded that teachers "demonstrate a willingness to understand the cultures and background realities of their students and school community" (p. 11), in order "to view the school and broader society through the eyes of their students and the communities the staff served" (p. 13). The schools' CPD programme was focused on knowing the community in terms of its language background and wider context and culture. Their research was conducted in five schools across England including Birmingham, which had 'substantial number' of students from minority ethnic backgrounds.

In 2004, a TTA-commissioned review identified strategies which could be used by teacher trainees and newly qualified teachers to raise the attainment of pupils from culturally diverse backgrounds (Parker-Jenkins et al., 2004). This recommended that the:

> government should ensure that all providers actively enskill future teachers for the challenges presented by working with pupils from culturally and linguistically diverse backgrounds, and that this should be a substantial core and not a separate additional, one-off module … and that teachers need to be encouraged to engage with issues of racism.
>
> (p. 47)

In response, the commitment on diversity was reiterated in the revised teacher standards (TDA, 2007). These spoke of the importance of responding to learners' diverse needs and overcoming potential barriers to learning. It was seen as incumbent on ITT to enable trainees to take a practical account of diversity and promote equality and inclusion in their teaching, including in the choice of resources. Teachers were asked to "understand children's religious and cultural influences" (C18); "promote equality in their teaching" (C19); "make links between in-school learning and learning in out-of-school contexts" (C37) and to "have extensive knowledge of equality" (E6). However, the gaps in diversity preparation of trainee teachers remained. Hick et al. (2011) reported that, in response to the question: "How good was your training in preparing you to teach learners from minority ethnic backgrounds?", 43% of primary and 44% of secondary NQTs answered 'good or very good'. Since then, the situation is likely to have worsened as a result of deracialisation in ITT. The revised Teachers' Standards (DfE, 2011) deliberately omitted issues such as equality, diversity and inclusion from teacher training discourse. Teacher training had now become solely focused on classroom management competencies but in a colour-blind way (Lander, 2013). Consequently teachers were being treated even more as 'technicians or applied scientists' (Crozier, 1999a). This meant that trainee teachers were unsure and lacking in confidence about how to talk about equality and diversity issues in their work or to understand how to tackle the inequalities that schools as public institutions may perpetuate. They thus relied on their 'ethnocentric everyday world' (Troyna, 1994). A similar problem was reported by Hick et al. (2011): race equality was addressed in a minimalist way on ITT courses and many teacher education courses generally devoted only a single session to race equality issues. This left teachers uncomfortable when engaging with issues related to racial differences and racism. They were reported, by their pupils, to have an under-appreciation of the impact of everyday racism. Hick et al. (2011) pointed out that short, one-off lectures were not viewed by most interviewees as an effective way to engage students on topics like race equality and racism. ITT providers were found by Lander (2013) to "labour to include the subject of 'race' and ethnicity within the teacher education curriculum" (p. 2). Anecdotal evidence has confirmed that diversity has more or less disappeared from ITT programmes. One ITT provider has communicated to me that their students currently have one 2-hour session on race, ethnicity and gender. That session is under threat because of other 'priorities' on ITT and the movement within teacher training away from universities into schools (Race,[2] 2015, email). The TTA (2000) had recognised that, like others, trainee teachers "may hold mistaken or stereotypical perceptions of groups from particular social, religious or cultural backgrounds" (p. 59). It was possible that this was now the case. With little or no coverage of equality and diversity on ITT courses, it was not surprising to read that teachers had 'tabloid knowledge of Islam' (Bloom, 2011). This was a reference to Revell's research (2012) who had found that Islam was misrepresented in education and that teachers' understanding of it was largely formed by the media. This meant that there was now a greater need for schools to provide such training, including to newly qualified teachers, as a part of their CPD programmes.

Teachers' understanding of Pakistani pupils' heritage; the current picture

Pakistani students in my study were asked for their opinion on the issue of teachers' understanding. More than two-thirds, 68.4%, of the questionnaire respondents agreed of its importance. During the interviews a majority of the students spoke of the benefits of teachers having such understanding. They indicated that it was central to the teaching and learning process. In their view this would enable the teachers to form good relationships with their pupils and be more responsive to the needs of the students. Academy pupil Waheed pointed out that it was important for teachers to understand the different needs of the students they were teaching. For Community pupil Faisal such understanding would lead the students to 'get on' with the teachers and lead to greater confidence to ask them questions during lessons:

> If they don't understand me then I can't get on with (them). I can't ask them anything, I can't talk to them, like, they won't understand me, like if I ask them for something, homework or something, they wouldn't be able to help.

For Community pupil Saleem there were general benefits of such understanding by teachers; such as greater student engagement – being made to feel welcome, coping with difficult situations and the teachers bridging the home and school worlds of the pupils – as well as benefits in particular teaching situations:

> In science, we are supposed to examine a liver. They didn't want to bring a, a pig's liver because it would affect, like our Islamic background. So they brought us a sheep's liver instead.

Community pupil Razaq explained that where teachers had such understanding, it would help them to avoid causing offence and respect the pupils. Community pupil Israr explained that teacher–pupil relationships extended to informal conversation:

> When you meet teachers in the playground, you can talk to them; it could be more than work as well. You can talk to them about, about things you've got in common, like football.

For Academy pupil Majid, understanding by teachers of pupil heritage would enable them to avoid having superficial relationships: "If the teachers understand your background they can have a laugh, make jokes even". Academy pupil Ibrar explained that he liked having a good relationship with his teacher; "I can talk to them about the events that may have happened on the weekend".

For Moll et al. (1992) teachers' understanding of their students' background and cultural context would enable them to avoid having 'thin' and 'single stranded' relationships with the students, whereas for Bhatti (1999) it would enable the teachers to talk about normal things with their students. Academy pupil Majid pointed out that when they had teachers who understood them at a deeper level, they felt more comfortable around those teachers. "If you are having problems at home, you could probably talk to the teachers. Otherwise you might keep the problem to yourself". For Community pupil Amir, teacher understanding of pupils' background was central to the pupils' sense of belonging to the school and feeling welcome: "you feel *invited* (original emphasis)". Academy pupil Khalad pointed out that such understanding enabled the teachers to connect the school and home worlds of their pupils; they would be in a position to "ask good questions about things outside school", thus lessening the discontinuities between the two worlds which for Ogbu (1982) was a particular problem for students from disadvantaged backgrounds, such as Pakistanis.

The parents also saw the value in teachers understanding their Pakistani pupils' cultural and religious background. Grammar parent Shahida explained that teachers needed to be familiar with intricacies of the Pakistani culture as this would help them understand their pupils' day-to-day behaviour. Grammar parent Wali pointed that without the necessary understanding the teachers would not be able to bridge the values of the school with those of the home and create congruence for the students. This would mean the children would not have to leave their home culture at the school gate, which is a problem that is particularly faced by minority and Muslim children. Community parent Zaman explained the value of schools employing teachers from the local community which would help to link the pupils' school and home worlds:

> Some teachers are from the local area so they have an even deeper understanding, of the realities of the local community. They walk up and down the same streets and shop in the same shops ... so that means they understand the area. These teachers have an advantage over the others. Someone from outside the area wouldn't know what they know.

The teachers in the research outlined the reasons for, and benefits of, such understanding, the responsibility of the school and its likely impact on pupil outcomes. By far the most comprehensive response came from Community teacher Abid. He outlined the following benefits of such understanding:

- It helps with teaching:

  If you can relate a topic to maybe their background or something they have understanding of, it helps you with your communication generally as well.

- It helps to link school and home lives of students:

  We find that our school values are linked in what they might learn at the mosque and from their family. It's linking all they know; it can make a difference.

- It helps to knock down teacher–pupil barriers:

  Sometimes they might find it a little bit difficult to engage with a teacher who they are not comfortable with. It can take a teacher a few weeks to overcome the barrier. Maybe it's a lot easier for me; I am the same background as them. Having the (cultural) understanding can help the teacher to communicate better. Once they're used to a teacher, they'll open up and be more relaxed around the teacher. It could also be when walking around the corridor, out in the playground, just having a general conversation; the kids want to ask you something; being able to relate to them, it just helps with that relationship building with the kids.

* It helps in pupil engagement:

If you have an understanding of the pupils' background, it helps with engagement in the lessons. If you can relate your teaching to their home lives – Islamic heritage, country of origin – it can make a difference. You might say "so how does the lunar calendar link with the orbit".

Grammar teacher Steve stressed the importance of teacher–pupil relationships which for him were critical in the teaching and learning process as well as for general interaction between teachers and pupils. For him, good relationships made it easier for the teacher to deliver a good lesson. He also thought that 'small talk' between teachers and pupils was an important way of building such relationships. However, this was not something that would be possible if the teachers did not have an understanding of their pupils' day-to-day lives. Furthermore, he pointed out that teachers needed to understand their pupils' cultural heritage so to avoid causing offence by 'putting your foot in it'. He went on to reiterate Community parent Shahida's comment:

It's very important. Say a pupil says: "I can't do my homework because my great uncle passed away". Now in the English culture this may not be important; it's such a distant relative but for the Pakistani pupil it's a close relative. We know all the family have to go so the homework may not be done.

Academy teacher Jean explained that understanding by teachers made a 'huge difference' for pupils; they may feel more supported and may, consequently, respond in a different, better, way. She shared the example of an Y11, who was under pressure by his mother to go to a grammar school but he was not convinced by this:

When he realised I understood his situation he beamed at me; it made that relationship that bit different.

Academy teacher Zahida also thought that understanding the pupils' background was critical for teachers, given its likely impact on their learning. For her, understanding what has been referred to as 'funds of knowledge' (Moll et al., 1992) was central to the whole educational process:

And, if I want to reach the children I'm teaching, it's important for me to know where they're coming from. And, they come to me, they're diverse, they're rich in different ways; it's important for me to know, to have knowledge of that.

She pointed out that it was the teachers' responsibility to enable the students to reach their potential; something they were unlikely to be able to do if they did not understand the pupils:

> If I really don't know enough about their culture and background, am I really going to be able to motivate them, inspire them, really engage them? Ideally, I want to be able to go into the classroom and say: "actually, I know what you're about and I'm going to use that to our advantage; for you to achieve, get you to your full potential".

For Academy teacher Jean, such understanding made a difference to the pupils. In some roles it was even more critical. She explained that for teachers in the behavioural or pastoral team, the cultural knowledge might influence how they address some of the issues, such as how to accommodate Muslim students' needs while they were fasting. For her, it was the school's responsibility to provide such training.

Some of the teachers in my research appeared to have a very low level of understanding of their Pakistani pupils and their cultural and religious background. Possibly the most extreme example of this was provided by Academy teacher Jean. During the interview with me she spoke of 'Ramadam', instead of Ramadan, when referring to the month of fasting. I double checked, without letting her know the reason for doing so. She repeated the mistake. The Pakistani teacher interviewees outlined the current level of understanding amongst their peers, of the heritage of the Pakistani pupils. They confirmed that the level of the understanding was poor, thus confirming Bloom (2011), who had said that teachers had a 'tabloid' understanding of Islam. Academy teacher Mehboob, in response to whether his colleagues had an understanding of Pakistani boys' cultural background, replied: "The honest answer is: no, they don't. Absolutely not". He explained that school and home, for Pakistani pupils, were two separate worlds, causing them to lead a double life.

> So in answer to your question: do members of staff truly (his word) *understand* (gives added emphasis) Pakistani boys and their culture, I don't think they do. Some do but most don't.

This was backed up by his colleagues. Academy teachers Zahida and Jean, who pointed out that their school did not offer any opportunities for the staff to acquire such understanding:

> I've been here 13 years. We've never as staff had anyone explain the minority culture; no. (It's) what you pick up. I mean because I teach

RE, I know all the religious backgrounds.

Academy teacher Jean.

Academy teacher Mehboob explained that the 'commuter teachers' (Reed, 2009), who lived away from their multicultural schools, were less likely to understand their Pakistani pupils, while those who were from the local community were likely to have greater understanding:

> Teachers may live outside Birmingham so really they've not had to mix with people of the ethnic minority. Local teachers have a good idea what kids do when they go home, what their typical day is like. I think the majority of teachers don't really understand the lives the average Pakistani boy lives, what he does when he gets home.

He spoke of the demographic changes which were taking place in Birmingham generally and at Academy, leading to the 'cultural environment' at Academy, to increasingly have more of a Pakistani 'feel'. However, he believed that such changes were only noticed by teachers with the necessary understanding of the pupils' cultural background:

> You will see a lot of Pakistani boys who are more confident in their Pakistani-ness.[3] You will see them using 'ethnic' words. They may just talk amongst themselves, they'll shake hands; very cultural things. They'll all take the day off for Eid (festival). They may even use swear words in their own language. Those subtle nuances, I think, I can pick out very quickly when I see boys communicating. I can see how their Pakistani side is coming out. To the untrained eye, maybe this won't be obvious.

The role of the school as enabler

With Lander (2013) as a backdrop – that trainee teachers were not being prepared with an understanding of ethnic diversity – I explored how the teachers were acquiring such knowledge. Community teacher Abid explained that teachers who were from outside the 'super-diverse' (Vertovec, 2007) Birmingham often had little or no understanding of the cultural background of the students. However, once at the school they may pick up some understanding from students and their fellow teachers. Academy teacher Jean also stated that where one lived played a part in this respect:

> For some staff who've come from elsewhere and some who don't live here (and a lot don't), such understanding can be a problem.

For Community teacher Linda, the source of her cultural understanding was her personal background of growing up in Rockhill, a mainly Kashmiri/

Pakistani area. She explained that she had had a very positive experience of coming from that community. She had made Pakistani and other Asian friends and had participated in cultural activities with them such as attending weddings. She also pointed to learning from her peers and from the general multicultural school environment.

I explored the role of the school, following Blair's advice (2002) – that schools should provide CPD for teachers on diversity. With this backdrop, my teacher interviewees made a number of suggestions as to what schools should do. Community teacher Abid suggested that teachers, especially when they first arrived at the school, could be asked to learn about the Pakistani pupils and their wider community. Academy teacher Zahida pointed out that there was a great deal the school could do to raise the teachers' awareness of the cultural background of the Pakistani pupils, such as by inviting local diversity experts to deliver training in the school. I asked, in the time she'd been at the school (eight years), what had the school done to raise awareness of the staff:

> cultural awareness does not appear on the CPD agenda. No. No. There's nothing.

The teachers identified a number of areas where they needed to understand their Pakistani pupils. For Academy teacher Mehboob, this would include matters such as the pupils' participation in madrassah classes. Or it may be to understand what the boys did in their spare time, given that many came from poor families: "As teachers, I think the more information you have, the better it is". Grammar teacher Steve identified a number of areas which in his view were important for teachers to understand, in relation to their Pakistani pupils:

> What does it mean when they have to fast, especially in those hot summer months? A pupil maybe away because of some religious or cultural requirement. I should know about that. I may be asking a pupil to do cross-country running and they may be fasting. What does it mean for our Muslim pupils when we celebrate Christmas, a Christian festival? Do we do enough for their festivals?

Picower (2009) identified a number of issues for White teachers working in diverse schools. She implored them to explore Whiteness and its relationship to teaching, pointing to the dangers of such teachers maintaining advantage she referred to as 'White supremacy'.[4] In order to become successful with students from minority backgrounds, she saw it as imperative that White teachers developed cultural competence and socio-political consciousness, with critical awareness of the role of culture, power and oppression. She suggested to ITT providers to "make a commitment to transform themselves in order to interrupt the hegemonic understandings of pre-service teachers by implementing strategies, programmes, and reforms with this objective" (p. 211). Picower also argued for more teachers from minority backgrounds to be recruited into the profession.

Pakistani teachers as a resource

Kohli and Pizarro (2016) have drawn attention to the particular role of minority teachers. They spoke of such teachers as 'advocates' for their communities, a resource for their non-minority colleagues and a bridge between the minority community and the school. Basit and Santoro (2012) spoke of minority teachers as 'cultural experts' who can translate for their ethnic majority colleagues. Community teacher Abid explained:

> Staff will ask me questions, in relation to cultural or religious practices. This sort of thing helps them to have some idea that the young people have demands on their time such as going to the mosque. Yeah. I'm more than happy to help. Sometimes it's easier to learn from a colleague.

Academy teacher Mehboob explained that their background was a particular source of understanding for him and his Pakistani colleagues:

> I have a good handle on Pakistani culture. I have a strong connection with Pakistan. I speak Urdu, quite fluently[5] and Punjabi; I speak both languages.

Community teacher Abid also spoke of being a resource for his non-Pakistani peers:

> I've had staff come to me and ask: "what does this mean? You tend to share what you know".

However, as in Kohli and Pizzaro's research (2016), there was little or no use made of the cultural expertise of the Pakistani teachers in my study. Academy teacher Zahida pointed out that she had not been used as a cultural resource. I asked how she would respond if the school did ask her to use her cultural knowledge for the benefit of her colleagues:

> Well, I would be quite, quite excited. . . . I would be happy to do that. I think it's an important thing that, at the moment, has, perhaps been overlooked.

Kohli and Pizarro (2016) advised schools to ensure that minority teachers have a place on school leadership teams and to seek advice from them on school policy matters. Such advice would be equally relevant to my study. They suggested to schools to invest in minority teachers. They also drew attention to the marginalisation and alienation of minority teachers especially those who have few peers at their school from their own ethnic background. This was the case of Grammar teacher Masood. He was employed in a part-time role and was the only Pakistani teacher at Grammar. I asked him: in the time you've been here, how have you found being the only Pakistani, Muslim teacher? He asked: officially or unofficially? I explained that all data gathered were confidential and would be anonymised. He then responded: "Ok. It's predominantly a White school. The staff are White". (He then went a bit quiet, almost a whisper). "I came here and it was difficult". I prodded further; to which he responded:

> There are still some prejudices there which I can see but they cannot see. I can see some of them. Like racism for example. You can spot it. You can realise 'oh right'. I can. But for someone who is not brown or different colour or black whatever, they can't spot it. For them it's not there, it's nothing.

I asked: how does it express itself?

> Ignorance. I am seen as a lesser being; they look down on me. Because on things I can talk about, things I know, they'll not talk to me. I'm a cricket coach. They won't ask me they'll go to someone else. It's a lack of respect. I have to go out of my way to show them I'm a good teacher whereas with the others they don't have to. Others cut corners, they might be late for lessons and they're still ... Ok. I see them standing there 'chaa pee ray' (drinking tea), without a worry in the world.

Throughout my career I also had often found myself as one of the few Pakistani or ethnic minority teachers and feeling that I had to perform to higher standards of expectations. Consequently, I would work hard on, say, making presentations while my White colleagues would be much more relaxed; they would just scribble something on 'the back of an envelope'. So conscious I was of being one of a few Black and Asian advisers that I felt the burden of responsibility on my shoulders. I asked: "Is there anything else you'd like to say?" He explained the double standards practised in the school, using an Urdu phrase:

> Woh, siyahee jo meray nama-e-ehmal mein thee un-ki zulf mein lehra-ee to husan kehlai. (That blot on me, when it was in her attire, it was called beautiful.)

Impact on pupils' performance of teachers' understanding

Teacher understanding of their pupils' background is not just a 'nice to have' but important for the difference it can make to educational standards. For Academy teacher Mehboob, teachers with cultural understanding would be able to get even more out of the Pakistani pupils and make a bigger impact on their educational achievement:

> By getting on the right side of the kids, you can change their attitudes and then change your results, maybe by 5%. It's do-able. Just, by, you know, having that little handle on the culture and knowing what makes these kids tick. What would make the pupils focus more on their work? What would improve their behaviour? The more information you have like this, the better. I think if you have a cultural understanding; what's happening in their home the way they think; what they value; how they value things; I think you can do it.

For him, having the cultural understanding and knowing how to connect with the pupils was a useful tool in a teacher's armoury, to get the pupils to study when they were in the classroom.

Pupil interviewees saw a clear link between teacher understanding (of pupils' heritage) and pupils' performance in the learning process. Community pupil Khadam pointed out that it was easier to talk to teachers who were known to understand the pupils. "Otherwise, you wouldn't want to talk to them. You just go to their lesson and then move on to another. You don't feel as comfortable with them. You just go to their lesson and that's it". Grammar pupil Hamzah pointed out that where a teacher was known to understand them, the pupils were more likely to pay attention:

> You'll feel at ease with them. Next time you have a problem or have a need you'll feel more ... comfortable ... to go to them.

Community pupil Pervez stated that the closer a pupil feels to the teacher "the more likely you are to learn from them" while Academy pupil Khalad pointed out that "you put more effort into what they are teaching you and stuff like that". Academy pupil Imran explained that there were times when a pupil's life outside of school needed to be considered such as when setting them homework. He explained it in relation to him going on jamaat, preaching and discipleship trips, over a weekend. This meant he was not able to complete his homework which had been set on the Friday and which was due to be handed in on the following Monday. The teacher could not understand why he had not done the homework; they had no appreciation of jamaat:

> If the teachers understood about jamaat, they would give more time for assignments. It feels easier in lessons with a teacher who has such understanding.

These comments suggest that pupils are more satisfied with their schooling and happier if they felt more understood by the teachers. Although, it cannot be stated with any certainty, it is plausible that it might lead to greater pupil engagement with schooling and even more parental support for education and improvements in academic performance of Pakistani boys.

Notes

1 www.ncte.org/cee/positions/diverselearnersinee
2 Senior Lecturer in Education. I had met him at an education conferences. So I emailed him to seek his views on this matter.
3 According to Tim Boyes, CEO of Birmingham Education Partnership, "Pakistani children behave differently on their patch from when they go to school away from their area. They don't own their identity, language or enjoy their Pakistani-ness". He then went onto point out that the behaviour of the children was worse in such schools, "because they know they are some distance from their uncles and brothers and imams".
4 Explained by Gillborn (2005). He saw education policy as "an act of White supremacy" (p. 498).
5 He then spoke in Urdu to demonstrate his competence.

Bibliography

Alexander, K. & Entwisle, D. (1987). School performance, status relations, and the structure of sentiment: Bringing the teacher back in. *American Sociological Review* 52(October) 665–682.

Andrews, J. & Yee, W. (2006). Children's 'funds of knowledge' and their real life activities: Two minority ethnic children learning in out-of-school contexts in the UK. *Educational Review* 58(4) 435–449.

Antidote: Newsletter. (2010, March). www.antidotenews.org.uk/?p=307 Accessed 31.10.2012.

Archer, L. (2010). 'We raised it with the head': The educational practices of minority ethnic middle class families. *British Journal of Sociology of Education* 31(4) 449–469.

Basit, T. & Santoro, N. (2012). Playing the role of 'cultural expert': Teachers of ethnic difference in Britain and Australia. *Oxford Review of Education* 37(1) 37–52.

Bhatti, G. (1999). *Asian children at home and at school: An ethnographic study.* London: Routledge.

Birch, S. & Ladd, G. (1997). The teacher: Child relationship and children's early school adjustment. *Journal of School Psychology* 35(1) 61–79.

Blair, M. (2002). Effective school leadership: The multi-ethnic context. *British Journal of Sociology of Education* 23(2) 180–191.

Bloom, A. (2011). The teachers with a tabloid grasp of Islam. *Times Educational Supplement,* 16 September.

Brighouse, H. (2007). Equality of opportunity and complex equality: The special place of schooling. *Res Publica* 13 147–158.

Bullock Report. (1975). *A language for life.* www.educationengland.org.uk/documents/bullock/bullock1975.html Accessed 10.3.2016.

Byrne, B. (2009). Not just class: Towards an understanding of the whiteness of middle-class schooling choice. *Ethnic and Racial Studies* 32(3) 424–441.

Callanan, M., Kinsella, R., Graham, J., Turczuk, O. & Finch, S. (2009). *Pupils with declining attainment at Key stages 3 and 4.* London: Department of Children Schools and Families.

Caplan, N., Choy, M. & Whitmore, J. (1991). *Children of the boat people.* MI: University of Michigan Press.

Chowdry, H., Crawford, C. & Goodman, A. (2009). *Drivers and barriers to educational success: Evidence from the longitudinal study of young people in England.* London: Department for Children Schools and Families.

Coles, M. (2004). Education and Islam: A new strategic approach. *Race Equality Teaching* 22 41–46. Stoke-on-Trent: Trentham Books.

Conteh, J. (2012). Families, pupils and teachers learning together in a multilingual British city. *Journal of Multilingual and Multicultural Development* 33(1) 101–116.

Crozier, G. (1999). Is it a case of 'we know when we're not wanted'? The parents' perspective on parent-teacher roles and relationships. *Educational Research* 41(3) 315–328.

Crozier, G. (1999a). The deracialisation of initial teacher training: Implications for social justice. *Race Ethnicity and Education* 2(1) 79–91.

Damon, W. & Colby, A. (1996). Education and moral commitment. *Journal of Moral Education* 25(1) 31–37.

DCSF. (2008). *Raising the attainment of Pakistani, Bangladeshi, Somali, and Turkish heritage pupils: The national strategies: Secondary.* London: DCSF.

DCSF. (2009). *The Extra Mile (Primary): Achieving success with pupils from deprived communities.* London: DCSF.

Delpit, L. (1995). *Other people's children: Cultural conflict in the classroom.* New York: The New Press.

Demie, F. & Lewis, K. (2011). White working class achievement: An ethnographic study of barriers to learning in schools. *Educational Studies* 37(3) 245–264.

Desforges, C. & Abouchaar, A. (2003). *The impact of parental involvement, parental support and family education on pupil achievement and adjustment.* London: Department for Children Schools and Families.

Deslandes, R. (2001). *A vision of home-school partnership: Three complementary conceptual frameworks.* www.ernape.net/articles/2001002Fsession1/Deslandes.pdf Accessed 14.2.12.

DFE. (2011). *Teachers' standards: Guidance for school leaders, school staff and governing bodies.* www.gov.uk/government/uploads/system/uploads/attachment_data/file/301107/Teachers__Standards.pdf Accessed 10.3.2016.

DFES. (2004). *Aiming high in mainly white areas.* London: DFES.

DFES. (2006). *Excellence and enjoyment: Learning and teaching for bilingual children in the primary years, unit 3: Creating an inclusive culture.* London: DFES.

Eggleston, J., Dunn, D., Anjali, M. & Wright, C. (1986). *Education for some.* Stoke-on-Trent: Trentham Books.

Essed, P. (1990). *Everyday racism.* Canada: Hunter House.

Evans, G. (2007). *Educational failure and working class White children in Britain.* Basingstoke: Palgrave Macmillan.

Gay, G. & Howard, T. (2000). Multicultural teacher education for the 21st century. *The Teacher Educator* 36(1) 1–16.

Gillborn, D. (1997). Racism and reform: New ethnicities/old inequalities? *British Educational Research Journal* 23(3) 345–360.

Gillborn, D. (2005). Education policy as an act of White supremacy: whiteness, critical race theory and education reform. *Journal of Education Policy* 20(4) 485–505.

Goodall, J. (2012). Parental engagement to support children's learning: A six point model. *School Leadership & Management: Formerly School Organisation.* 33(2), 133–150.

Gorard, S. & See, B. (2011). How can we enhance enjoyment of secondary school? The student view. *British Educational Research Journal* 37(4) 671–690.

Haertel, G., Walberg, H. & Haertel, E. (1981). Socio-psychological environments and learning: A quantitative synthesis. *British Education Research Journal* 7(11) 27–36.

Harrow SACRE. (2013). *Guidance on offering space for prayer and reflection in school.* www. harrow.gov.uk/www2/documents/s108380/sacre Accessed 22.3.2018.

Hick, P., Arshad, R., Mitchell, L., Watt, D. & Roberts, L. (2011). *Promoting cohesion, challenging expectations.* Research Report. Manchester Metropolitan University.

Hoque, A. (2018). Third-generation British Bangladeshis from east London: Complex identities and a culturally responsive pedagogy. *British Journal of Sociology of Education* 39(2) 182–196.

Hughes, M. & Pollard, A. (2006). Home: School knowledge exchange in context. *Educational Review* 58(4) 385–395.

Klein, G. (2007). When will they ever learn? in Richardson, B. (ed.) *Tell it like it is: How our schools fail Black children.* London: Bookmarks Publications.

Kohli, R. & Pizarro, M. (2016). Fighting to educate our own: Teachers of color, relational accountability, and the struggle for social justice. *Equity & Excellence in Eucation* 49(1) 72–84.

Kohli, R. & Solorzano, D. (2012). Teachers, please learn our names!: Racial microaggressions and the K-12 classroom. *Race Ethnicity and Education* 15(4) 441–462.

Lander, V. (2013). Initial teacher education: Developments, dilemmas and challenges. *Race Ethnicity and Education.* DOI: 10.1080/13613324.2013.832917.

Lareau, A. & Horvat, E. (1999). Moments of social inclusion and exclusion: Race, class and cultural capital in family-school relationships. *Sociology of Education* 72 37–53.

Leadbeater, C. (2008). *Relationships and the public good.* www.charlesleadbeater.net/cms/xstandard/With1.doc Accessed 01.2.2012.

Lee, C. (2001). Is October Brown Chinese? A cultural modeling activity system for underachieving students. *American Educational Research Journal* 38(1) 97–141.

Markose, S. (2008). *Home literacy practices of immigrant families and cultural discontinuity: Two case studies.* International Educational Research Conference, Freemantle, Australia.

Marshall, E. & Toohey, K. (2010). Representing family: Community funds of knowledge, bilingualism, and multimodality. *Harvard Educational Review* 80(2) 221–241.

Meer, N. & Modood, T. (2007). *The political and policy responses to migration related diversity in Britain's education system: A European approach to multicultural citizenship: Legal political and educational challenges.* EMILIE.

Melhuish, E., Phan, M., Sylva, K., Sammons, P., Siraj-Blatchford, I. & Taggart, B. (2008). Effects of the home learning environment and preschool centre experience upon literacy and numeracy development in early primary school. *Journal of Social Issues* 64(1) 95–114.

Merry, M. (2005). Cultural coherence and the schooling for identity maintenance. *Journal of Philosophy of Education* 39(3) 477–497.

Michael, S., Dittus, P. & Epstein, J. (2007). Family and community involvement in schools: Results from the school health policies and programs study 2006. *Journal of School Health* 77(8) 567–579.

Moll, L., Amanti, C., Neff, D. & Gonzalez, N. (1992). Funds of knowledge for teaching: Using a qualitative approach to connect homes and classrooms. *Theory into Practice* 31(2) 132–141.

Murray-Harvey, R. (2010). Relationship influences on students academic achievement, psychological health and well-being at school. *Educational and Child Psychology* 27(1) 104–115.

Murrell, P. (2000). Community teachers: A conceptual framework for preparing exemplary urban teachers. *The Journal of Negro Education* 69(4) 338–348.

Noordhoff, K. & Kleinfeld, J. (1993). Preparing teachers for multicultural classroom. *Teaching & Teacher Education* 9(I) 27–39.

O'Connor, E. & McCartney, K (2007). Examining teacher-child relationships and achievement as part of an ecological model of development. *American Educational Research Journal* 44(2) 340–369.

OECD. (2011). *Lessons from PISA for the United States, strong performers and successful reformers in education.* OECD Publishing.

Ogbu, J. (1982). Cultural discontinuities and schooling. *Anthropology & Education Quarterly* 13(4) 290–307.

Parker-Jenkins, P., Hewitt, D., Sanders, T., Brownhill, S., Lall, R. & Keeling, J. (2004). *What strategies can be used by initial teacher training providers, trainees and newly qualified teachers to raise the attainment of pupils from culturally diverse backgrounds?* London: University of London.

Picower, B. (2009). The unexamined whiteness of teaching: How White teachers maintain and enact dominant racial ideologies. *Race Ethnicity and Education* 12(2) 197–215.

Pigott, R. & Cowen, E. (2000). Teacher race, child race, racial congruence, and teacher ratings of children's school adjustment. *Journal of School Psychology* 38(2) 177–196.

Pomeroy, E. (1999). The teacher-student relationship in secondary school: Insights from excluded students. *British Journal of Sociology of Education* 20(4) 465–482.

Race, R. (2015). *Diversity as a priority in ITT.* Email communication, 12 March.

Ranson, S., Martin, J. & Vincent, C. (2004). Storming parents, schools and communicative inaction. *British Journal of Sociology of Education* 25(3) 259–274.

Reed, W. (2009). The bridge is built: The role of local teachers in an urban elementary school. *The School Community Journal* 19(1) 59–75.

Revell, L. (2012). *Islam and education: The manipulation and misrepresentation of a religion.* Stoke-on-Trent: Trentham Books.

Rhamie, J. & Hallam, S. (2002). An investigation into African-Caribbean academic success in the UK Race. *Race Ethnicity and Education* 5(2) 151–170.

Richardson, R. & Wood, A. (2004). *The achievement of British Pakistani learners.* Stoke-on-Trent: Trentham Books.

Robertson, L. (2006). Learning to read 'properly' by moving between parallel literacy classes. *Language and Education* 20(1) 44–61.

Sahin, A. (2013). *New directions in Islamic education.* Leicestershire: Kube Publishing.

Shalabi, D. & Taylor, M. (2011). A multiple case study on parents' perspective about the influence of the Islamic culture on Muslim children's daily lives. *The Journal of Multiculturalism in Education* 7 1–30.

Sleeter, C. (2001). Preparing teachers for culturally diverse schools: Research and the overwhelming presence of whiteness. *Journal of Teacher Education* 52 94–106.

Strand, S. (2007). *Minority ethnic pupils in the longitudinal study of young people in England.* London: DFES.

Sue, D., Capodilupo, C., Torino, G., Bucceri, J., Holder, A., Nadal, K. & Esquilin, M. (2007). Racial microaggressions in everyday life: Implications for clinical practice. *American Psychologist* 62(4) 271–286.

Swann Report. (1985). *Education for all.* London: HMSO.

TDA (Teacher Development Agency for schools). (2007). *Professional standards for teachers in England from September 2007.* www.rgs.org/NR/rdonlyres/061E9742-9A39-4DD3-AF6A-6F758B1200CB/0/CGT_Online_TDA_standards_framework.pdf

Thomson, P. & Hall, C. (2008). Opportunities missed and/or thwarted? 'Funds of knowledge' meet the English national curriculum. *The Curriculum Journal* 19(2) 87–103.

Troyna, B. (1994). The 'everyday world' of teachers? Deracialised discourses in the sociology of teachers and the teaching profession. *British Journal of Sociology of Education* 15(3) 325–339.

TTA (Teacher Training Agency). (2000). *Raising the attainment of minority ethnic pupils: Guidance and resource materials for providers of initial teacher training.* Surrey: TTA.

TTA. (2003). *Qualifying to teach: Professional standards for qualified teacher status and requirements for initial teacher training.* London: TTA.

Tyler, K., Uqdah, A., Dilihunt, M., Beattty-Hazelbaker, R., Conner, T., Gadson, N., Henchy, A., Hughes, T., Mulder, S., Owen, E., Roan-Belle, C., Smith, L. & Stevens, R. (2008). Cultural discontinuity: Toward a quantitative investigation of a major hypothesis in education. *Educational Researcher* 37(5) 280–297.

Vertovec, S. (2007). Super-diversity and its implications. *Ethnic and Racial Studies* 30(6) 1024–1054.

Walker, A., Dimmock, C., Stevenson, H., Bignold, B., Shah, S. & Middlewood, D. (2005). *Effective leadership in multi-ethnic schools.* Nottingham: NCSL.

Warikoo, N. (2004). Race and the teacher-student relationship: Interpersonal connections between West Indian students and their teachers in a New York City high school. *Race Ethnicity and Education* 7(2) 135–147.

Warren, M. (2005). Communities and schools: A new view of urban education reform. *Harvard Educational Review* 75(2) 133–173.

Whitty, G. (2001). Education, social class and social exclusion. *Journal of Education Policy* 16(4) 287–295.

Wilson, C. (2009). The relation among parental factors and achievement of African American urban youth. *The Journal of Negro Education* 78(2) 102–113.

8 A culturally responsive education for Pakistani students

The focus of the research

I began this study with the aim of identifying ways of reducing the number of Pakistani pupils, especially boys, leaving compulsory schooling without the benchmark qualifications. I posed my research question: what factors underlie variation in educational achievement amongst Pakistani boys in Birmingham? Might any of these factors contribute to an achievement gap relative to White British students? In order to answer this main question, I explored whether religion was important for the boys and how did that impact on their educational outcomes and processes. Here, I attempted to understand what Pakistani parents want from education for their children. I explored with the boys and their parents the important qualities in a teacher (e.g. ethnic match, cultural understanding etc.). It has been pointed out that education of Pakistani children, boys and girls, is impacted on by their religious affiliation, including religious prejudice, Islamophobia, the failure of schools to support their religious identity, the impact of supplementary schooling and their daily exposure to values different from those of the home (Halstead, 2005). In places such as Birmingham the issues are taken to a particularly different level. For many years Muslim children have been the largest pupil religious group in the city and Pakistani children are near to becoming the largest pupil ethnic group. One way of looking at this situation is by asking the following question: what would an education system look like if it was designed with their particular needs in mind? With this in mind I investigated how schools were accommodating the cultural heritage of Pakistani boys (e.g. religious observance etc.). While I was conducting my research, the wider Birmingham community and its schools were affected by the Trojan Horse affair. It is likely that the controversy will go on impacting education for many years to come and may even repeat itself if steps are not taken to prevent it.

The most significant finding from the study is multifaceted. Confirming previous research it has been shown that education is highly valued by the Pakistani students and their parents and both place a great deal of importance on their religion, Islam. Education, for the parents, means both 'deen and dunya', religious and 'of the world'. The parents demonstrated, through the way they guided their boys' lives, their belief that compulsory schooling left significant gaps in the boys' education. This led the boys to be sent to, parallel with their compulsory schooling, madrassah classes where they spent a significant amount of their out-of-school time. This points to a possible challenge for the education system and the Pakistani community: to help raise the boys' attainment by enabling them to *increase* their school-related work such as participation in extracurricular activities and 'intervention' or 'catch-up' opportunities provided for students who are seen by teachers to need additional input. The activities provided can have other wider benefits too. It is here that the students are able to spend informal time with a range of fellow students, including those from different ethnic groups and develop 'meaningful contact', thus generating greater community cohesion. Another impact of religion was possibly in the area of boys' learning habits and style. This was a likely result of the very different pedagogical style employed at madrassahs, when compared with what the boys experienced in their state schooling – passive and uncritical learning, little or no focus on understanding of what they were reading and teacher-centred learning.

Homework was an area of need flagged up by this research. Pakistani pupils were found to face 'weighted scales' of homework. A small number of the students reported not having a quiet place in which to do their homework. However, a much larger number reported that they did not have people in their family who they could turn to for help when completing their homework. This problem was faced by pupils across the board, though more so by those who were from poorer families. This appeared to be the main area where being poor had an impact on Pakistani pupils. The other situation where we could see the impact of poverty was in relation to parental strategies utilised in Islamic religious education (IRE). The wealthier Grammar parents used their economic power to employ personal Quranic tutors who came to the pupils' home. This was not something done by the parents at the other two schools. Grammar parents were also better organised in their provision of madrassah education for their boys. They had done so by organising religious classes at the weekend so that it did not impact on the boys' schooling or participation in extracurricular activities. A few of the students reported that they had to spend too much time in their madrassah classes which interfered with their school work. While I did not specifically investigate this, based on earlier research, it is quite likely that their homework also suffered as a result of the boys' involvement in such classes; after having been to madrassah they did not have the time or energy to complete their homework. As homework does not have to be 'home work' (Cosden et al., 2001), i.e. done at home but could be completed 'at places other than home' (DFEE, 1998), the extended day spoken of by, the then Education Secretary, Michael Gove (DfE, 2014) may be the answer. In Gove's view this would be particularly helpful for those children who come from homes where it is difficult to secure the peace and quiet necessary for study and where parents are not able to help them in the tasks set.

A majority of Pakistani students and many of their parents considered it important for teachers to have an understanding of the Pakistani heritage. However, this was found not to be a priority for teacher training or professional development within the schools researched. Consequently, this left the teachers lacking a full understanding of their students' heritage. While the schools were found to accommodate some religious needs of their Pakistani students such as providing prayer facilities, teachers' poor understanding of the pupils' heritage meant they were not able to effectively bridge the students' lives at school and beyond. A related finding was the make-up of the teaching workforce. For a sizeable number of students it was important to have teachers from their own ethnic and religious background. Much of the literature on the subject also thought such diversity to be a good idea. However, in all three schools researched, Pakistani teachers were substantially under-represented amongst the workforce, compared to the proportion of Pakistani pupil population.

A responsive education service

It has been the aim of this study to identify ways for the education service to respond to the particular needs of Pakistani students, so that more of them achieve the benchmark qualifications and receive a rounded education within their religious and cultural context. There is much within general educational policy and practice that is potentially transferrable to the current study. Concepts such as multicultural education, culturally relevant pedagogy and community education have much to offer in this respect. I have drawn on the principles that underpin these concepts in order to respond to the needs and issues that have been flagged up by the wider literature as well as the findings of this research.

Multicultural education

Research has highlighted a number of measures which can be implemented by schools to raise the attainment of underachieving ethnic minority pupils. Tikly et al. (2006), in a report for the Department for Education, spoke of the wider 'conditions of success' in dealing with the needs of underachieving pupils. These included willingness of the governors and senior management, especially the Head Teacher, to address race equality issues in the school and commitment to mainstreaming initiatives to raise achievement. "Where schools have begun to make race equality an essential part of their normal activities – through professional development work; the routine gathering and analysis of ethnically based data; and targeted programmes of support – impressive changes are evident" (p. 74). Given that schools have to provide for the needs of many groups the authors pointed out that taking such an approach on race equality for one group need not mean excluding other groups of pupils. Instead "it means making a concern for race equality a central part of *all* (original emphasis) of the school's quality assurance processes" (p. 74). Indeed, they go on to point out that once strategies are effectively mainstreamed "they can have a positive impact on the achievement of *all* (my emphasis) groups" (p. 74). This kind of approach was once taken by Birmingham. Ofsted (2002), in its inspection of Birmingham local education authority (LEA) recognised that much had been done with schools to overcome the educational effects of high degree of disadvantage. Consequently, it was held up as an example to others of what can be done, even in the most demanding urban environments. The LEA's work on combating racism was found to be very good, and involved a lot of effective initiatives. For example, the local authority had convened its own commission following the death of Stephen Lawrence. The commission's report was critical of aspects of the local authority's work but they took on board the commission's recommendations. One of these was asking schools to monitor racist incidents using the LEA form and guidelines. Schools Link Advisers checked that forms were completed and submitted to the LEA. Using the benchmark 'Success for Everyone', schools had in place a race equality policy and action plan, tailored to an individual school's needs. For this they were issued a model, which I had written in my role as Equalities Adviser. The LEA also undertook a range of work – including developing curriculum material, organising conferences, and maintaining linkages with ethnic minority groups – which to Ofsted represented effective action to embed equality issues within the mainstream, and to tackle racism.

In the British context, multicultural education has been the main vehicle for addressing educational inequalities and underachievement. It placed an emphasis on equality of opportunity as well as equality of outcome with the general curriculum on offer being inclusive and provided by a teaching workforce that reflects the diversity of the wider society. For the DFES (2004), the institutional context played a critical role; "practical support that a school is able to provide to its pupils is more likely to succeed if it is undertaken in a context where issues of equality and diversity are central to the school's basic systems and processes" (p. 8). Numerous others have arrived at a similar conclusion (Swann Report, 1985; Blair & Bourne, 2000; DFES, 2003; Banks, 2006; Tomlinson, 2008; Gillborn, 2008). There was also isolated opposition expressed towards multicultural education. A recent example of this was a speech by Phillips (2005) in his criticism of multiculturalism, pointing out that it led to segregation of ethnic and racial groups. However, Modood (2013) responded to the debate by pointing out that multiculturalism had been misunderstood.

It is worth remembering here that with the Coalition government in 2010, came the era of 'absent presence' (Apple, 1999) of a number of priorities relevant to this study. For example, the Education Secretary, Michael Gove de-prioritised community cohesion as 'peripheral' (Harrison, 2010). We can see the evidence of its marginalisation in the current teacher standards (DfE, 2011) which, unlike the previous standards, makes no reference to it. Previously, community cohesion was also central to inspection of schools by Ofsted (DCSF, 2007).

Culturally responsive pedagogy

Similar to multicultural education is the concept of culturally responsive pedagogy (CRP) (Ladson-Billings, 1995; Villegas & Lucas, 2002; Richards et al., 2006; Hayes & Juárez, 2012; Gay, 2013). To deliver it effectively, the pedagogy needs to be based upon, and proceeds from, the cultural perspectives of the group of people for whom it is designed, in our case Pakistani pupils. The pedagogy builds on the ideas of Moll et al. (1992) and their concept 'funds of knowledge', which can enable teachers to connect with their pupils as whole beings. It rejects the deficit-based beliefs that some teachers may hold, especially about minority students and operates from a standpoint of recognising student strengths, seeking to build on them (Yosso, 2005).

CRP uses the cultural knowledge, prior experiences and frames of reference of the students to make learning encounters more relevant to, and effective, for them. According to Richards et al. (2006), a number of dimensions of CRP interact in the teaching and learning process and are critical to understanding the effectiveness of the pedagogy: (a) institutional, (b) personal, (c) instructional and (d) systemic. The institutional dimension refers to the policies and values of the school as an organisation. The personal refers to the processes teachers must engage in to become culturally responsive. Here, it is worth reminding ourselves of the concept 'teacher identity as pedagogy'; who they are matters just as much as what they do (Swann Report, 1985; Morgan, 2004). This, therefore, has implications for the ethnic background of the teachers as well as the extent of their cultural competence. The instructional dimension refers to the resources, strategies and activities utilised while the systemic dimension addresses the socio-political context within education and society over time while simultaneously fostering students' abilities to achieve high levels of academic success and cultural competence.

CRP recognises that students whose cultural knowledge is most congruent with mainstream ways of knowing and being are more likely to experience cognitive comfort and better educational outcomes in schools; what Reay (2004) describe as the 'habitus' of the pupils fitting the 'field' of the school. It thus sets out to reduce the discontinuities between their home and school lives. By building bridges of meaningfulness between home and school experiences, the different worlds of the students can be connected, i.e. in-school learning with out-of-school living and learning. CRP, therefore, can be a means for improving achievement by teaching diverse students through their own cultural filters. In order to do so, it requires teachers to understand the cultures represented in their classroom and to relate to their students at a deeper level, as social and cultural beings connected to a complex social and cultural network. However, to do so would necessitate the teachers to visit the neighbourhoods and homes of the students in order to appreciate where the students live, what is important to them and what and who they care about. This is not something that happens in schools serving Pakistani communities. Here many teachers are 'commuters' who live away from the area and come in and out of the school in their cars without connecting with the people who live in the community that surrounds the school. Once teachers have the cultural understanding, they will be in a better position to use the families and communities as a resource. Lipman (1995) spoke of culturally relevant teaching that "uses the students' culture to help them achieve success" (p. 203). Culturally relevant teachers "build upon students' cultural and experiential strengths to help them acquire new knowledge" (p. 203). Such teachers demonstrate 'connectedness' with students and extend relationships beyond the classroom.

Community education

In order to respond to the findings of this study, it would require collaboration between the state school system and the parents and the wider Pakistani Muslim community. The philosophy of community education and 'community school' offers a possible model which could be utilised here (Grainger, 2003). Such schools are outward facing, rather than insular and inward-looking. They do not separate learners from their context but work in partnership with the wider community; with the clear intention to fully utilise its resources. Nisbet et al. (1980) see such schools as 'community plant' whose use should not be restricted to one age group only or to certain hours and days. For them the key elements that characterise such schools include mutually supportive relationships between, and sharing of facilities by, school and community and community-oriented curriculum and community involvement in decision-making and management of schools. The concept of 'community education' is similar to what was described by the government as Schools Plus (DFEE, 2000). The then Minister for School Standards, Estelle Morris, had stated that "School Plus activities can make a real difference to the lives of pupils and others in the community" (p. 1). They spoke of a two-way partnership – "community in the school and the school in the community" – with both willing to and being comfortable in working in the other's 'space'. They provided examples of links between schools and their communities (DFEE, 1999). Elsewhere (DCSF, 2008), schools were asked to offer madrassahs the use of their premises. Furthermore, it was recommended that Ofsted should consider how examples of effective community activity can best be highlighted through inspections, both of schools and local education authorities.

Local curriculum

The RSA (2012) 'area based curriculum' project has offered similar ideas to community education. Instead of asking 'what should the curriculum include', in their view, the starting question should always be "who should determine what the curriculum includes"? An area based curriculum for them helps to create connections with the communities and cultures that surround the school and to distribute the education effort across the people, organisations and institutions of a local area. It helps to open up the school space for conversations with local communities about the purpose of education in order to help create a national curriculum, but the one which has local dimensions (Tomlinson, 2008).

The RSA proposed a way forward for schools to develop a 'school curriculum' in partnership with their communities: local businesses, heritage and cultural organisations, faith communities and parents. Earlier, Waters (2007), the then Director of Curriculum at the QCA, had stated that while it was important to have a common national core within the curriculum "there also needs to be a regional or local dimension and an element unique to each school" (p. 3). This could provide a model in the context of this study in helping to design an education service which meets the needs of an ethnic minority (Pakistani) within the context of the society overall. Leat (2015) similarly spoke of 'community curriculum making', which recognises the benefits for schools to develop some of their curriculum with community partners, using their resources. It would be a powerful statement indeed for such a curriculum to be developed by Birmingham schools in partnership with the Pakistani community. In the new education landscape of academies, it would be possible for a multi-academy trust to embark on such a project for their group of schools. Local teachers and others who have a good understanding of the community would clearly be an asset in such a venture.

More effective education of Pakistani boys

There are numerous examples within education of targeted work to address educational underachievement of specific groups, such as the many strategies aimed at addressing underachievement of Black pupils and the education of White working class children (Burden, 2013; Strand, 2013; House of Commons, 2014). I believe such a targeted approach is necessary in education policy and practice to raise Pakistani boys' attainment. For it to be successful, it would need to be embedded within the school improvement system and be 'ecological' (Finigan-Carr et al., 2015; Iruka et al., 2015) with a focus on a range of areas and issues, inside school and in the wider lives of the boys. This is based on a belief that children develop over time within interrelated systems that exist at levels proximal and distal to the child (O'Connor & McCartney, 2007). According to Feinstein (2004), to address inequalities requires investment in pre-school provision as well as enhanced investments throughout school. Elsewhere Feinstein (2003) has argued for provision of adaptive and informed services, personalised to the developmental needs, in our case, of Pakistani children. He spoke of 'progressive universalism' which requires understanding the diverse needs and aspirations of children and families, "with extra, targeted resources available to address those developmental needs not met by the standard, whole class school system" (p. 218). For him, the interventions might be school-led or involve support for out-of-school activities.

Ladson-Billings' (2006) explained that a focus on the achievement gap was misplaced. In her view, what was needed instead was to look at the 'education debt' that had accumulated over time, comprising historical, economic, socio-political and moral components. In relation to Pakistani children, the debt has accumulated over many years. It has been known, since at least the early 1990s, that Pakistani children, especially boys, were underachieving. The question that arises is whether enough has been done to help address the problem. We know of at least one occasion (Strand et al., 2010) when the highest authority in education, the Department for Children, Schools and Families, deliberately excluded Pakistani children from a policy intervention in order to avoid presenting a more negative picture on education of Muslims. We also know that the Birmingham Council predicted (BSLC, 2001) without any backing evidence that low attainment of Pakistani children would sort itself out and BRAP Chair Warmington (House of Commons, 2002) failed to represent the problem of Pakistani underachievement to Parliament when she had the chance to do so. It is also likely that there have been times when Birmingham schools did not act to address underachievement of their Pakistani pupils when they could have done so, thus committing a 'sin of ommission'.

Foster (1990) had pointed out that equality of opportunity only had meaning if those who began with unequal chances had unequal investment; arguing that they needed to be compensated through positive discrimination – through the provision of additional resources. "The idea is that additional educational resources should be provided in schools not just to those who are disadvantaged by virtue of home background, but to those students who fail, for whatever reason, to achieve certain minimum standards" (p. 187). But such ideas are not new. Many years ago Bowles (1968) had said that "achievement of equality of educational opportunity requires inequalities in the amount of resources devoted to the education of black children and White children, and of rich children and poor children" (p. 90), as "equal school inputs will not produce equal school outputs" (p. 95). However, he pointed out that such a policy response was controversial as "it will involve favouring the interests of the poor and the powerless to the detriment of the interests of those better endowed with wealth and influence" (p. 99). In the post-Trojan Horse times such an approach, though highly necessary, is certainly likely to be controversial in relation to Pakistani children.

Tough (2006) similarly explained that if we wished to close the education gap between disadvantaged children and their advantaged peers, we would need to not provide the same education for disadvantaged children that advantaged children received, but one that was considerably better. There are a number of ways of doing so for Pakistani boys. The legislative framework for this is provided by the Equality Act 2010. The law has put in place the Equality Duty on public sector bodies as well as specific duty on specified bodies, such as schools. In the context of schools the equality duty helps to focus attention on performance gaps between groups of pupils. The Equality and Human Rights Commission (EHRC, 2012) spelt this out with two examples relating to underachievement. After analysing its data the academy school in one example concluded that its Bangladeshi pupils were underachieving compared to other pupils when previous attainment was taken into account. Given the large numbers of Bangladeshi pupils the academy decided this was a priority. They decided to set an equality objective to tackle the underachievement identified. In order to achieve this, they planned to undertake a range of activities including study skills support, mentoring, additional classes and higher education visits. They pointed out that the activities "are lawful positive action measures that contribute to meeting the duty to have due regard to advancing equality of opportunity" (p. 6). Another example referred to challenges which prevented some ethnic minority pupils from participating in extracurricular activities and interacting with pupils outside of their own ethnic group. These ideas have the potential of being applied to the situation of Pakistani children in Birmingham. Instead of 'educational drift',[1] where things are left to chance, such purposeful process of change is more likely to address the issue of their underachievement.

Taking a strategic approach with the end in mind

In the past government has advised that local authorities should have a clear strategy for enhancing the achievement of minority ethnic pupils, as a part of their Education Development Plan (DFES, 2004). It was suggested that LA inspectors should support schools, such as in the analysis of data, action-planning and target setting. Tikly et al. (2002), in their report for the DFES, similarly advised that local authorities should support schools in their effort to raise achievement, by providing training, resources and sharing good practice. Given that the achievement of Pakistani pupils is not an issue for one school, but one affecting education across Birmingham, requires a strategic approach; one that is underpinned by a spirit of 'transformative accommodation' (Shachar, 2004) and 'additive bilingualism' (Peal & Lambert, 1962). Moreover, I am suggesting that the 'logic model' of policy intervention (Kellogg Foundation, 2004) should be adopted here. This was implemented by Birmingham Children's Services for a brief period. The model starts with the end in mind and works backward, i.e. what outcome do we desire and how will we attain it. Its elements are resources, activities, outputs and (short, intermediate and long-term) outcomes. However, here it is necessary to point out that, within the current education landscape, such a task falls on more than one body. The education scene is very different now. Whereas previously local education authorities were the 'middle tier' – between schools and central government – as a result of the government's academy programme, their role has been reduced (DFE, 2010; Hill, 2012). Much of the work done previously by local authorities has either stopped altogether or has become the domain of others, such as Multi-Academy Trusts (MATs). This is an education organisational structure which usually has within it a number of academy schools. The trust acts as the accountable body for the schools. Ninestiles MAT is one such, Birmingham-based, schools structure, which I am familiar with, through my role as a Director and later as Academy Councillor and School Governor. It has, within it, seven schools – three secondary and four primary – plus one sixth form college. It has adopted an equality and diversity policy (Ninestiles MAT, 2016). With reference to staffing, the policy aspires for its workforce profile to broadly reflect the community it serves. It commits the organisation to promote a positive narrative around equality, continually monitor the situation and take positive action to provide encouragement and support to individuals and groups (such as the Pakistanis in this case). The policy commits the Trust to "(viii) take positive action to provide encouragement and support to individuals and groups whose progress has been limited by ... stereotyping and cultural expectations". The policy is supported by an appendix 'Equalities Framework-Working Document'. This further commits the Trust to know its community and ensure they are equally involved in its affairs. On staffing matters, it commits the Trust to "understands its local labour market, the barriers faced by those from vulnerable or marginalised individuals and groups, and the impact these have on achieving a diverse workforce" (1.19). It commits them to demonstrate movement towards greater equality in the Trust workforce profile compared with previous years, "including increasing the levels of previously under-represented groups at all levels of the organisation" (2.19). The overall aim here is to ensure that the "the organisation's workforce profile broadly reflects the community it serves/local labour market" (3.19). The Trust has taken the first step on the journey of implementation of its policy. It gathered and published the data, in response to my Freedom of Information request (Table 8.1). Time will tell what action is taken to address the under-representation of Pakistanis in the Trust workforce when compared with Pakistanis in its pupil population.

More broadly, with reference to Pakistani underachievement I am suggesting that, like the historical Birmingham achievement action plans (BCC, 2003), this should be treated as a multifaceted process. Here, ways were identified in which the local authority could intervene, such as through work with schools, provision of services to underachieving groups and strategic leadership and

Table 8.1 Pakistani pupils and staff in the schools and college within the Ninestiles Multi-academy Trust – 2018

School	Pupils %	Staff %
Erdington Hall	46	26
Pegasus	1	0
The Oaklands	18	7
Yarnfield	43	5
Cockshut Hill	26	3
Lyndon	8	3
Ninestiles	42	5
Solihull Sixth Form College	27	1

management. But that was then. It is possible that, within the new education landscape, the response to Pakistani boys' education would result in more than one plan, from a number of bodies (e.g. Birmingham Education Partnership, multi-academy trusts, single schools and academies).

Ceci and Papierno (2005) observe that where gap-narrowing interventions were universalised – given not only to the group of children who most need assistance but also to the more advantaged group, the gap can get even bigger. In my view this can be avoided by implementing targeted Positive Action strategies for Pakistani children who underachieve. Here, the work of two Birmingham schools provides examples. Broadway Academy has a significant Pakistani pupil population whose attainment is lower than other pupil groups. According to a paper the school had produced for the Lead Ofsted Inspector (Broadway, 2016), it was acknowledged that "Pakistani students' attainment was much lower than the national ... and this became an acknowledged area for improvement". It was pointed out that through targeted intervention, the school had managed to make improvements. In its plan for the academic year – 2015–2016 – the strategies included inviting to the school local and national British Pakistani role models and working in partnership with parents. The problem was clearly being treated as a mainstream matter. It was an integral part of the school's performance management priorities: "*All* (my emphasis) staff to have a performance target relating to Raising Achievement of Pakistani pupils" (Broadway, 2015). The other school, Holyhead (2018), has begun to investigate the underachievement of Pakistani boys. Utilising my doctoral research they set up a working group. They undertook research through a questionnaire and interviews with Year 11 and Sixth Form Pakistani boys. Their research highlighted three areas that required action: parental engagement, mentoring and role models. Based on the findings, the school is currently in the process of developing a whole school strategy on raising achievement. Central to their approach is an attempt to tap into the cultural influences of their students in order to use them to close any attainment gaps. This is based on the assumption that a host of factors – individual, home related and school related – account for some of the registered differences in the educational outcomes among groups. Recent conversations with Birmingham education practitioners have confirmed this in relation to Pakistani pupils. It would appear that there is a diverse picture in terms of needs. As well as the previous list one may add other factors which may impact on educational progress – where the pupils' family comes from, the size of their extended family, how big they are as an ethnic group in their community or school or the mosque they worship at. All of this points to a need for further localised research.

Improving madrassah education

This study began with the assumption that by Year 11 Pakistani boys would not be participating in after-school religious classes. However, this was not the case.

Given that education for Pakistani boys and their parents is considered broader than what is on offer within the state school system, suggests an obvious area where interventions need to be made. By doing things better and differently for their deen, religious education, improvements can be made in the dunya, of the world, education. One way of maximising the impact of madrassah education would be to have in place effective curriculum and teaching. I would like to suggest to the Pakistani parents and community that they heed the advice of respected Muslims such as Brohi (1979), Sahin (2005) and Sai (2017) and attend to the pedagogical issues related to the Islamic Religious Education. Mogra (2007) had said that curriculum development within madrassahs had not been given sufficient priority. It is time this was given the attention it deserves. He had reviewed resources which had been produced by a Council of Religious Scholars in South Africa but which could be useful in the British context. A more relevant set of materials could be the ones produced by An Nasihah Publications. According to their website[2] they have been in existence since 2008. Recently they have produced 'enjoyable', 'child friendly' and 'age-appropriate' resources. According to their launch video, the materials have been designed specifically for the young Muslims of today which draw on mainstream ideas of education such as Bloom's Taxonomy.

Once steps have been taken to properly resource the provision of madrassahs and the recruitment and training of their staff, it would be helpful to bring their work within the education inspection framework as recommended by Birdwell et al. (2015). They reported a similar approach being taken within the Scottish system. A significant driver of this policy was the recognition that non-formal learning and community organisations played a significant role in the development of young people. By developing a similar model of inspection in England, Ofsted could look at the 'big picture' of children's learning (Waters, 2007; Bartlet et al., 2008) than that which has a narrow, purely school-based, focus. As in Scotland, a dual community and school inspection process would encourage cooperation between schools and non-formal education providers.

Incorporating madrassah education within the state system

Research (Richardson & Wood, 2004) has shown that school and madrassah are often experienced *separately* by many of the Pakistani and other Muslim children. It is possible that there are benefits of the two working together. Cherti and Bradley (2011) recommended that there should be greater partnership between the two systems of education, especially to facilitate the training of staff and to create greater coherence in the lives of the children. The DFES (2004) had reported that 'most effective schools' had actively developed relationships with parents, local community and supplementary schools. In pointing out its benefits, it was stated "sharing of experience and knowledge between mainstream and supplementary schools can bring significant and mutual benefits to both, e.g. through better cultural awareness, curriculum enrichment and coordinated support in and out of school that focuses on the needs of the child" (p. 11). Later, the DFES (2007) had cited examples of good practice where schools had established close links with madrassahs, "through inviting teachers to attend training, sharing attainment data on pupils and providing resources to the supplementary schools" (p. 16).

Two recent reports offer some possible ways forward in this respect. The first (Nwulu, 2015) showed that supplementary schools helped to nurture the culture, heritage and language(s) of the children who attend them:[3] 85% of schools were found to teach culture and heritage and 79% community or mother tongue languages. Religious teaching was offered by just under half of the supplementary schools, with Islam (52%) being the most commonly taught religion. According to the report, the supplementary schools act as a bridge between the children and their parents and the wider community. The schools help to reflect the identity of children and provide positive role models and host culturally familiar spaces where children can be themselves. For Nwulu, wherever possible and appropriate, mainstream schools should open up professional learning opportunities to staff from supplementary schools and for teaching schools alliances (TSAs)[4] to extend their CPD offer to supplementary schools. Furthermore, it was recommended that the state schools should consider using Pupil Premium funding to support partnerships with supplementary schools. More generally, it might be worth exploring some of the European models of practice in supporting madrassah education at school (Berglund, 2015). The second report, which concerned the work of the non-faith supplementary school sector (Ramalingham & Griffith, 2015),[5] recommended greater complementarity and coordination between madrassahs and the mainstream education system. For them this would help the state sector to become better engaged in their communities.

> In doing so, they can raise the capacity of those communities, and of parents, to take ownership of their children's education. They can help ensure that out-of-school learning and enrichment opportunities are high-quality, and open and accessible to all pupils, particularly those who need them the most.
>
> (p. 4)

The report provided a roadmap for how the state sector could engage with supplementary schools, which could offer a model of practice for Birmingham.

Given that the madrassah system plays such a major part in the lives of Pakistani boys, it is legitimate to discuss its role in improving their levels of attainment. While one encounters isolated examples of good practice,[6] the system overall continues to offer a poor service – lacking structured and accredited curriculum and staffed by low-paid and unqualified teachers who are often not checked for safeguarding. Given that this impacts on the education of large numbers of Muslim children (not just those from the Pakistani community), it calls for improvement at a system level. A small number (nearly one third) of the Pakistani pupils stated that what they learnt in their madrassah classes should be taught at the school. A few parents supported this too. One parent suggested that this extra-religious teaching could be delivered through classes held at the school before or after the normal day such as those held in the extended schools model (Cummings et al., 2007; Dyson & Kirstin, 2014).

One way of making improvements in this context would be through the resourcing of madrassahs. They are usually poorly resourced (Nwulu, 2015). If they are to improve their standards and make a contribution to Pakistani children's achievement then they will need external help. Warraich and Nawaz (2005) had recommended the setting up of a Muslim-led resource unit for the development of curricula in madrassahs. In addition to teaching the Quran, they saw it important for the madrassah curricula to complement the work of the state education system. Coles (2008) recommended that madrassahs should be supported to enable the development of effective links with mainstream schools. Here, the National Resource Centre for Supplementary Education (NRC)[7] could be a model. This may help to ensure that madrassahs meet minimum standards, with basic policies and procedures to protect and support children. Madrassahs could be helped in producing curricula on Islam and training of their teachers. Based on the NRC model, there could be a range of training programmes for all involved in the supplementary schools.

The education of Pakistani children could be improved through partnership of schools and madrassahs to deliver homework and other school-related provision at the madrassah or IRE at after-school homework clubs, as suggested by Scourfield et al. (undated). This could be modelled on the kind of provision the middle class Pakistanis had established. There is potential here to explore the provision set up by the Pakistani community in Slough (Shah et al., 2010). Also the Swedish example could be transferred here; there, once the children have studied the Quran and basics of Islam, the remainder of their time at the madrassah is devoted to the Swedish national syllabi. Whichever option is pursued, it would require investment into the infrastructure of madrassahs and capacity building of other community organisations within the Pakistani community.

Reducing madrassah attendance

Pakistani young people clearly have long learning days. As well as attendance at school they spend significant time at madrassah in the evening. In addition, some may also attend a madrassah or mosque before school. This raises the question whether their time is being spent efficiently and effectively. Could steps be taken to improve what they do during this time, such as make their madrassah learning more complementary to what they do at school? Strand (2013) suggested that in order to address ethnic differences at age 14 "a key focus should be on processes occurring during the primary school phase" (p. 215). Could we similarly focus on the primary phase, in the provision of madrassah education? This would mean that by the time the Pakistani children start their secondary education they might have completed their Quranic and Islamic learning, thus freeing them to concentrate more of their time and energy on their non-religious, dunyavi, education and development.

Given that the madrassah education in the UK exists to fill a gap in what is seen as essential for them by their parents, i.e. knowledge and understanding of their religion and the Holy Quran and competence in mother tongue, the challenge for the state education system, in areas such as Birmingham, could be to help remove the gap, so the Muslim children do not need to attend madrassah for such long periods of their lives.

For Muslims, the Quran has a central place in their belief system. Although it is on occasion read without being understood, understanding it is seen to be critical if it is to be used as a guide for actions. However, it is recognised that it is impossible to reach the desired understanding without prior study of the language in which it has been revealed, Arabic. A case could be made here for the maintenance of the Arabic language given that it is the language of the Quran, and therefore the language of Islam. Swann Report (1985) was "wholeheartedly in favour of the teaching of ethnic minority community languages, within the languages curriculum of maintained secondary schools, open to all pupils whether ethnic minority or ethnic majority" (p. 406). A number of Birmingham schools already offer Urdu as a part of their normal curriculum, including at GCSE level. Now, a few also offer Arabic. Community, one of the schools in my study, has provided Urdu as a part of its normal languages curriculum. At the time of my research, it was about to start offering Arabic as well. Could such provision be expanded across Birmingham?

Warraich and Nawaz (2005) stated that madrassahs should provide accredited courses, such as Islamic Studies at GCSE. This would provide an incentive for children undertaking such study and help to 'synergise' the work of the mosques and madrassahs with the state education system. One Birmingham school, Queensbridge, has for many years offered Islamic Studies as a GCSE subject. Some of the students progress from this to the A level course at Cadbury Sixth Form College, also in Birmingham. If more schools made available such provision then a case could be made with the Muslim community to reduce the amount of time its young spent in madrassah classes. The schools could also offer such a qualification in partnership with local madrassahs. It would be reasonable to expect the teaching in this context to be done by Muslim teachers. However, given the shortage of such teachers, the job may initially have to be done by non-Muslim teachers. This was the case in both Queensbridge and Cadbury where the teachers were Christian and it had raised no objections from the Muslim community. Berkson (2005) identified a number of challenges that can arise in such a situation, especially one relating to the question of authenticity. He suggested the way to overcome this would be through the involvement of imams and other visiting speakers from the Muslim community (Lewis, 2006). A more long-term strategy would require the recruitment and training of Muslim teachers such as through the type of scheme identified by Campbell and Felderhof (2007). This would be achieved through a system-wide collaboration, involving the Department for Education, individual schools, MATs, the local authority and the Pakistani community.

Madrassah at school

Reference has been made to extended schools interventions which addressed barriers to learning and achieved positive outcomes for disadvantaged children, as seen by a narrowing of the gap in attainment for FSM and non-FSM children (Cummings et al., 2007; Dyson & Kerr, 2014). Their development had resulted in directing funding to a number of schools to enable them to offer additional services, over a longer day. The schools offered, generally between 8 AM and 6 PM, additional activities and services to some or all of the children, families and local communities, including access to study support, adult learning and a range of extracurricular activities. For the QCA, extended hours provision can bring far-reaching benefits – to the school, to students, to families and the community in general (Bartlet et al., 2008). Within the US, the KIPP schools operated a similar long learning day (Lack, 2009). They asked students to commit to arriving at school from 7.25 AM and remain there until 5 PM. Based on the principle "more time in school equals more success in life", the KIPP schools have also been reported to operate a longer learning week (through the organisation of Saturday schools) and longer learning year – three weeks of planned programme during the summer. The attendance at these additional activities form a part of their community's – teachers', students' and parents' – contract. While there, the students are exposed to extracurricular and enrichment activities. Schools and the Pakistani parents could explore these options for their young people, both for 'madrassah' teaching and as an opportunity to catch-up with school work. This type of approach within the state education sector was seen as desirable by Michael Gove, Education Secretary. In a speech (DfE, 3 February 2014), he stated that state schools, like their independent peers, should offer a school day 9 or 10 hours long. For him this would make time for "after-school sports matches, orchestra rehearsals, debating competitions, coding clubs, cadet training, Duke of Edinburgh award schemes and inspirational careers talks from outside visitors, just like in independent schools". Although, it is possible that the particular education of Pakistani children was not what Gove had in mind, his model does provide a framework within which more culturally and religiously appropriate activities could be provided for Pakistani youngsters. Schools could, for example, include the teaching of the Quran in their menu of activities. There has been isolated support for taking such an approach. One Birmingham school, Arden Primary, already offers an after-school opportunity for its Muslim children to learn the Quran and Islamic Studies. This practice could be spread more widely.

Sinnot, the General Secretary of the National Union of Teachers was reported (Garner, 2008) as being supportive of the idea of schools inviting in imams (and rabbis for Jewish children), to provide IRE. In his view this would help to better 'accommodate' Muslims within the education system. Here, it is worth referring to CORAB (2015), which called on the government to:

> expect publicly funded schools to be open for the provision of religion–or–
> belief-specific teaching and worship on the school premises outside of the

timetable for those who request it and wish to participate; this would be in line with the autonomy of young people and their human right to freedom or religion or belief.

(p. 82)

Research has shown that 'summer learning effect' is an issue which affects the education of disadvantaged children (Lauer et al., 2006; Kim & Quinn, 2013). Slates et al. (2012) pointed that school environment is a compensatory factor for disadvantaged students; "without schooling, [they] fall behind, which implies that resources available to them and their family environments account for the shortfall in their learning during the summer months" (p. 166). They recommended a structured response to addressing the 'summer learning effect' such as through increased availability of books through libraries. While I did not investigate this issue during my research, there is anecdotal evidence, gained over many years of living amongst the Pakistani community in Birmingham, which shows that 'summer learning effect' is possibly an issue for Pakistani students. A better use of the summer (and other) school holidays could thus make a positive difference to their education. At the least, the schools could provide their premises so the parents could organise before/after school and holiday learning programmes – including religious instruction classes. This would be possible at a school such as Community, which is open, during the evenings and weekends, all year round for a range of leisure and education activities for adults and young people.

Teachers and their role

Teachers play a critical role in the education process. Who they are as well as their knowledge level are both important. Pakistani pupils were asked whether it was necessary for them to be taught by teachers from their own religious or ethnic group. The majority said that it did not matter who the teachers were or their backgrounds. Amongst the interviewees – boys and their parents – there was an equal split. Half of them stated it was important to have Pakistani teachers, while the other half said it did not matter what background the teachers were; the quality of their input was the key. However, here it is necessary to point out that all the Pakistani boys and their parents considered it important for the teachers to have an understanding of Pakistani heritage. It is also necessary to point out that, given the overwhelming support in the literature reviewed for diversity in the teaching workforce, this is a matter that will require some attention by Birmingham schools. A number of reasons have already been cited previously for having a diverse teaching workforce. Of particular relevance here is the concept 'inclusive diversity' where it is not just important for Pakistani pupils to be taught *directly* by Pakistani or Muslim teachers but more an indirect benefit; by having them on the staff, to see them around the school and have occasional contact with them (Ross, 2001). As to what to do, previous initiatives and efforts could be revisited in order to use as a model for increasing Pakistani and Muslim teacher diversity. Given the significance of religion and increasing incidence of Islamophobia

(Lopez, 2011), the presence of Pakistani Muslim teachers is even more perti-
nent, including as a guard against 'stereotype threat' (Steele & Aronson,
1995). This problem had been reported by Abbas (2004). In his research conducted amongst Pakistani Muslims in Birmingham he had reported their negative experiences at the hands of their White teachers.

The Birmingham initiatives to increase teacher diversity included the course
developed within the MERITT scheme, from Birmingham Education Department (BCC, 2008) and Westhill College of HE to help train Muslim teachers
(Campbell & Felderhof, 2007). These initiatives could help to recruit local
people into the schools (Reed, 2009). This could be as teachers as well as
to a range of other non-teaching roles. During my many years working as a
Schools Adviser I noticed that there were often more ethnic minority staff in
support roles – teaching assistants, learning mentors – than the numbers
employed as teachers. It could be the case that some of the support staff may
wish to become teachers. Helping them achieve that goal would be an
example of Positive Action. A course of this type was on offer at Loughbor-
ough University until a few years ago, which was popular with minority
ethnic teaching assistants especially amongst Pakistani females with caring
responsibilities (Davies, 2016). Wilshaw, the then head of Ofsted, supported
'positive discrimination' when he was reported as saying that if the ethnic
mix of pupils is very diverse, "it's important to have a staff which reflects
that" and "headteachers faced with equal candidates for a teaching post
should consider 'positive discrimination'" (Coughlan, 2015). Of course, we
do not know whether and how having a diverse teaching workforce and, in
particular Pakistani teachers, would make a difference to raising educational
standards for Pakistani children in Birmingham. This is something for future
researchers to explore.

There is also the issue of teacher understanding of their Pakistani students'
heritage. A number of the pupils had stated that it was important for teachers
to have an understanding of the pupils' heritage. A number of teacher interviewees, too, saw such understanding to be central to the teaching and learning
process and for raising standards. In the light of this it is highly important that
individual schools, Teaching Schools Alliances, and bodies such as Birmingham
Education Partnership enable teachers to gain such understanding so that a
"positive account is taken of the faith dimension of Muslim pupils in education
and schooling" (MCB, 2007, p. 17). This is now an even greater need given
that such matters related to diversity have been de-prioritised in initial
teacher training.

Given the significant presence of religion in this study teachers will need
to have increased knowledge of Islam. One way of achieving this would be
through a 'funds of knowledge' (Moll et al., 1992) approach, where teachers
go out into their community, especially to learn about the 'Islamic funds of
knowledge' (Shalabi & Taylor, 2011). Imams and other community learning
champions could play a key role here as a resource (DFEE, 2000; Lewis,
2006). Through my education consultancy work, I came across an example

of this, though not in Birmingham. A primary school in Bristol had devoted a whole CPD Day to facilitate its teachers visiting their mainly Somali Muslim parents in order to learn from them.

A particular need to address here is the acquisition by teachers of religious literacy. This was defined as "the skills and knowledge required to engage in an informed and confident way with faith communities" (DCLG, 2008, p. 33). Earlier, religious literacy was described as

> skills in understanding and assessing religious statements and behaviour; discerning the difference between valuable and harmful aspects of religion and religions; appreciating religious architecture, art, literature and music without necessarily accepting all the beliefs that they express or assume; and making reasonable accommodation between people holding different religious and non-religious worldviews.
>
> (GLA, 2007, p. 9)

Griffiths-Dickson (2015) likened such literacy "to the religious equivalent of emotional intelligence; a matter of knowledge, but also an ability to be informed, aware, at home with diverse religions; the ability to conduct oneself well when questions of faith and belief come to the fore". Recently CORAB (2015) has reiterated the need for religion and belief literacy especially amongst those in educational establishments.

Given the size of the task at hand, especially in areas such as Birmingham, it may benefit the system to employ specialist teachers who would have particular expertise and responsibility for raising the attainment of Pakistani pupils in particular and education of Muslim children at a general level. Bhopal and Rhamie (2014) had suggested that local authorities should be encouraged to develop such teacher posts for diversity. At a general level, Ameli et al. (2005), in answering the question what schools do British Muslims want, recommended that the state education system should provide accommodation of religious needs, use students' faith identity to raise attainment (such as in the benchmark GCSE qualifications), improve education about Islam, institute religious awareness training for staff and governors and offer better teacher training on diversity.

Religiously inclusive curriculum practices

MCB (2007) published guidance for schools to guide them in their work with (Pakistani) Muslim children. In their view an inclusive curriculum requires the full accommodation of the pupils' religion such as through provision of space and facilities for daily prayers. This would help to challenge the majoritarian narratives that often shape the school curriculum (Fránquiz et al., 2011). The guidance was well received. Tim Brighouse, the previous Chief Education Officer for Birmingham and now a Schools Commissioner for London schools, was a 'chief guest' at its launch. He endorsed the guidance in these words: "I could tell you 500 schools in Birmingham would welcome this document and that's in Birmingham alone. And I can tell you another 3,000 schools in London would welcome this document. I read it cover to cover. I think it's a fantastic document".[8] Schools were also advised to develop curriculum materials and perspectives that reflected Muslim contributions to the contemporary world (Coles, 2008). Ofsted (2004) provided an example of a school serving a mainly Bangladeshi Muslim population where the mathematics department acknowledged the Islamic contribution to the subject. DES (2006) spoke of teachers making use of resources that reflected the pupils' heritage, such as "studying literature by Muslim authors and highlighting contributions made by Muslim scientists and mathematicians" (p. 14). An example of accommodation of Muslim pupils' needs was provided by DFEE (2000a), where schools timed their homework clubs to fit with the students' madrassah classes. Elsewhere, DES (2007) provided examples of Muslim-friendly school practices, including holding whole school *iftari* (the meal served when the fast is broken) during Ramadan, involving parents and community members and utilising local imams as academic mentors. They also referred to schools liaising with the local mosque to work with families where attendance had been an issue.

Within responsive schools, there is a focus on the development of the 'whole child' and needs of all students are accommodated within a spirit of respect for cultures, religions and languages of groups such as Pakistanis and Muslims (Coles & Chilvers, 2004; Coles, 2008). There are high expectations of all pupils, with monitoring of their achievement and targeting specific areas of need. Education is seen as a partnership, which encourages and facilitates active and full involvement of parents and the wider community, in this case of Pakistani heritage. Responsive schools provide for their staff opportunities to understand the culture and background of their students and have a policy for recruitment and retention of staff with similar cultural and ethnic backgrounds to those in the pupil population.

Further role of the Pakistani parents and the Pakistani community

The Pakistani family has generally been found to have a positive influence on their children's education. My research has found parents to have respect for education; something which they passed on to their children. This was verified by the boys during the interviews. The family was also a source for role models for the boys, a number of whom reported looking up to their parents, siblings and members of the extended family. However, it would appear that there is room for improvement. A number of students reported that their family responsibilities interfered with their education. This was more of an issue for the boys than girls. This may be something for parents to reflect on. Some students said they lacked a quiet space to do homework. This may have been due to the family culture within which many Pakistanis live their lives; there is always something going on – a death, a celebration, a visit from relatives –

which can distract from or disturb children doing their school work. This is an area that deserves attention.

Beyond individual parents there are possible areas for consideration by the Pakistani community. One reason for the neglect of Pakistani underachievement has been a lack of pressure from within the community. While they have campaigned on matters such as the religion-related needs of their children to be accommodated by the education system, at a general level they have been 'accommodating' of the system with little or no participation in 'the politics of protest' (Dench, 1986; Grosvenor, 1997). One reason for this lack of community action could be an absence of appropriate community-based Pakistani organisations. To fill this gap would require schools and the community to work together in the capacity building[9] of parents and teachers so that they can together exploit and generate education-based community social capital. According to Warren et al. (2009), this can be a particular need in disadvantaged communities where parents may lack relevant skills and knowledge and a sense of power and self-efficacy. They argue that when organisations are authentically rooted in community life, they can be a resource for schools in providing better understanding of the culture and assets of families. "As go-between, they are well situated to build relational bridges between educators and parents and act as catalysts for change" (p. 2214). From my knowledge of Birmingham, I know there are many individuals and some organisations in the Pakistani community who could potentially make a valuable contribution to ITT, schools' CPD programmes and act as a curriculum resource.

Generally, little attention has been paid to the role of communities in education and the influence they have or could have on educational outcomes. This much has been acknowledged by the Department for Education (DCSF, 2009) but sadly little has been done to address the gap in our understanding. It continues to be an under-researched area. Smith et al. (1992), in their research on social capital, did, however, point out that family and community can compensate for each other's shortcomings.

A possible model of schools–Muslim community partnership is provided by Woods et al. (2013). Their case study centred on the 'Tower Hamlets Story' where there was a system-wide focus on local education and, the mainly Muslim, Bangladeshi community working together to raise educational standards and increase the number of Bangladeshi staff in the schools. The potential of the larger community to participate in the preparation of teachers for diverse contexts is also yet to be realised. For Picower (2009), this could be as in-class guest speakers, mentors, or panel participants or offering sites for field trips and placements. This would be a way of challenging hegemonic stories by building empathy and new understandings. As well as imams there are likely to be many more people in Pakistani-Birmingham who may already fulfil the role of 'Community Learning Champions' and who could be a resource for teachers and schools. However, in order to achieve such a partnership–relationship would require a certain level of trust, of the kind that exists between Community and the Muslim religious leaders in the locality. Woods et al. (2013)

stressed the importance of building partnerships, trust and capacity with school leaders but also informed partnerships with parents, community groups and governors. They saw such communities of active trust, engagement and advocacy bringing about school improvement.

> High levels of trust seem to exist between school professionals, the community and the Local Authority so when there are problems and difficulties they are sorted out together rather than through conflict and confrontation.
>
> (p. 50)

In the case of Birmingham such a relationship between the education system and the Pakistani community is some distance away. There is a large trust deficit, as a result of the Trojan Horse affair, which would need to be made good before any partnerships can be established. Furthermore, such trust would need to be made good before implementing some of the ideas suggested here.

Notes

1 After 'multicultural drift' (Parekh, 2000).
2 www.nasihah.com
3 The report, within the UK context, was produced under the guidance of an expert group of practitioners, policymakers and academics, with expertise around BME achievement or supplementary schools.
4 Teaching schools are outstanding schools that work with others to provide high-quality training and development to new and experienced school staff www.gov.uk/govern ment/uploads/system/uploads/attachment_data/file/474309/Teaching_Schools__the_ school_perspective.pdf Downloaded 9.6.2016.
5 A qualitative report, also within the UK context, where data were gathered through study visits.
6 www.phf.org.uk/wp-content/uploads/2015/06/Paiwand-case-study.pdf Downloaded 1.12.2015.
7 www.supplementaryeducation.org.uk/supplementary-education-the-nrc/ Accessed 2.12.2015.
8 www.iccuk.org/page.php?section=media&article=22 Accessed 15.10.2016.
9 Capacity building, according to Labonte and Laverack (2001), describes a "generic increase in community groups' abilities to define, assess, analyze and act on health (or any other) concerns of importance to their members" (p. 114).

Bibliography

Abbas, T. (2004). *The education of British South Asians*. Basingstoke: Palgrave Macmillan.

Ameli, S., Azam, A. & Merali, A. (2005). *Secular or Islamic? What schools do British Muslims want for their children?* (Volume 3 of the British Muslims' Expectations Series). Summary of a report by for the Islamic Human Rights Commission.

Apple, M. (1999). The absent presence of race in educational reform. *Race Ethnicity and Education* 2(1) 9–16.

Banks, J. A. (2006). *Race, culture and education*. London: Routledge.

Bartlet, S., Devlin, B., Hadfield, M., Jopling, M., McGregor, D. & Worrall, N. (2008). *QCA big picture of the curriculum: Component playlists*. Wolverhampton: University of Wolverhampton.

BCC. (2003). *Asian heritage achievement action plan: 19 December 2003 revision.* BCC. Education Department.

BCC. (2008). *A guide to MERITT trainees and participating schools.* BCC. Education Department.

Berglund, J. (2015). *Publicly funded Islamic education in Europe and the United States.* Washington: Centre for Middle East Policy.

Berkson, M. (2005). A non-Muslim teaching Islam: Pedagogical and ethical challenges. *Teaching Theology and Religion* 8(2) 86–98.

Bhopal, K. & Rhamie, J. (2014). Initial teacher training: Understanding 'race', diversity and inclusion. *Race Ethnicity and Education* 17(3) 304–325.

Birdwell, J., Scott, R. & Koninckx, D. (2015). *Learning by doing.* London: Demos.

Blair, M. & Bourne, J. (2000). *Making the difference: Teaching and learning strategies in successful multi-ethnic schools.* London: DFEE.

Bowles, S. (1968). Towards equality of educational opportunity. *Harvard Educational Review* 38(1) 89–99.

Bradbury, M. & Kellough, J. (2011). Representative bureaucracy: Assessing the evidence on active representation. *The American Review of Public Administration* 4(2) 157–167.

Broadway Academy. (2015). *Improving the outcomes for Pakistani heritage students.* Copy supplied to me. Birmingham.

Broadway Academy. (2016). *Briefing paper for Lead Ofsted Inspector.* www.broadway-academy.co.uk/info/briefing-paper-for-lead-ofsted-inspector/. Accessed 16.8. 2016.

Brohi, A. K. (1979). Education in an ideological state in al-Attas, S. M. (ed.) *Aims and objectives of Islamic education.* Jeddah: Hodder and Stoughton/King Abdulaziz University.

BSLC (Birmingham Stephen Lawrence Commission). (2001). *Challenges for the future-race equality in Birmingham.* Birmingham City Council: Report of the Inquiry Commission.

Burden, R. (2013). Written evidence to education committee inquiry: *Underachievement in education by White working class children – WWC 03.* London: House of Commons.

Campbell, W. & Felderhof, M. (2007). A pioneering experiment: A report on Islamic studies within a teaching qualification. *Journal of Beliefs & Values* 28(3) 297–308.

Ceci, S. & Papierno, P. (2005). The rhetoric and reality of gap closing-when the 'have-nots' gain but the 'haves' gain even more. *American Psychologist* 60(2) 149–160.

Cherti, M. & Bradley, L. (2011). *Inside Madrassas.* London: IPPR.

Coles, M. (2008). *Every Muslim child matters.* Stoke-on-Trent: Trentham Books.

Coles, M. & Chilvers, P. (2004). *Curriculum reflecting experience of African Caribbean and Muslim pupils.* London: Department for Education and Skills.

CORAB (Commission on Religion and Belief). (2015). *Living with difference.* Cambridge: The Wolf Institute.

Cosden, M., Morrison, G., Albanese, A. & Macias, S. (2001). When homework is not home work: After-school programms for homework assistance. *Educational Psychologist* 36(3) 211–221.

Coughlan, S. (2015). *Ofsted 'positive discrimination' call.* BBC News, 7 January.

Cummings, C., Dyson, A., Muijis, D., Papps, I., Pearson, D., Raffo, C., Tiplady, L. & Todd, L. (2007). *Evaluation of the full service extended schools initiative: Final report.* London: Department for Children Schools and Families.

Davies, A. (2016). Personal email, 23 July.

DCLG (Department for Communities and Local Government). (2008). *Face to face and side by side.* London: DCLG.

DCSF. (2007). *Guidance on the duty to promote community cohesion.* London: DCSF.

DCSF. (2008). *Raising the attainment of Pakistani, Bangladeshi, Somali, and Turkish heritage pupils: The national strategies: Secondary.* London: DCSF.

DCSF. (2009). *Breaking the link between disadvantage and low attainment: Everyone's business.* London: DCSF.

Dench, G. (1986). *Minorities in the open society.* London: Routledge & Kegan Paul.

DES. (2006). *Minority ethnic achievement project (MEAP): Raising the achievement of Pakistani, Bangladeshi, Somali and Turkish heritage pupils: Evaluation of phase 1 2004–2006.* London: DFES.

DES. (2007). *Raising the attainment of Pakistani, Bangladeshi, Somali, and Turkish heritage pupils: Secondary national strategy for school improvement: A management guide.* London: DFES.

DfE. (2010). *The academies programme.* London: National Audit Office.

DfE. (2014). *Michael Gove speaks about securing our children's future.* www.gov.uk/gov ernment/speeches/michael-gove-speaks-about-securing-our-childrens-future Accessed 17.4.2018.

DfE. (2011). *Teachers' standards: Guidance for school leaders, school staff and governing bodies.* www.gov.uk/government/uploads/system/uploads/attachment_data/file/301107/Tea chers__Standards.pdf Accessed 10.3.2016.

DFEE (Department for Education and Employment). (1998). *Homework: Guidelines for primary and secondary schools.* London: DFEE.

DFEE. (1999). *Raising standards: Opening doors: Developing links between schools and their communities.* Nottingham: DFEE.

DFEE. (2000). *Schools plus: Building learning communities.* Nottingham: DFEE.

DFEE. (2000a). *Removing the barriers: Raising achievement levels for minority ethnic pupils.* London: DfEE.

DFES. (2003). *Aiming high: Raising the achievement of minority ethnic pupils.* London: DFES.

DFES. (2004). *Aiming high: Supporting effective use of EMAG.* London: DFES.

DFES. (2007). *Ensuring the attainment of Black pupils.* Nottingham: DFES.

Dyson, A. & Kerr, K (2014). Out of school time activities and extended services in England: a remarkable experiment? *Journal for Educational Research Online* 6(3) 76–94.

Dyson, A. & Kirstin, K. (2014). Out of school time activities and extended services in England: A remarkable experiment? *Journal of Educational Research Online* 6(3) 76–94.

EHRC (Equality and Human Rights Commission). (2012). *Public sector equality duty guidance for schools in England.* London: EHRC.

Feinstein, L. (2003). Not just the early years: The need for a developmental perspective for equality of opportunity. *New Economy.* London: IPPR.

Feinstein, L. (2004). Mobility in pupils' cognitive attainment during school life. *Oxford Review of Economic Policy* 20(2) 213–229.

Finigan-Carr, N., Vandigo, J., Uretsky, M., Oloyede, E. & Mayden, B. (2015). 'You can't help a child if you don't know something yourself': A qualitative study of barriers to education in an underserved West Baltimore community. *The Journal of Negro Education* 84(3) 298–310.

Foster, P. (1990). *Policy and practice in multicultural and anti-racist education.* London: Routledge.

Franquiz, M. (2011). Challenging majoritarian tales: Portraits of bilingual teachers deconstructing deficit views of bilingual learners. *Bilingual Research Journal: The Journal of the National Association for Bilingual Education* 34(3) 279–300.

Garner, R. (2008). Schools should use imams and rabbis in classes. *The Independent,* 25 March.

Gay, G. (2013). Teaching to and through cultural diversity. *Curriculum Inquiry* 43(1) 48–70.

Gillborn, D. (2008). *Racism and education: Coincidence or conspiracy?* London: Routledge.

GLA (Greater London Authority) (2007). *The search for common ground - Muslims, non-Muslims and the UK media*. London: GLA.

Grainger, J. (2003). Schools and the community in Gelsthorpe, T. & West-Burnham, J. (eds.) *Educational leadership and the community: Strategies for school improvement through community engagement*. Harlow: Pearson Education.

Griffiths-Dickson, G. (2015). Making your own mind up on role of religion and belief in UK. *The Tablet-the International Catholic News Weekly*, 16 December.

Grosvenor, I. (1997). *Assimilating identities*. London: Lawrence and Wishart.

Halstead, M. (2005). British Muslims and education in *Muslims in the UK: Policies for Engaged Citizens*. Hungary: Open Society Institute.

Harrison, A. *Schools inspections slimmed down*. BBC News 23.9.2010. Accessed 3.7.2018.

Hayes, C. & Juárez, B. (2012). There is no culturally responsive teaching spoken here: A critical race perspective. *Democracy & Education* 20(1) 1–14.

Hill, R. (2012). *The missing middle: The case for school commissioners*. London: RSA.

Holyhead School. (2018). *Response to Freedom of Information request*. www.whatdotheyknow. com/request/455400/response/1103771/attach/3/Iqbal%20FOI%20Jan%202018.pdf? cookie_passthrough=1 Accessed 17.4.2018.

House of Commons. (2002). *Education in Birmingham*. The Stationery Office: Education and Skills Committee.

House of Commons. (2014). *Underachievement in education by White working class children*. London: The Stationary Office.

Iruka, I., Curenton, S. & Gardner, S. (2015). How changes in home and neighbourhood environment factors are related to change in Black children's academic and social development from kindergarten to third grade. *The Journal of Negro Education* 84(3) 282–297.

Kellogg Foundation (2004). *Using logic models to bring together planning, evaluation and action*. Michigan: Kellogg Foundation.

Kim, J. & Quinn, D. (2013). The effects of summer reading on low-income children's literacy achievement from kindergarten to grade 8: A meta-analysis of classroom and home intervention. *Review of Educational Research* 83(3) 386–431.

Labonte, R. & Laverack, G. (2001). Capacity building in health promotion, Part 2: Whose use? And with what measurement? *Critical Public Health* 11(2) 129–38.

Lack, B. (2009). No excuses: A critique of the Knowledge Is Power Program (KIPP) within Charter schools in the USA. *Journal for Critical Education Policy Studies* 7(2) 126–153.

Ladson-Billings, G. (1995). Towards a theory of culturally relevant pedagogy. *American Educational Research Journal* 32(3) 465–491.

Ladson-Billings, G. (2006). From the achievement gap to the education debt: Understanding achievement in U.S. *Educational Researcher* 35(7) 3–12.

Lauer, P., Akiba, M., Wilkerson, S., Apthorp, H., Snow, D. & Martin-Glenn, M. (2006). Out-of-school-time programs: A meta-analysis of effects for at-risk students. *Review of Educational Research* 76(2) 275–313.

Leat, D. (2015). 'Turning Schools Inside Out': Developing Curriculum with Community Partners. BERA Blog 6 August. https://www.bera.ac.uk/blog/turning-schools-inside-out-developing-curriculum-with-community-partners. Accessed 3.8.2016.

Lewis, P. (2006). Imams, Ulema, and Sufis: Providers of bridging social capital for British Pakistanis? *Contemporary South Asia* 15(3) 273–287.

Lipman, P. (1995). Bringing out the best in them: The contribution of culturally relevant teachers to educational reform. *Theory into Practice* 34(3) 202–208.

Lopez, F. (2011). Towards a definition of Islamophobia: approximations of the early twentieth century. *Ethnic and Racial Studies* 34(4) 556–573.

MCB (Muslim Council of Britain). (2007). *Meeting the needs of Muslim pupils in state schools* http://www.religionlaw.co.uk/MCBschoolsreport07.pdf. Accessed 10.3.2016.

Modood, T. (2013). *The strange non-death of multiculturalism.* Max Weber Lecture no 2013/03. Italy: European University Institute.

Mogra, I. (2007). Moral education in the makātib of Britain: A review of curriculum materials. *Journal of Moral Education* 36(3) 387–398.

Moll, L., Amanti, C., Neff, D. & Gonzalez, N. (1992). Funds of knowledge for teaching: Using a qualitative approach to connect homes and classrooms. *Theory into Practice* 31(2) 132–141.

Morgan, B. (2004). Teacher identity as pedagogy: Towards a field-internal conceptualisation in Bilingual and second language education. *International Journal of Bilingual Education and Bilingualism* 7(2–3) 172–187.

Ninestiles MAT. (2016). *Equality and diversity policy.* Adopted by Directors at their meeting 9 February and recorded in the Minutes of the meeting. Birmingham.

Nisbet, J., Hendry, L., Stewart, C. & Watt, J. (1980). *Towards community education: An evaluation of community schools.* Aberdeen: Aberdeen University Press.

Nwulu, S. (2015). *Beyond the school gates.* London: RSA.

O'Connor, E. & McCartney, K. (2007). Examining teacher-child relationships and achievement as part of an ecological model of development. *American Educational Research Journal* 44(2) 340–369.

Ofsted. (2002). *Inspection of Birmingham local education authority.* https://reports.ofsted.gov.uk/sites/default/files/documents/local_authority_reports/birmingham/012_Local%20Authority%20Inspection%20as%20pdf.pdf

Ofsted (Office for Standards in Education). (2004). *Achievement of Bangladeshi heritage pupils.* London: Ofsted.

Parekh Report, (2000). *The future of multi-ethnic Britain.* London: Profile Books.

Peal & Lambert (1962). The relations of bilingualism to intelligence. *Psychological Monographs* 76(27).

Phillips, T. (2005). *After 7/7: Sleepwalking to segregation.* www.jiscmail.ac.uk/cgi-bin/webadmin?A3=ind0509&L=CRONEM&E=quoted-printable&P=60513&B=-_%3D_Next Part_001_01C5C28A.09501783&T=text%2Fhtml;%20charset=iso-8859–1&pending= Accessed 20.1.2017.

Picower, B. (2009). The unexamined Whiteness of teaching: how White teachers maintain and enact dominant racial ideologies. *Race Ethnicity and Education* 12(2) 197–215.

Ramalingham, V. & Griffith, P. (2015). *Saturdays for success.* London: IPPR.

Reay, D. (2004). 'It's all becoming a habitus': Beyond the habitual use of habitus in educational research. *British Journal of Sociology of Education* 25(4) 431–444.

Reed, W. (2009). The bridge is built: The role of local teachers in an urban elementary school. *The School Community Journal* 19(1) 59–75.

Richards, H., Brown, A. & Forde, T. (2006). *Addressing diversity in schools: Culturally responsive pedagogy.* Arizona State University: NCCREST.

Richardson, R. & Wood, A. (2004). *The achievement of British Pakistani learners.* Stoke-on-Trent: Trentham Books.

Ross, A. (2001). *Towards a representative profession: Teachers from the ethnic minorities: Conference paper.* London: London Metropolitan University.

RSA. (2012). *Area-based curriculum.* London: RSA.

Sahin, A. (2005). Exploring the religious life-world and attitudes toward Islam among British Muslim adolescents in Francis, L., Robbins, M. & Astley, J. (eds.) *Religion, education and adolescence: International empirical perspectives.* Cardiff: University of Wales Press.

Sai, Y. (2017). Teaching Qur'an in Irish Muslim schools-curriculum, approaches, perspectives and implications. *British Journal of Religious Education* 40(2) 148–157.

Scourfield, J. (undated). *Bringing up Muslim children.* Cardiff: Cardiff University .

Shachar, A. (2004). *Multicultural jurisdictions.* Cambridge: Cambridge University Press.

Shah, B., Dwyer, C. & Modood, T. (2010). Explaining educational achievement and career aspirations among young British Pakistanis. *Sociology* 44(6) 1109–1127.

Shalabi, D. & Taylor, M. (2011). A multiple case study on parents' perspective about the influence of the Islamic culture on Muslim children's daily lives. *The Journal of Multiculturalism in Education* 7 1–30.

Slates, S., Alexander, K., Entwisle, D. & Olson, L. (2012). Counteracting summer slide: Social capital resources within socioeconmically disadvantaged families. *Journal of Education for Students Placed at Risk* 17 165–185.

Smith, M., Beaulieu, L. & Israel, G. (1992). Effects of human capital and social capital on dropping out of high school in the South. *Journal of Research in Rural Education* 8(1) 77–87, Winter.

Steele, C. & Aronson, J. (1995). Stereotype threat and the intellectual test performance of African Americans. *Journal of Personality and Social Psychology* 69(5) 797–811.

Strand, S. (2013). The limits of social class in explaining ethnic gaps in educational attainment. *British Educational Research Journal* 37(2) 197–229.

Strand, S., Coulon, A., Meschi, E., Vorhaus, J., Frumkin, L., Ivins, C., Small, L., Sood, A., Gervais, M. & Rehman, H. (2010). *Drivers and challenges in raising the achievement of pupils from Bangladeshi, Somali, and Turkish backgrounds.* London: DCSF.

Swann Report. (1985). *Education for all.* London: HMSO.

Tikly, L., Haynes, J. & Caballero, C. (2006). *Evaluation of aiming high: African Caribbean achievement project.* London: DFES.

Tikly, L., Osler, A., Hill, J., Vincent, K., Andrews, P., Jefreys, J., Ibrahim, T., Panel, C. & Smith, M. (2002). *Ethnic minority achievement grant: Analysis of LEA action plans.* Norwich: HMSO.

Tomlinson, S. (2008). *Race and education.* Berkshire: Open University Press.

Tough, P. (2006). What it will really take to close the education gap. *The New York Times*, 27 November.

Villegas, A. & Lucas, T. (2002). Preparing culturally responsive teachers: Rethinking the curriculum. *Journal of Teacher Education* 53(1) 20–32.

Warraich, S. & Nawaz, I. (2005). *'Preventing extremism together' working groups.* London: The Home Office.

Warren, M., Hong, S., Rubin, C. & Uy, P. (2009). Beyond the bake sale: A community-based relational approach to parent engagement in schools. *Teachers College Record* 111(9) 2209–2254.

Waters, M. (2007). *The big picture of the curriculum.* London: QCA.

Woods, D., Husbands, C. & Brown, C. (2013). *Transforming education for all: The Tower Hamlets Story.* London: Tower Hamlets Council.

Yosso, T. (2005). Whose culture has capital: A critical race theory discussion of community culture wealth. *Race Ethnicity and Education* 8(1) 69–91.

Index

Page numbers in bold indicate tables on the corresponding pages.

Printed in Great Britain
by Amazon